Bob Spence lays out a proven game plan in an a[...] afford to be played. His experience and wisdom applied to hiring the right people is deep and rich. Reading his book is the next best thing to sitting with him and listening to him, which I have done many times. I have watched him over the past 20 years live this methodology out. If you want to have the right people in place to grow your organization, implementing the wisdom in this book must be an everyday practice.

— Brent Long, Brent Long, Executive Coach and
Founder of Long On Life

Every talent pro knows the cardinal sin of hiring is failing to get stakeholders aligned upfront on the "who" and "what" you're looking for. Skip this critical step and you might as well sell tickets to your recruitment circus. But Bob Spence offers the antidote with his structured system for defining the ideal candidate profile and mapping required competencies. By achieving unity on the target upfront through candidate scorecards and formalized criteria, you'll bring a laser focus to your hiring process. With Spence's brilliant approach to your game plan, you'll attract bullseye candidates instead of regretting those inevitable mis-hires.

—Aimee Houde, Director of Recruiting Services,
OneDigital | Resourcing Edge

Bob Spence's new book, A Game Plan for Hiring the Right People *is ground breaking. I read a ton of books for our weekly broadcast and this book was a page turner. It is the best book on hiring ever written and you will not be able to put it down. This Game Plan will change everything about the way you hire!*

—Jim Brangenberg, Author, Speaker, Podcaster/
Broadcaster, iWork4Him

My first thought as I read Bob's book was, I wish I had heard of Bob's Choosing Winners System years ago. We all want to hire high performers but equally as important, we need to make sure they integrate well with our existing team and align with our corporate mission and culture. Bob has created a powerful systematic process that gives you all the tools you will need to hire, onboard and retain the person that fits that profile perfectly.

—Deborah Robinson, Walt Disney World,
Disney Vacation Club Sales Manager

Bob Spence's latest book mirrors his profound understanding of Brighton's culture and his unwavering dedication to assisting clients in selecting top-tier leaders. Having partnered with us since 1989, he brings over three decades of invaluable experience to the table. As the architect of the Choosing Winners System, Bob provides unparalleled insights into finding the perfect fit for every role. His objective evaluation criteria have consistently proven his expertise, often validating his recommendations when others, myself included, have doubted."

—Laura Young, President, Brighton Collectibles

A GAME PLAN
for HIRING
the *Right People*

THE POWER OF A DISCOVERY PROCESS

BOB SPENCE

EABooks Publishing
Your Partner In Publishing

Cover design: Robin Black
Cover photo: iStock/Panuwat Dangsungnoen
Author photo: from the author's personal library

ISBN: 978-1-963611-23-6
LCCN: 2024910200

EA Books Publishing, a division of
Living Parables of Central Florida, Inc. a 501c3
EABooksPublishing.com

TABLE OF CONTENTS

Preface

"THE NEED FOR A HIRING SYSTEM"

For years, I have presented seminars about my five-step hiring process, the Choosing Winners© System, and using it with clients to help them find the right fit and match as they seek a new key leader for the organization.

Managers make hiring a whole lot more difficult than it is in real life. The single greatest problem is that managers refuse to devote the time and effort necessary to improve their hiring success. They all look for the magic potion, the single test that will tell them who to hire. Guess what? That single test is a myth, regardless of who tells them that a certain assessment tool will tell them whom to hire.

I developed my concepts about hiring while working as a school principal and superintendent. I studied as much as I could about people, behavior, and how to interview. I talked to everyone I could about their approach to hiring.

The person with the most positive influence on me was Ken Cardinal. Ken developed numerous structured interview practices, and he taught me how to interview. Using structured interviewing techniques teaches you how to discipline yourself as an interviewer.

Ken described hiring as a discovery process. I found that with a discovery process mindset, I could focus on the interviewee's responses and learn more about the person. In hiring/interviewing, you want to learn all you can about the potential employee before you make the job offer. After the offer and acceptance, it is too late to learn about the new hire. Unfortunately, most managers do not do this, and after the person begins working in the company they see that the person really is not a good fit for the job.

When you hire the wrong person, this costs your company at least three times the mis-hire's annual compensation. And remember, as the Book of Proverbs (a Biblical book of wisdom) notes in 26:10, (ESV): "Like an archer who wounds at random, is he who hires a fool or any passer-by."

Most managers are not disciplined and do not use a hiring system. You will be more successful with a system than without. I do know that you will be far more successful with a system that everyone in the company supports and follows without exception. (Including the president!) If you are not disciplined and do not follow a set system, you will never achieve the hiring success your team deserves.

INTRODUCTION

People have repeatedly asked me when I would write a book about my Choosing Winners System©. I put it off year after year and now have taken on the challenge of writing the book.

I think part of my struggle was wondering, "How do I make the system interesting and not another dry book about interviewing?"

I decided the best way was to write the book in a story format. In this book you will walk with a leadership team that needs to hire a new operations professional. The team consists of eight members, and their company is a small manufacturing company in the Midwest, Howell Precision Manufacturing—a family-owned company with annual sales of about $50 million. Let's begin by meeting the members of the leadership team.

Leadership Team Members

Ron Howell is president and co-owner, with his brother and two sisters, of Howell Precision Manufacturing. He is the only family member who works in the company, but the siblings are on the board of directors. The father started the business thirty-five years earlier. Ron is in his mid forties, married to his wife, Cindy, and the father of two boys and two girls. He is an elder at his church.

Ralph Long has been the CFO for five years. He is known as a very frugal manager, although Bill Johnson, the marketing director, calls him cheap. Ralph is fifty-eight years old and has been married for thirty-five years. He is president of the local community service club. He also collects coins.

Bill Johnson is marketing director and has been with the company for seven years. The team refers to him as Mr. Practical. Like Ralph, he is in his fifties. He lost his wife of nearly thirty years to cancer two years earlier. He really enjoys playing golf and attends the church in which Ron Howell is an elder.

Sally Hawkins is director of sales and has been with the company for nine years. You never have to wonder where she stands on any issue, as she is very direct. Sally is in her late thirties and married to her childhood sweetheart. They have no children. She serves as the leader of women's ministries in her church.

Susan West is the director of human resources and has been with the company for six years. She is the intellectual of the team. She is forty years old, divorced, and a single mother with three children. She is a member of a quilting group and enjoys making quilts, including prayer quilts for her church.

Sam Brown, the technology manager, has been with the company for three years. He is twenty-eight years old and is the youngest member of the team. He loves music and is a member of a small band, performing at local clubs in his spare time. He also plays his guitar on the worship team at his church. He is married but has no children.

Linda Martin is the manufacturing manager and has been with the company for ten years. She is 51 years old and began her career in manufacturing as a machine operator. She has never married, but is raising her three nephews. She took them in when her sister and husband died in an automobile accident several years earlier.

Charlie Richardson, the operations manager, is leaving the company after ten years to become the president in another local company. He is a forty-nine-year-old accomplished operations professional who is a skillful trainer and enjoys coaching others. He is married, and his wife is a realtor in the community. He leads the men's mentoring program at his church.

Mary Foster is Ron's assistant and one of her tasks is to keep the minutes of the meetings. She has been with the company for five years. She is the older sister of Ron's wife. She and her husband of twenty years also own and operate a local coffee shop. She enjoys helping at the shop when she can, and she loves baking. She is Sally's assistant leader for the Women's Ministry at their church.

While reading this book you will see how a hiring system works through the eyes of this Howell Manufacturing leadership team. You will watch while they conduct a brainstorming session for their open position, director of operations.

Of course, this is not an actual company and the people are not real. I have created these characters to help you understand the intricacies of a hiring system and how it works.

You will also get to know the team members and their thoughts and desires. You will see that they are a team that works well together. You will be with them as they face ups and downs and deal with some serious issues and events. You will also meet members of other teams in the company and see how they handle an ethical situation.

You will go with the team as they decide the *who*, *what*, and *ticket* for this very important position. You will learn how they conduct telephone screening, including the questions they use. You will also learn how to do an effective one-to-one interview and use an interview day to get to know and compare your top candidates.

I hope you enjoy reading the book, but more than that, I hope your eyes are opened, and you learn the value of having a set hiring system.

Chapter 1

A KEY LEADER RESIGNS

Howell Precision Manufacturing was founded about thirty years ago by George Howell, father of the current company president, Ron Howell. The company has been very successful and actively supports the local community through activities and donations. Ron is meeting with Ralph Long, the CFO, and Charlie Richardson, the operations manager, reviewing the monthly financial reports.

"Sales are up about twelve percent this month," Ralph said. "Our budgeted expenses are right on target. It is a good year!"

"Linda has done a great job keeping our manufacturing costs within budget," Charlie said. "She is really developing into a strong leader, and she has achieved zero employee turnover for the past two months."

"Make sure we recognize her at the next team meeting," Ron said. "Charlie be sure to give her the $500.00 gift card."

"Will do," Charlie responded. "Thanks, Ron. I know she will appreciate it."

"Well guys, it's been fun," Ralph said, "but I need to go back to my office and take care of a couple of things before the weekly leadership team meeting."

"See you at the meeting," Ralph said.

As the door shut behind Ralph, Ron turned to Charlie and asked, "Do you think it is time to tell the team about your decision?"

Charlie hesitated. "Yes, it is time." He said. "I do keep having second thoughts. This is a tough decision."

"I appreciate that," Ron said. "And as much as I agree with your decision, on the other hand, I wish it were different."

Charlie said. "I will let everyone know at the meeting this afternoon."

"Speaking of which," Ron said, "we need to get to the conference room, or we will be late. You know how much I detest being late."

"I do," Charlie said. "I will never forget when you told me if you got to church at 9 o'clock for a 9 o'clock service, you are late. I think about that every Sunday as I push my wife out the door to get to church at 8:50."

Both laughed as they walked into the conference room and over to the coffee dispenser, where Bill, the marketing director, and Sally, the director of sales, were already conversing.

"How do the numbers look?" Bill was asking Sally.

"Not bad, but they could be better," she replied. "My new reps are not learning very quickly, and I am not seeing in them what I thought I saw when I did the interviews last month."

Bill asked, "Not seeing what?"

Sally paused for a moment and replied, "I thought they had drive. It looks like their drive went the other direction."

Bill asked, "What are you doing to get them going?"

"I talked to Ron, and he recommended two things. He thought that for one thing, I should bring a sales trainer in and secondly, set up a coaching plan with them."

Bill thought for a moment. "I agree with Ron. I had a similar situation when I started here seven years ago, and Ron had me do the same thing. If I were you I would get it going."

They moved to the conference table where other team members had taken seats. Ralph the CFO, Linda the manufacturing manager, and Sam, the technology manager, arrived at the same time. Everyone stopped talking as Ron said, "Good morning everyone. This will be a busy meeting and the week ahead looks to be really packed for us. Let's go over everyone's reports, and then Charlie has an announcement."

"Sally, how our sales?" Ron asked.

"As you and I discussed," she said, "I have some serious concerns about my new hires, but I am pleased that we are right on target with our sales. This quarter we matched our goal, and the previous quarter, we exceeded it."

"Bill, how about marketing?" Ron continued.

"The website update is just about complete and ready to go live," Bill said. "We are making good progress on lining up presentations with some new contacts for our sales team, and I will give Sally that information this afternoon. We are hitting our goals throughout the department."

"Linda how about manufacturing?" Ron asked.

"First, I want you to know that our manufacturing leaders' team is great and doing a top-notch job," she said. "We are on schedule with a healthy backlog, inventories are where we want them to be, and we are very pleased with our quality goals being met."

"Ralph how about our finances?" Ron asked.

"Receipts are on target, and right now we only have two delinquent accounts," he said. "At the end of the last quarter our profit margin matched our goal. Things are going so well that I might have to take some time off."

"I canceled all of your PTO, Ralph," Ron joked.

"So no time off," Ralph looked melodramatically at the ground. "Okay, I will put my ball and chain back on and keep working. Could you at least add a few links so I can move better?"

"Don't do it, Ron. We need to make sure the chain is tight," Bill interjected.

"Sam, your report," Ron said.

"As Bill mentioned, the updated website is about ready to go live, and we have been working hand-in-hand with marketing to finish it," Sam replied. "We have installed more security measures, and I have written new training guides for new hires."

"Your turn Susan," Ron said.

"My HR team has been reviewing policies pertaining to HR issues and finding we are in compliance with the key issues. We have also done our benefit study and found that our prices are well within industry lines and competitive with other companies."

"Charlie, how about operations?" Ron asked.

"I have been mentoring my team, and I am really pleased with their progress. We are meeting all of our goals."

"Thanks for the reports everyone," Ron said. "Charlie, are you ready to make your announcement?"

The room became still. All eyes were on Charlie.

"As you know I am very direct, so I will get right to it," Charlie said. "I am leaving the company, effective at the end of the month."

Dead silence shrouded the room. No one had expected this. Charlie had been in charge of Operations for ten years and everyone liked him. He continued, "I have an opportunity to be president in another company, and the offer is too good to turn down."

Susan asked, "Can you tell us the company? Will you have to move someplace else for the job?"

"You know the company well. It's one of our customers," Charlie answered. "It is Specialty Products, Inc., and since they're here in town, I don't have to move!"

Everyone was genuinely excited that Charlie was moving up to be president, but you could sense some sadness in the air.

Ron allowed the group a few minutes to learn more from Charlie and then said, "I am adding an item to our agenda. We need to hire a new operations leader. Since we have already received updates and reports, let's talk about hiring our new operations leader. How do we want to handle this?"

"Well I assume we need to post the opening," Sally said. "Recently I hired some new sales reps, and Susan helped me post the openings, so I understand how it works. I can get this posted on several Internet sites after our meeting."

Ralph quickly joined in. "Let's not go crazy with a lot of postings. They are not cheap."

Bill added, "Let's keep it short and to the point."

Susan then added, "Do we have any job specifics? Who will be reviewing the resumes? Who will be in charge? Who will do the interviews?"

"I assumed you would since you are HR," Sally responded.

"I do not have time. I am in the middle of helping Linda hire several manufacturing positions," Susan said. "I think a position at this level should be handled by Ron. Right Ron?"

Ron paused and then said, "We have not had a new member on the leadership team since Sam joined the team five years ago. Charlie has been with us a long time. This is really a big decision for us. We cannot get it wrong."

The room grew quiet again as the team members thought about what Ron said.

Bill broke the silence. "Do we need to get a headhunter to do this for us?"

"Isn't that expensive?" Ralph asked. "I worked with a recruiter once, and it really cost a lot. I don't recall the percentage of the new hire's salary they used, but it was not cheap. By the way, the guy we hired only lasted six months. There was nothing in the way of a guarantee either."

"It is important to note that headhunters do not do any assessments or testing," Linda said. "Candidly, they only shuffle resumes and then move into a sales role, selling their candidate to us, so they can collect their check."

Bill, being very practical, chimed in, "How about we just contact our CPA and corporate attorney and have them send us some referrals? We can let our social media contacts know we are looking for an operations professional. I am sure they have lots of friends."

Linda added, "So we get all these referrals; who is in charge? Who will review the resumes, and what is our process? Without our effective manufacturing processes, we would not have quality products, and we would all be working somewhere else."

"Linda makes an excellent point," Ron said. "If we value our manufacturing processes so much, why not undergo a process for hiring the right person to join our team? Don't we tell our community that we value our people? We do. If we truly believe that, how do we live it? Since we need to fill Charlie's position, this is a good time for us to finally develop a hiring process. I want Susan, Linda, and Charlie to serve with me on an off-line group to come up with some ideas for a hiring process. We will report back to the group next week."

This team is struggling.
A process is critical to their success!

Chapter 2

GETTING READY TO HIRE

The next morning Ron met with the planning team to begin developing a hiring process.

"First, thank you for your willingness to be part of this challenge," he told them. "Let me begin by sharing an example that I believe will get us energized and ready to work."

Ron continued, "Assume that you are building a house. First, you would have the plans for the building, study them, and prepare for construction. You would then implement the plan and begin building the house, taking care to follow the plan and do each task systematically. Sometimes you may deviate from the plan due to new information and then prepare a change order modifying the plan. You make sure the plumbing and electrical connections are all in place before you hang the drywall. You have to have all the right parts in the right places in order to have the right house. And of course you have to have the building inspector pass approval! In my mind, this is the same process we follow to hire the right person. Anyone want to react to that?"

"That makes a lot of sense to me," Charlie said. "Let me share something I read about in *Good To Great* by Jim Collins. He wrote, 'The executives who ignited transformations from good to great did not first figure out where to drive the bus and then get people to take it there. No, they first got the right people on the bus (and the wrong people off the bus) and then figured out where to drive it. Great vision without great people is irrelevant.'"

"I have a question," said Linda, jumping in. "What role do our company core values, mission, and vision statements play in a hiring process?"

"Good question, Linda," said Ron. "They all are a critical part of a hiring process, and we want to hire people who share our values and believe in our mission and vision."

"It might help if we take a minute to review our core values," Susan suggested.

Ron added, "A consultant I heard speak recently said that if you do not have core values that all the team members own and internalize, you will never make a good hire."

Linda said firmly, "I agree with him. I was drawn to this company by the core values, and the company's positive reputation in the community. And the fact it has been family owned and operated for over thirty-five years was very important to me also."

"We are super glad you are here!" Charlie added, and everyone agreed.

Ron lifted a piece of paper from the table. "Let me read our core values." He began to read.

WE are a team. WE . . .

- are like a family, and we always support and respect each other.
- are focused, productive and get things done.
- believe open communication is vital to our success and achieving results.
- leave our egos at the door and are more concerned about others than self.
- believe that dependability and compassion drive our relationships.

WE are creative. WE . . .

- are enthusiastic, challenging, and accept responsibility.

- are comfortable in tough discussions and debates.
- are not satisfied with the status quo and look for a better way.

WE are a team. WE . . .

- are like a family and we always support and respect each other.
- are focused, productive and get things done.
- believe open communication is vital to our success and achieving results.
- leave our egos at the door and are more concerned about others than self.
- believe that dependability and compassion drive our relationships.

WE . . .

- are problem solvers and results driven.
- have clear expectations and a strong focus on quality.
- are prepared and organized, embracing our processes and systems.
- operate from integrity, doing what we say.

"Thanks, Ron," Susan said. "It is really helpful to hear our core values and to understand that we need to always keep these in mind—not only in this hiring situation, but in all our work and interactions."

"I want to go back to *Good To Great* for a minute," Charlie replied. "If I remember it correctly, Collins said you have to focus first on the *who*, and then on the *what*. I think he meant that it is most important to know the person, who he or she is, and then worry about what the person does."

Susan responded, "Charlie I am also familiar with that book! I especially like the way the author said, as you quoted a few minutes ago, that it is important to not just get the right people but to also have them in the right seats on the bus."

"So, how do we do that?" Linda asked.

"I think that brings us back to developing a process, right, Ron?"

"That's right," Ron replied, "I have some ideas to share, but please do not view these as set in concrete. I simply want to get our minds focused on this, and I need input from everyone."

Ron began, "Since we are seeking to find an operations professional, as I commented earlier, I want to use this position as the model for our process. From what I have read and garnered from the consultant and some of the members of my peer group, it is important for us to identify the behaviors, values, characteristics and traits we want in our new team member.

"For example, we might want someone who is a people person, a strong relator, driven, and has integrity. Those ideas are to get our minds open and ready to seek ideas. We can use Charlie as a model for our discussions. What do you think about this plan?"

"It makes sense to me," Susan replied. "I just am not sure how we come up with the desired behaviors. I guess we could put Charlie in front of the room and share how we have seen him behave all of these years. He's done a great job, and maybe the best answer is to find a way to clone him."

Everyone laughed and Charlie got up and took a model's pose.

"Do we also list the less than perfect behaviors he has shown over the years?" Linda asked with a mischievous grin. Everyone laughed again, as Charlie faked a frown.

"Well," Charlie said. "We definitely have the ball rolling!"

"Yes we do," replied Ron. "Now let's focus on getting a process. We will need input from all of you and the other members of the leadership team. I also want input from Charlie's direct reports. By the way, Charlie, have you told them you are leaving the company?"

"Not yet," he replied. "Tomorrow morning, I will announce it during our weekly team meeting. I am sure this will surprise them, and I know they will have a lot of questions. Most of them have been with me for all of my ten years with the company."

"That's good, Charlie," Ron said. "I want you to start thinking about *who*—not a specific person—but the traits and values you believe would be the best fit and match for us. Think about our core values, mission, and vision statements and how they impact whom we need to hire. With, the who, we really need to focus on behaviors, values, and characteristics.

"Brenda Ross, an employee of a member of my peer group, told me that at her company, Mid-Town HVAC, they brainstorm together the qualities they want in a new hire. I think that makes sense. So, let's get the leadership team together and meet tomorrow at 1:00 p.m. Come prepared for a brainstorming activity."

The meeting ended, and Susan and Charlie walked out together.

"Are you still making quilts?" Charlie asked.

"I am," Susan answered. "Thanks to Sally, I am now making quilts for her church. Instead of finishing a quilt the standard way, what they call quilting, we put ties in the quilt. Then, at Sally's church, they announce who is receiving the quilt, and people stop by the quilt table and tie a knot, while saying a prayer. They call these prayer quilts."

"I need to tell Connie about this," Charlie said, "She loves making quilts; I am sure making prayer quilts would be perfect for her."

"Please do," She said. "I imagine she would enjoy it. In fact, I can invite her to our next quilting meeting."

"Thanks, Susan, I will definitely tell her, but an invitation from you would be meaningful," he said. "I am on my way right now to a mentoring session with one of the young men in our church. Our church has a program in which men mentor other men."

"That sounds great," Susan replied, "Do you have a program for women?"

"We do," Charlie replied. "I will email information about both programs. See you tomorrow."

Coe values are the foundation of a successful hiring system!

Chapter 3

BRAINSTORMING THE WHO

Ralph and Bill were walking down the main hallway on their way to the Leadership Team meeting.

"So Bill," Ralph broke the silence. "Did you score a hole in one last evening?"

"Do you need to ask?" Bill replied. "No."

"Well, were you close?" Ralph pushed.

"Depends on what you describe as close," Bill said. "Would twenty feet be close?"

"I don't think so," Ralph replied. "However, I do not play golf. But in darts, 'close' means right on the edge of the center circle."

Just then Sam joined them.

"Hey Sam," Ralph said, "Are you a golfer?"

"I have never played golf." Sam answered.

"So you never played golf?" Ralph asked.

"No," Sam replied. "My band has played at golf tournament events for charity for several years, but that is as close to golf I have ever been. Does that count?"

"Not hardly. However, the Chamber of Commerce is sponsoring a golf tournament for a charity, asking local companies to send a team and maybe you and your band could help with the set up. What do you think?" Bill said.

"I like it," Sam said.

"Me too, Ralph said. "Take charge, Bill. Find some guys for the team."

They arrived at the conference room right on time for the meeting.

All the staff members were in their seats in the conference room exactly at 1:00 p.m., showing their excitement and commitment to learn about and create a new hiring process.

Ron started the meeting. "Before we begin brainstorming, I want to share a story with you. I believe this will help you focus on the *who*."

Ron cleared his throat. "While on a business trip, I had some down time, so I stopped for a cup of coffee. As I entered the shop, one of the shop's associates exclaimed with a big smile, 'Welcome to our shop. How are you doing today?'

"'I'm doing great,'" I told her. "As I ordered my cup of coffee, I said to her, 'You sure seem to be happy today.' As she filled my coffee cup, she glanced at me and said, 'I'm happy every day!'

"Her smile was so contagious that I smiled back at her and said, 'You must really like this job.' She smiled again and said, 'I love this job.'

"I asked her, 'So, why do you love this job?' As she set my cup of coffee on the counter, she answered, 'The pay and benefits are good, and as a single mother of three, that is really important to me. But it's more than that.'

"She suddenly grew serious and thoughtful. After a moment, she said, 'This company gave me my dignity.' I waited for a moment and asked, 'Your dignity?'

"Tears welled up in her eyes. 'I told you I was a single mother with three kids. I don't know for sure who fathered any of them. I was a prostitute,' she explained. 'This company came to the safe house and offered several of us a chance. I was the only one who took it. Now I am able to be a true mother, caring and loving while supporting my girls.'

"With tears in my own eyes, I said to her, 'You obviously feel good about yourself and your girls.' That big, winning smile returned to her face as she wiped away the tears. 'I really do, and guess what I did last week.'

"Not willing to risk a guess, I replied, 'I have no idea. Tell me what you did.' Almost dancing with joy, she said in a strong, proud voice, 'I got my GED!'

"My tears came back, and before I could say a word, she said with unrestrained joy, 'Guess what tonight is?' Being overwhelmed by the joy I was blessed to share with her, I said, 'Tonight?' She exclaimed, 'My first class at the junior college!'"

Ron said, choking back a catch in his throat, "That is a true story. I will never forget her. It still tugs at my emotions. Would any of our associates say that? That our company gives them dignity? I don't have that answer, but if they did, would they tell that to others? I think the example shows how important it is to be part of a company that genuinely cares about its people. By the way, she eventually became a store manager."

Ron looked around the room and switched gears. "I asked my assistant, Mary, to be the scribe for our brainstorming, so I can be part of the group and not have to write things down," he told the group. "She will write everything on the white board, then she will take a photo so she can refer to it, as we focus on deciding who we want as our new operations leader."

Ron continued, "When I spoke with Brenda Ross at Mid-Town HVAC, she said after they have brainstormed the position, they write a position profile."

Linda waved a finger to get Ron's attention. "That is a totally new term for me," she said. "Can you explain what a Position Profile is?"

"Sure," Ron replied. "First, it is not a job description, but more like a road map or a specification sheet. In researching hiring processes, I have found that a position profile spells out a description of the ideal person, the person's specific duties and responsibilities, and the experience, education, and skill sets needed for a person in the role."

Ralph asked, "I think I understand what you mean by a position profile, but how does this brainstorming work?"

"Glad you asked," Ron said with a smile. "In brainstorming, there are no wrong answers. Think about the ideal person for our operations position. Then share the words or phrases describing the ideal candidate—think of behaviors, values, traits, and characteristics. Once we have fully exhausted our ideas, Mary will take all of the words and phrases and write a narrative describing the ideal person. She will share it with all of us, and we will have a chance to edit these."

"Just to be clear," Linda said. "We want to only list those items pertaining to the *who*—not responsibilities or requirements. Is that correct?"

"Yes," replied Ron.

"It is words or phrases, right?" Ralph asked.

"Yes," replied Ron. "Keep in mind that we are defining the ideal person to be our new operations professional. We are focusing first on whom we want, as far as values, behaviors, traits and characteristics. Actually, this is the most important part. And like Collins wrote in his book, it is all about the *who*."

"Understood," said Ralph. "Mary, I am going to get us started. I want someone who has high integrity, values accountability, and believes the CFO is the most important person on the team."

Instantly, everyone laughed.

"Strike that last part. Just keeping the mood light," Ralph added with a big smile.

Bill quickly parried, "I have, for all these years, assumed the marketing leader was the most important person. So glad you clarified this for me." More laughter filled the room.

Susan spoke up next. "Being the lowly HR person, I would like for Mary to please list these words and phrases: people person, sensitive, and responsive to others' needs."

Sam contributed next. "As the one who keeps your computers running, I think this person needs to be detail-oriented, well organized, and prepared at all times."

Then Bill chimed in. "It sounds like we are all important! Mary, please list customer oriented, very strategic in thought processes, gets stuff done, and is loyal to the team."

"Hold on a minute," Sally interjected, "It sounds like we are creating a perfect person who walks on water!"

"A consultant told me that in preparing for hiring a new key leader, you need to set a target with the bulls-eye being the perfect person," Ron began. "As you interview and assess candidates you need to identify those who are closest to the bulls-eye, knowing that no candidate will be perfect. And Sally," he added, "described a key leader as one who walks on water. The Bible tells us in Matthew 14 that only Jesus could walk on the water, while his disciple Peter did go a few steps. By the way, if any of you had been on a raging sea in a boat, would any of you have left the security of the boat?"

Everyone nodded and Charlie said, "To get out of the boat you would have to have absolute trust in your leader and believe you could do it. Peter was okay until he took his eyes off of Jesus. There is a powerful message in that example for us as we seek a new team member."

Sally added, "I see the *who* as the foundation. Jesus referred to Peter as the rock, the foundation of the church. In our hiring efforts, the *who* is the foundation for this position. If we do not get the *who* correct, everything will crumble."

Charlie added, "I agree, Sally. If we set a target, we will have a measuring stick to assess candidates and find the best match. Also, I believe we can identify the vulnerabilities of candidates and be prepared to deal with those on day one."

Bill broke into the discussion. "What are vulnerabilities? Weaknesses?"

"Yes," Charlie responded. "Everyone has weaknesses. However, as I have learned over the years, people respond better when I suggest areas in which they might be vulnerable. They want to know more. However, if I suggest weaknesses, they become defensive and want to explain away behaviors.

"The same is true for us. We need to keep our focus on vulnerabilities and not weaknesses as we interview candidates. All candidates have strengths, and all of them have areas of vulnerability."

"Well then," Sally spoke up, "I want to add to our list a team player, a team leader, goal-oriented, an executor of plans, and motivational."

"Charlie," Ron interjected, "you appear to be thinking really hard!"

"Well, sitting here knowing I am leaving, I have been thinking about the traits and values that were most important to me in my role," Charlie said. "It is important that this person be optimistic, a leader, a coach, and driven by a mission of helping others—in other words, this person absolutely must be a servant leader."

"We are making a lot of progress," Ron said. "I would like to add some values and characteristics I believe to be important. I believe this person should be able to challenge my ideas and opinions; is opportunistic; values the worth and dignity of all people, while being detailed; can still see the big picture; values profitability; is honest as the day is long; and really cares about others."

"Ron," interjected Bill, "I would like to add that the person have a sense of humor, be positive, and is a strong communicator."

"Thanks, Bill," Ron said. "I think we have a strong list, so let's pause and consider who we are describing as the ideal leader.

"Next, I want to go through the list one item at a time and discuss what it means in our culture. As we do this, we will probably add more words to describe our ideal leader. Mary, please take a marker of another color and write down what we add to each item. As we do this, let's watch for threads of behaviors, values, characteristics, and traits by linking words that are similar."

THE WHITE BOARD

High integrity	Values accountability	People person	Sensitive
Responsive to needs	Detail-oriented	Well organized	Prepared
Customer-oriented	Strategic thinker	Gets stuff done	Loyal to the team
Team player	Team leader	Goal-oriented	Executor
Motivational	Optimistic	A leader	A coach
Helps others	Servant leader	Challenges Ron	Worth & dignity others
Opportunistic	Sees big picture	Values profitability	Honest
Cares about others	Sense of humor	Positive	Strong communicator

The team completed the exercise and discovered they had five threads that encompassed all of their descriptors: (1) Leadership; (2) Strong Value System; (3) Responsive; (4) Coach; and (5) Organized.

"I have a question," Ron said. "We reviewed our core values earlier. Do these descriptors, and even the threads, match our core values?"

The conference room was so quiet you could hear a pin drop. Ron let them think for a couple of minutes before speaking.

"What do you think?" Ron nudged.

"I believe they do match up with our core values," Susan answered Ron. "Sitting here thinking about our core values and how they apply to hiring has been the most valuable part for me in this discussion. We should have done this a long time ago."

Ralph spoke next. "I am more of a hard-issue guy than one who deals well with the soft issues. However, this exercise has really been helpful. Honestly, I have not spent much time over the years thinking about our core values. I don't oppose them. I just never considered the impact that core values have on us as individuals and the company, and the powerful impact on the hiring process. And, yes I agree with Susan."

Susan then added, "You are not alone Ralph. Many—and I mean many—companies and their people do not understand the impact of core values, assuming they have some. Core values impact everything we do in a company. Whether it be decision-making, problem-solving or relationships, core values make all the difference"

"I spend most of my time in the manufacturing area, working with the people who produce our products," Linda said. "As I am sitting here thinking about our core values, I am doing a personal assessment as to how well I demonstrate these values to the folks in manufacturing. I am going to review these with my planning team at our meeting next week so they are fully aware of our core values. And, yes, I agree with Susan and Ralph."

"I agree they are a match," Sally said. "If we were to hire someone who is not consistent with our core values, just think about the damage they could do in a short time; relationships negatively harmed; loss of good employees; and perhaps even a good customer."

Sam joined in the conversation. "I do agree, it is a match. And as I thought about this, I remembered a verse from a recent Bible study.

Proverbs 27:17, in the ESV version, says, 'Iron sharpens iron, and one man sharpens another.' That is all about coaching, in my thinking."

"Sam, I had heard that verse several times, but never connected it to coaching," Bill commented. "That is a great observation. I agree we have a match. And as I reviewed the core values and the descriptors in our who brainstorming, I remembered a Bible verse Ron shared with me to demonstrate servant leadership. I think it is from Philippians and goes like this, 'Do nothing from selfish ambition or conceit but in humility count others more significant than yourselves.' Is that from Philippians, Ron?"

"It is," Ron answered. "Chapter 2, verse 3. And that is the foundation of what is now called servant leadership in business. There is no question but that we need a servant leader in our operations position. After all, the man leaving is indeed a servant leader, and we need one to replace him."

Charlie smiled and said, "Thanks Ron. This discussion is making me realize how much I love this company and the people who work here. I agree we have a match."

Bill quickly jumped back into the discussion. "Well then, Charlie, maybe you need to consider not leaving! Not only would we be happy to have you stay, but we would also be relieved of having to do a hiring process."

Everyone grinned.

"I agree with the match and declare it unanimous," Ron said. "I really appreciate your candor and taking time to think about how important our core values are to not only this search, but overall to our company."

"Unfortunately," Charlie replied, "far too few companies have stated core values, and even those that do are not applying them to their leadership and work. As I leave, I am taking with me some important values that I intend to cultivate in my new assignment. I am thankful to all of you for the support you have given me through the years, and how much I have learned from you."

"We will miss you, Charlie," Linda said. "Don't be a stranger."

"I won't!" Charlie replied.

Ron paused and then said, "I think we have a good picture of who we want as our new operations leader. Good work, everyone. Now we need to focus on duties and responsibilities. We will use the same method we did for defining the *whom*. But first, let's take a fifteen-minute break."

Several quickly checked their email and voice mail messages, while others filled their coffee cups.

Linda and Mary were standing next to each other, and Mary asked, "How are your three boys?"

"They're all doing well in school and growing like weeds!" Linda responded.

"Where do they attend school?" Mary asked.

"At the Christian School Academy," Linda said. "Ron recommended it, and he was so right. They are also getting involved in athletics. Before I go on and on about the boys, let me ask you how the coffee shop you and your husband own is doing."

"Great!" Mary replied. "As they say in the business, we are brewing!" She paused as Linda smiled in response. "We are doing really well. And I do appreciate the support of the team. All of you are such good customers."

Sam, who was standing near to them, said, "Mary I just love the shop. I really appreciate that you have let my band play at the shop several times."

"Your band is fantastic," she replied. "Our customers love it when you play, and our coffee and sweet treat sales really increase!"

Ralph joined them and said, "I heard that, Mary, and as Sam's agent I am requesting a fair part of the increase for him and the band."

Everyone laughed and then Linda said, "With that, let's get back to our seats and keep working on the brainstorming."

Successful hiring *is all about the WHO:*
values and behaviors!

Chapter 4

BRAINSTORMING THE WHAT

Following the fifteen-minute break, the team reconvened in the conference room.

"Before we begin the brainstorming for the duties and responsibilities, I want to share an article with you that I believe supports the results of our brainstorming the *who*," Ron said, "I think you will agree."

Ron passed around copies of this article to team members, asking them to focus on the key traits of a leader.

THE IDEAL LEADER
By Bob Spence, HR Consultant

The ideal leader is one who has:

(1) **A clear sense of purpose.** This person should have a well-thought-out personal mission statement and a clear and focused personal vision, which he or she can openly share with others. The person should be able to actively encourages others to do the same.

(2) **Personal core values.** These should be clearly developed, written down, and displayed for the person and others to see. This person makes decisions, solves problems, builds and

---

maintains relationships, coaches team members—all governed by their core values.

(3) **A sense of and support of accountability for self and others**. The person takes ownership for all personal actions and holds others accountable for their actions. The ideal leader understands and supports the value of timely and effective performance evaluations, based on metrics.

(4) **Servant Leadership.** This is a leader who understands that the development of the team members is priority one. A servant leader is a coach and, at times, a mentor—depending on the needs of the team member. This one values team work and actively supports and works toward building and maintaining a high performing team. He or she places others above self. (Philippians 2)

(5) **Exceptional communication skills**. An ideal leader is articulate, well spoken, an excellent writer, and an active listener who knows and uses active listening techniques, while focusing on the needs of the one who is speaking.

(6) **Clear objectivity**. A leader who is objective weighs all the information and options, seeks others' input and involvement, possesses an anticipatory set, able to plan for the unexpected, and is a logical thinker. The person should be calm and patient in demeanor, but also have a proper sense of urgency.

(7) **The Ability to execute.** An ideal leader is strategic in thinking and planning and understands that planning without action is an exercise in futility. The person should be organized in thought and action, with a strong focus on step-by-step positive progress. He or she gets things done!

After allowing time for the team to read the article, Ron asked, "What do you think?"

"Ron, that is really consistent with the five threads we discovered in our brainstorming," Charlie said. "It could easily be a model for all of us to follow as leaders."

"I agree," Susan added. "It is simple, yet powerful."

Bill said, "I want to frame it and hang it on the conference room wall!"

"I think all of us need to share this with our teams," Ralph said. "Tell them this is what the leaders of this company strive to be. If we take time to explain it to them, it may help them in their own lives."

"Ron," Linda asked, "Do you know the author?"

"I do not," Ron said. "I got the article from Brenda Ross, who I mentioned earlier. This author also created a hiring system called, The Choosing Winners© System. In fact, I was doing some research on hiring systems, and thanks to Brenda, I remembered that he spoke to our peer group several months ago. We are actually following his system with the brainstorming."

"Do you have any more information about his system?" Susan asked. "We have talked about establishing our own hiring system—would this author's ideas be helpful?"

Ron replied, "I think so. Right now let's keep focused on our task at hand—finding a new operations leader. We need to brainstorm what the author calls the *what* criteria, and then we will brainstorm the '*ticket* criteria'. After that we can dive into evaluating The Choosing Winners© System."

"Can you elaborate more on this system?" Susan asked.

Ron replied, "Maybe a little. I am still reading about it and talking to Brenda, who uses it, but I do know it teaches five steps, and I remember the first step is called 'Define' and the second step, 'Score.' I have also learned the system takes time to learn, and it is not a hiring shortcut. But, more later."

"Thanks, Ron," Susan replied. "That is helpful."

Ron turned to Mary and said, "Are you ready to keep our notes?"

"I am," Mary replied.

"Great," Ron said. "Let's brainstorm what this person will do and be responsible for as our operations leader. Someone get us started."

"I will get us started," Charlie replied. "This person will be responsible to supervise, evaluate, and coach members of the operations team."

Susan added, "Also, making the hard people decisions and hiring the right people for the team."

"Hard people decisions?" Ralph asked.

"What I mean is," Susan added, "knowing when the new hire is not working out as we planned, and after helping the person, knowing when it is time to make a change."

Ralph responded, "Okay, got it. And I can only assume deciding who to hire is a hard decision based on the facts not emotion?"

Susan nodded.

"Ron," Linda asked, "Are you still considering joining the Entrepreneurial Operating System network and using those processes in the company?"

"What is EOS?" Bill quickly inquired.

"It is a system of business concepts, tools and principles to aid the business in achieving its desired results." Ron replied. "I had a lengthy conversation with one of their implementers. I am impressed with what I am learning. I also spoke with Tom Matthews, a member of my peer group, who is using this EOS system, and he said his company, TM Construction, is sold on the process. Essentially, it is a process to keep the team focused on the important issues."

"Would this person play a key role in the EOS system?" Linda asked.

"Yes," Ron replied. "For example, part of the process is a weekly planning meeting that they call an L10 meeting, which is structured and has specific objectives. From what I have learned, it is a highly efficient and effective method for tracking company priorities. I would see this person leading that weekly meeting. Not sure we should add it to the responsibilities at this time, and but we can add it later. Let me think about that."

"I think this person needs to carry on what Charlie has done," said Sam. "This leader needs to maintain the motivating environment Charlie created and continue to make sure the team members are involved in decision-making, planning, and implementation."

Bill interjected, "Good point Sam. Not bad for a techie!"

Everyone laughed, and then Bill continued on a serious note. "I believe this leader has to be responsible to enforce the accountability processes that are now in place. Of course, this person has the ability to make changes if deemed necessary."

"Since this person is coming in with different perspectives, why not have them review the existing systems and processes," Sally said. "Maybe they can offer insights and recommendations as to keeping our processes the same or making changes."

"That's a great idea Sally," Ralph said. "I don't think we have done that in the past five or so years. It is probably long overdue, and it would also help the new leader to get to know the company and the people."

Linda asked, "Charlie, have you been in charge of contract documents and working with our attorney to make sure everything is correct?"

"I have, Linda," Charlie responded. "I think we need to list this as one of the responsibilities for the new leader. We need to include contracts with customers and vendors."

Sally said, "We cannot forget customer service. In the past we discussed moving customer service to a different department. That team has reported to Charlie, but do we want to keep it in operations?"

"Let's think about that for a minute," Ron said. "Do we want to make a change now with the new person? As Sally said, we have discussed having this department report to another department, specifically sales. Any opinions about that?"

Charlie responded, "I think we need to give this some serious discussion, but I do favor moving it to sales under Sally."

"Why?" Bill asked.

Charlie answered, "To be honest, I have not really done much with customer service. My Assistant actually has handled all aspects of it and she has done a good job. In reality, she has been our customer service leader."

"Does that mean if we move customer service to my department, your assistant comes with it?" Sally asked with a smile.

Charlie laughed and pointed a finger at Sally. "Not so fast! I am still here. However, with the new leader coming in, it might be a good time to make the switch and move customer service and my assistant to Sally's department. That way the new leader can select his or her own assistant."

"Sold, Charlie," Sally exclaimed. "It's a deal!"

"Not so fast," Ron interjected. "We need to spend more time evaluating this change and seeing if it really makes sense."

"Thanks, Sally," Charlie said, "I expect you to get with Ron and help him see the wisdom of this change."

Ron threw his arms up in the air. "I surrender."

Mary said, "I have the duties and responsibilities written on the white board. What is next, Ron?"

Ron replied, "We next go through the duties and responsibilities to determine what good performance looks like, so when we prepare the job description, we have what we need to write the performance metrics."

Susan asked, "Do we actually write the performance metrics now, in what we are calling a position profile?"

Ron replied, "As I understand this concept, the actual metrics will be written when I meet with the new operations leader during onboarding. I will meet with him or her, using the position profile as a base, and put together the job description. In being part of this, the new leader develops a sense of ownership for the metrics, since he or she has helped to set them and agreed to them. Any opinions?"

"While this is new to me, I really like this," Sally noted. "It is even something we can do with all of our current positions."

"We can now focus our attention on describing good performance. Before we jump into that, take a minute to check messages and grab some more coffee."

THE WHITE BOARD	
Responsibility/Duty Good Performance Is . . .	
Supervising operations team members	
Evaluating operations team members	
Coaching operations team members	
Hiring the right people for the team	
Maintain the motivating environment	
Involve team members in decision-making, planning and implementation	
Enforcing accountability processes	
Review existing systems and processes	
Contract documents	
Customer Service	

Have specific and clear responsibilities and duties.

Chapter 5

BRAINSTORMING GOOD PERFORMANCE

"We have the responsibilities and duties identified," Ron said. "Now we need to brainstorm what good performance looks like. I read in the materials about the Choosing Winners© System that most companies do not take time to clarify their expectations for the new hire. This means they do not describe what good performance will look like, assuming the right fit and match is hired."

"As I understand that system, the focus is on preparing for the hire we need. Then we put together material for a position profile, not a job description. The position profile can then be used to construct the job description with the new hire and his or her supervisor. The job description must have clear metrics for each responsibility."

"As I mentioned earlier, I really like that idea," Susan said. "We need to look at all of our job descriptions and make sure we have metrics as well as expectations. I am pretty sure most of our job descriptions are the old standard."

Linda chimed in, "Since we began this process and have talked about putting together a hiring system, I did a search for this Choosing Winners© System, and I like what I am discovering about it. Having performance metrics is mandatory. It is also recommended that the annual performance review be eliminated."

Ralph jumped in, "What? No annual review? Not sure I like that, but it would eliminate the annual sit down meeting to tell people what they did wrong all year."

"I agree, Ralph," Bill responded. "While I hate doing the annual reviews, people need to know how they are doing, and we need to measure performance."

Charlie spoke up, "If there is not an annual review, something must take its place. Can you enlighten us on that, Linda?"

"Sure," said Linda. "According to what I read, in place of an annual review are twelve monthly reviews. The manager meets with each direct report every week for thirty minutes to one hour for a one-to-one session. For the first three weeks of the month, the meetings are just to touch base and continued relationship building. During the fourth meeting of the month, the manager pulls out the job description and does a performance review based upon the specified metrics. At the end of the year, there is no need for an annual review. You have twelve reviews done."

"I have to admit, I find this most interesting," Ron said. "I can see several advantages to doing it this way. For example, if someone is having difficulty, you catch it early and can take corrective action with your coaching. If it is serious, you can put them on a PIP , a personal improvement plan, and perhaps help them become more successful."

"And," Sally added, "If they are not meeting expectations and the metrics, you can take action earlier to make a change."

Linda added, "In the materials, they describe the traditional annual reviews as being like having a box in which you spend all year dumping negative notes into the box, and at the annual review you open it and pour the negative contents all over the associate. Sound familiar?"

"Great discussion!" Ron interjected. "We obviously need to work on developing our performance review system. But, right now let's get back to the task at hand and brainstorm our expectations for our new operations manager. Who wants to start with some ideas?

"I can," Sam said. "When I read the first one on the white board, 'supervising operations team members,' to me, that means, first, that the manager has developed good rapport with the team as a whole and each member individually."

"Because of this, and the fact that the manager is on top of everything, we see a high-performing team that get things done and results are achieved."

Mary asked, "Would it be ok to summarize and write 'Strong team rapport and results achieved,' on the chart?"

"I could not have said it better myself," Sam replied with a big smile.

"Let me address the second one on the list—evaluating operations team members," Ralph said. "Evaluations are timely and effective, meaning that the leader gets them done, and they are accurate and helpful to the associate, not just written words to meet a deadline."

Mary asked, "Is it okay to write it as 'timely, accurate, and helpful'?"

"That works for me," Ralph replied.

"Let me offer an idea for the third one on the list," Ron said. "Coaching is really not the same as evaluating or supervising. With coaching, there is mutual respect between the manager, the coach, and the associate. The coach is a good listener, an active listener, who establishes trust so that the associate feels free to share feelings and concerns. Mary, as the wizard of words, how can we shorten that for the chart?"

Mary replied. "How about, 'Active listening and trust builder'?"

"I like that," Ron replied. "As a reminder, these are not to be exact metrics, but they serve as helps to help us find the right fit and match."

Susan then added, "I have some thoughts on hiring the right people. If the manager hires the right people for the team, we will see a high-performing team that focuses on getting results. So, the outcome for the manager is that by having hired the right fit and match for the team, the team achieves the goals and gets results."

"Will this work for the summary?" Mary asked. "'A high-performing team focused on results?'"

"Yes," Susan said.

"I find this next one, 'motivating environment,' to be challenging." Sam said. "I am not that good at creating a motivational environment, so I struggle with how to define good performance. My mentor told me years ago that I could not motivate anyone, but that it was my job to create a motivating environment. Just how do you do that and what does it look like?"

"Sam, it starts with respect and rapport," Ron said. "Show respect to your team, and they will respect you, assuming you are genuine and demonstrate integrity. The key is to get them involved in planning, decision-making, and implementing activities."

"Be a good coach, and also provide them with the training they need to be successful. If you want a motivating environment, and your team members committed to the team, get them involved. Tell them and show them how much you value them as people and team members. However, if you do not involve them, you will never get their commitment, and you will fail to create and maintain a motivating environment."

Mary asked Ron, "Then should I write 'Involved in decision-making'?"

Ron replied. "Not quite. I would write 'Involved and committed to the team.' And I would tie the next one to this motivating environment, if it is okay with the group."

Everyone nodded.

"Anyone have an idea for the next one, 'Accountability?'" Ron asked.

Charlie spoke up. "Let me take a run at this one. Accountability is crucial to the success of an organization. Without it, total failure occurs. And not only do you need a motivating environment, but it must also be built on total trust. Yes, you do have to enforce accountability standards. But honestly, if you are in the enforcement mode you might have some acquiescence, but you will eventually destroy the team. You have to make accountability one of your team's core values, and as the leader, you have to teach them what it is, why it is so important, and what it means to success as a team.

"And remember this, you must have buy-in from the team so all team members are involved in enforcement—not just the manager."

Mary looked at Charlie and said, "I need your help on this one!"

"No problem, Mary," he said. "I can be a little wordy at times. Write this on the board: 'Make accountability a core value.'"

"Being detail-oriented and an advocate for the rules, I will try to do the next one on reviewing existing systems and processes," Ralph said. "Companies need to continually review their systems and processes. If not, you get consumed, with a lot of stuff not needed any more. We have to learn how to end programs, projects, systems, and processes that no longer serve the needs of the organization. It makes a lot of sense to have a new person with new insights look at what we are doing. I think that I would put as the outcome, 'Makes recommendations to change, delete, or keep.'"

"Ron can you give me an example of this in the workplace?" Sally asked.

"I think a good example is when a company has a program in place and it is obviously not working as initially planned." Ron explained. "For whatever reason, the leader continues to hold on to it because they cannot give up. It might be a manufacturing process, a marketing plan or a sales plan for example."

Mary responded, "How about if I just list the three outcomes?"

"I am okay with that," Ralph said.

"I think I can lead discussion on the next one," Mary said. "'Accurate, complete and legal.'"

"Good call Mary. Direct and to the point like the acute documents. Ron said.

"Since we are not settled yet on the placing of customer service, I think we should hold on that one for now—except, let's list the outcome as 'outstanding service meeting customer needs.'"

"What's next, Ron?" Bill asked.

"We will now brainstorm the education, experience, and skills we are looking for with the new person. I saw that the Choosing Winners© System refers to this as the 'Ticket.' The description says it is referred to that way because if we want to go to a concert, a play, or an athletic event, we need a ticket to get in the door. In order to be considered for this job, candidates must have a ticket. Let's take a ten- to fifteen-minute break to refill coffee cups."

"Hey Linda, what do you think about this process so far?" Sam asked, as people pushed their chairs away from the table.

"I am really getting into this," Linda said. "I see tremendous benefits for our company. It's a lot like your band, Sam. Each of you has a specific instrument and specific notes to play at the right time to produce music people like to hear. If your timing is off, what happens to the piece?"

"It's destroyed." Sam said.

"Right," Linda said. "If we have all the right people, in the right places, with a clear understanding of the expectations, like the band, we play good music. Take out one aspect and we do not get any new gigs."

"I like your analogy," Sam said. "It makes a lot of sense and is easy to understand."

"I was listening to your analogy, Linda," Sally said, standing from the table. "I really like it. Thanks."

"I am anxious to get into what Ron called the Ticket," Linda said. "I have never seen so much clarity planning for a new hire in my whole career."

THE WHITE BOARD

Responsibility/Duty Good Performance Is . . .

Supervising operations team members	Strong team rapport and results achieved.
Evaluating operations team members	Timely, accurate, and helpful
Coaching operations team members	Active listening and trust builder
Hiring the right people for the team	High-performing team focused on results
Maintain the motivating environment	Involved and committed to the team
Involve team members in decision-making, planning, and implementation	
Enforcing accountability processes	Make accountability a core value
Review existing systems and processes	Change, delete or keep
Contract documents	Accurate, complete and legal
Customer Service	Outstanding service, meeting needs

Performance Standards are mandatory!

Chapter 6

BRAINSTORMING
THE TICKET

All the group members returned to the conference room with their coffee, ready to keep working on the task at hand, defining the role of Operations Manager.

The team was investing considerable time in the brainstorming process. However, should a mis-hire occur, dealing with fallout from that would take a whole lot more than the time spent in brainstorming the profile. Most authorities estimate that a mis-hire will cost a company at least three times the annual compensation of the mis-hire, not to mention the damage done to the culture.

"Here is how they recommend brainstorming the Ticket," Ron explained. "Anyone can give an item of education, experience, or skills, and Mary will write it on the white board. It does not matter which of you choose to add to the list. When we have all the items we wish on the list, we will go back, add any necessary explanations, and assign a priority."

"What do you mean by priority?" Sam asked.

"All items will be categorized as required, preferred, or desired," Ron explained. "For example, if we were doing this for a sales rep, you might put 'direct selling experience' on the list. You would not prioritize it at that time. After we have the total list, we will go back and set the priority, as I mentioned, at required, preferred, or desired. As we do this, keep in mind all requirements are must-haves. We will not contact anyone lacking any requirements."

"Before we jump into this, I want to share an observation," Ralph said. "In my many years, this is the most time and effort I have ever spent on planning for hiring a new team member. I have to admit I was skeptical about this process, but now I am convinced. As we prepare to brainstorm the Ticket, I think this is the only thing we focused on in our past hires. We were determined to identify all the experience, education, and skills we could while ignoring the people side.

"While we usually had some type of job description listing duties, we never talked about outcomes, or defining good performance. I cannot recall a time when we actually defined the characteristics, values, and behaviors we wanted in our new team member. So with that said, I would like to have three years of our industry experience on the white board."

"Thanks for sharing your observation, Ralph," Susan said. "I agree 100 percent with you, and while we began to define the operations manager role, I believe we are taking the initial steps to having a comprehensive hiring system. I would like to have five years of people management experience on the the board."

"And let me expand on that with five years of experience in operations," Bill added.

"I would like to add a bachelor's degree to the list," Sam replied.

"And I would like to expand that to a major in business," Linda added.

"I have a question, Ron," Sally said. "In describing our new leader, in the *who,* we had several things like strong communicator. Do we need to list those things on the Ticket, or are they covered as part of the *who* description?"

"Excellent question, Sally," Ron replied. "We do not need to list things like strong communicator on the Ticket. However, there might be some unique situations, and in those cases we will put a *who* item on the Ticket. If you are not sure, share the item with the team, and we will decide at that time."

"Thanks. That makes sense to me. I know this is not a sales position, but I want to add experience in sales for consideration," Sally said.

"For consideration let's add an MBA to the list," Linda added.

"We listed people management experience, but I want to also have experience in a senior level position," Bill added. "I would suggest five years as a minimum."

"Since we are a family-owned manufacturing company, I want to add experience working in a family-owned business for consideration," Susan said.

"Sally added sales experience, so I want to add marketing knowledge," Bill said.

"I can remember adding computer literate to job postings in the past, but I am not sure that is even necessary in today's world." Sam interjected. "However, I would like to add technologically savvy to the list."

"Are you keeping up with this rapid fire, Mary?" Ron asked.

"I am right here with you. I am very impressed with how well this is going, and I like what I am hearing," Mary replied.

"I know I am the CFO," Ralph began, "but I do think we should add that this person have an understanding of the profit and loss statement and budgeting processes."

"We are still discussing where the customer service will be, but I think it should be on the list for consideration," Charlie said. "Also, Ron, since you are taking a look at the EOS program, should we list knowledge and/or experience with EOS?"

"I agree," Ron responded. "Good point. I think we have a good list to work on and set the priorities. Let's begin with the three years industry experience and work our way down the list. And keep in mind we might eliminate an item or add an item."

THE WHITE BOARD

Education/Experience/Skills Required/Preferred/Desired

3 years our industry experience	
5 years of people management experience	
5 years of experience in operations	
Bachelor's degree	
Degree major in business	
Experience in sales	
MBA	
5 years senior level management experience	
Experience in a family-owned business	
Experience in marketing	
Technologically savvy	
Understands P&L and budgeting processes	
Experience with customer service	
Knowledge and/or experience with EOS	

"Are we wanting to narrow it down to our niche in manufacturing?" Ralph asked. "Or are we defining 'industry' as the manufacturing industry?

"I think if we narrow it to our niche, we will eliminate a lot of potential candidates," Sam added. "If it is the overall manufacturing industry, then I would make it a requirement."

"I agree," Ron replied. "Are we all in agreement? Show of hands?"

Everyone raised his or her hand, and Mary wrote, "required" on the white board.

"How about people management experience?" Ron asked.

"To me this is critical." Susan said. "We put a lot of thought into our description of the ideal leader, and managing people was key. In my opinion, this must be required."

Others nodded in agreement.

"We are looking for the right fit and match, that person who fits our culture," Linda began. "Knowing operations is a must. We do not have time to train someone, so I believe it must be required."

Ron responded, "These first three are critical, and I agree we must have them as required. We want a strong people person, a relationship team leader who fully knows operations and understands manufacturing. What about a degree?"

"Not sure how I feel about this." Sam said. "Correct me if I am wrong, but don't all of us now on the team have at least a bachelor's degree? And I think Ralph has an MBA?"

Ron spoke up. "That is correct, Sam. However, I am not that concerned about a degree. If anything I might make it preferred or change it to 'a degree or equivalent.'"

"Ron, I generally agree with you," Susan said. "If we add equivalent, we have to spell out how many years of experience are equivalent. We still can keep it required if we list degree or equivalent. We do not have to make it preferred."

Bill asked, "How many years would you recommend for equivalent, Susan?"

"If we do not require a degree, I would set the equivalent at seven years," Susan replied. "If we make it preferred, we do not establish an equivalent."

"Now I am confused," Ralph responded. "Is it required or not?"

Ron interjected, "Let's make it preferred and not have to deal with worrying about the equivalent stuff. Is that okay? Let's make the next one, a major in business, desired."

His coworkers nodded.

"Are we ready to move on?" asked Sally. Looking around and seeing that everyone seemed ready. "Since I added sales experience, I want to suggest we make it desired. It is obviously not critical for the operations leader, but it might be helpful."

"I agree," Bill added. "I put marketing experience on the list. I would like to make it desired also. Again, this would be helpful, but not that important."

"I can say the same for an MBA," Ralph added. "Make it desired."

Standing next to the white board, Mary turned, wrote 'desired' on all three items, and said, "Done. Are you ready to discuss senior management experience?"

"What is senior management?" Sam asked. "I have heard that many times over the years, but have never been really clear on what it is. I guess my perception of senior management is that these people are elderly and close to retirement."

He smiled as everyone acknowledged his sense of humor.

"Sam, I appreciate the humor!" Ron said. "While some senior managers might be elderly and close to retirement, that is not the definition. Another way people describe senior management is they will say, C-Level managers, meaning CEO, CFO, COO, etc."

"That means we only have one senior manager in our company?" Linda asked.

"Yep, and that would be me!" Ralph interjected. "Your friendly neighborhood CFO."

"Well that settles it," Bill said. "One Ralph is more than enough, so we can strike senior management from the list!"

Ralph laughed. "Bill, I never knew you cared! When we do the department budgets, I need to take a harder look at your submissions."

As the laughter subsided, Sally asked, "This might be a stupid question, but, Ron, are you a CEO?"

"No. Just company president," Ron replied. "I have zero interest in ever being a CEO. As you know, I am not fond of titles. I find titles can get in the way of relationships on a team. However, with that said, I think we keep it on the list."

Sam steps up and asks, "Why, then, is Ralph a CFO and not director of finance or lead accountant?"

"Simply stated," Ron began, "the bank."

"The bank?" Susan asked.

"Banks like titles, and they strongly believe companies of our size, and larger, need to have a CFO," Ron replied, "That is why Ralph is CFO and not some other title."

"And Ralph loves the title!" Bill said.

Mary spoke up. "Hey, team, I am standing here by the board. What are you going to do about the senior management item?"

"Ron basically said he doesn't like it, but he would keep it on the list," Charlie said, "Let's decide what priority it is."

"Is there any level below 'desired?'" Susan asked.

"No. With the group's approval we will make it desired. Give me a show of hands if you agree," Ron said, and paused to look at hands going up. "Write it on the board, Mary. And keep in mind that you may not have a senior manager title, but in my eyes, members of our Leadership Team are senior managers. The problem with calling people senior managers is that it creates borders and some holding that title use it for their own ego. I have no time or room in this company for senior manager attitudes. Leave the ego at the door and replace it with sincere humility. Let's keep on task."

"I never thought about this before," Charlie said. "I knew we were family-owned, but I have no idea how many of you previously worked in a family-owned business. I know I did several years ago, and obviously Ron has that experience. Prior to working here how many of you worked in a family-owned business?" Only Linda and Sally raised their hands.

Charlie continued, "Susan since you did not have experience in a family-owned business, were there some challenges or issues you initially faced here?"

"My position before coming here was in a larger company than ours, and it was a corporation," Susan said. "It was not an issue or a challenge, but with the openness of the people here, I had to learn to be less 'arm's length' in relationships. While I like it now, the informal atmosphere was really strange for me.

"For example, in my previous company, we always sent emails to our team members and seldom spoke to each other, except in meetings that were very structured—and no one would ever laugh like we do here."

"When I started here, I was sending emails and people did not send a reply to the email, but walked over to my office and answered verbally. I could never go back to the previous corporate environment."

"Interesting," Charlie replied. "How about you, Bill?"

"Well, all of a sudden I was no longer Mr. Johnson," Bill said, "Instantly I was just 'Practical Bill.' When I heard team members address our president as 'Ron,' and not as 'Mr. Howell,' I knew I was in a different world."

"I do have to admit I was somewhat shocked that the president of the company was called by his first name, not only by our team members, but also by workers in the factory."

"How about one more?" Charlie asked. "Tell us about your experience, Ralph."

"Well, I showed up day one in a white shirt, conservative tie, and full business suit. I stuck out like a banana in a tub of oranges. The next day I changed to a sport jacket instead of the suit. I still felt out of place. Now, look at me! Khaki slacks, a sport shirt, and comfortable shoes!"

"Why did you have a suit and tie outfit on Monday?" Sam asked.

"It's called banking relationships!" Ralph replied. "I had a meeting with our banker, and he not only wears a suit and tie, he also wears a vest."

"You are not serious," Linda replied.

"Oh, yes I am," Ralph insisted. "He fits the old stuffed-shirt caricature. I enter his office, sort of like the inner sanctum, and he greets me calling me Mr. Long. No 'How are you?' or any other greeting. Then, he points to a chair, and so I sit down. If I were to appear in my current attire, I would not be allowed in the inner sanctum."

"So what priority do we give experience in a family-owned company?" Ron asked.

"I was thinking 'desired,'" Linda said. "However, after hearing Susan, Bill, and Ralph, I think it is preferred. It's not something we would require, but it is indicative of who the person is and how well he or she will fit our culture."

"Let's have a show of hands," Ron said, "Is it preferred?" All hands went up.

"The next thing on the list is 'Technologically savvy.'" Susan said. "What exactly does that mean?"

Sam replied. "It does not mean software developer! But it means the person can get around on a computer and use basic programs and apps, and for example, can handle working with our customer relationship management software. I think it also means social networking."

"Sam, that makes sense to me," Susan replied. "Is everyone ok with Sam's description? So, Mary, please mark it required."

Mary said, "Done."

"I want to rate the next item," Ron said. "'Understands P&L and budgeting processes.' That should be required. I cannot imagine an operations manager who does not have that. Do you agree?" Everyone nodded.

Mary said, "We only have two items left, customer service and EOS experience."

"I think we can do this quickly," said Charlie. "As far as customer service, it is still up in the air as to whether this will be in the operation area or sales with Sally. I think with that in mind, we need to call it desired. Opinions?"

"That makes sense." Sally replied. "How do the rest of you feel? Give me a show of hands if you agree."

She looked at the raised hands and nodded in satisfaction.

"That brings us to the EOS item," Ron said. "This is something that is not immediate, but based on what I have learned about it, we may move toward it sooner than later. There is a book called *Traction* by Gino Wickham. I have ordered a copy of the book for each of you and would appreciate it if you would take time to read it over the next few weeks. I think at this point we can make this desired. Next, we can talk about sourcing the position. Let's take a thirty-minute break, and then talk about sourcing."

THE WHITE BOARD

Education/Experience/Skills Required/Preferred/Desired

3 years of industry experience (manufacturing)	Required
5 years of people management experience	Required
5 years of experience in operations	Required
Bachelor's degree	Preferred
Degree major in business	Desired
Experience in sales	Desired
MBA	Desired
5 years of senior level management experience	Desired
Experience in a family-owned business	Preferred
Experience in marketing	Desired
Technologically savvy	Required
Understands P&L and budgeting processes	Required
Experience with customer service	Desired
Knowledge and/or experience with EOS	Desired

Candidates must have all the requirements!

Chapter 7

SOURCING THE POSITION

Near the end of the thirty-minute break, Linda and Susan walked together toward the conference room.

"I really enjoyed the Ticket discussion," Linda said. "I learned a lot of things I did not know."

"I agree. I have enjoyed every minute of our brainstorming. I wish I had known about this much earlier in my career," Sally said. "I was at an HR coffee meeting last evening. About twenty members attend regularly. I told one person about our brainstorming. She shook her head and told me that she never devotes that much time to getting ready for a new hire. She said she uses three headhunters, and it saves her a lot of time.

"I asked her about their turnover, and she just gave me a stern look, got up, and moved away. I guess I hit a sore spot."

"You have to wonder how the headhunter culture survives." Linda responded. "My previous company used headhunters and our turnover was terrible. It will be interesting to see how we decide to do our sourcing."

Everyone was back in the room, and Ron began the meeting. "I want to discuss sourcing, but first I asked Mary to write a posting. Here is what she wrote for us to consider—follow along while I read it to you."

A Game Plan for Hiring the Right People

Operations Manager

We are seeking a leader who values the worth and dignity of others and always operates from the highest levels of integrity. Optimistic and goal-oriented, this person gets work done and knows how to execute the plan. A servant leader, this person really cares about others and is sensitive and responsive to their needs.

The responsibilities for this coach include, but are not limited to:
- supervising the operations team to include evaluating, coaching, and hiring the right people.
- involving team members in decision-making and planning.
- reviewing existing systems and processes.
- enforcing accountability processes.
- maintaining a motivating environment.
- handling contract matters including working with the attorney.

This strategic planner must have:
- 3 years of industry experience.
- 5 years experience managing people.
- 5 years experience in operations.
- be technologically savvy.
- understand the P&L and budgeting processes.

1. If you are a team leader/player who wants to be part of a dynamic group and contribute to the growth of the company, send us a narrative letter about yourself with your current resume.
2. "Notice the posting has four sections," Ron explained. "First is a summary of the *who;* second is a list of responsibilities, the *what;* third, the requirements from the Ticket; and fourth, an

invitation to apply. Also, we weave the *who* throughout the posting. What do you think?"

3. "Can't say I have ever seen a posting like this," Susan said, "and I have been in HR for more years than I will admit. But, it is intriguing."

4. "I like it," Bill said. "But where are the preferred and desired items?"

5. "It is optional as to whether you put them in the posting," Mary replied, "Most of the time those items are not included. From what I was told, it depends on the length of your posting as to whether you add them or not."

6. Ron asked the team, "Look at the first paragraph. Does it describe the person we are seeking for this role?"

7. The group studied the form and then Linda spoke first. "I think it does. Having servant leader in the description tells potential candidates a lot!"

8. "I agree," Sally said.

9. "I think we are doing a good job of communicating some of our values, too," Bill spoke next. "Including the goal-oriented, getting work done, and executing are key, and a candidate reading this should be clear on some of our expectations."

10. "It is not overdone," Susan said. "If we had included more descriptors the post would have been overwhelming."

11. "Then I take it the first paragraph meets your approval and we can move on to the responsibilities," Ron said and directed their attention to the next section.

"I like the phrase, 'include but are not limited to,'" Sam said. "The points we have listed, I think, give the candidates a good idea of what their role will be in our company."

"I agree," said Charlie. "It paints an excellent picture of the overall job responsibilities and leaves the door open to discussion. The lack of specificity, like 'enforcing accountability processes,' should cause a candidate to think and then ask us some specific questions. What they ask can tell us a lot about them."

Ron added, "Charlie, I had just read that exact concept in an article by Spence on LinkedIn. He wrote that when you are interviewing someone, you must give him or her time to ask questions and then you must write down what the person asks you. According to him, what he or she asks provides key insights into the person."

Jovial and practical Bill then spoke up, "What about the person who says they do not have any questions. What does that tell us?"

"Well," Ralph began, "it tells me it is time to move on to another candidate. It's like when a candidate comes to an interview without pen and paper. That also tells you a lot about him or her. At least that is my humble opinion."

"Quick!" Sam laughingly said. "Someone note that Ralph just became humble! There might be lightning bolts coming down, so use your duck-and-cover skills from grade school and get under the table."

Everyone laughed as Sam got under the table.

Ralph grinned and said, "I will give you that one, Sam. But know this: I like to get even, so be on guard."

Sam got back up on his chair amid more laughter.

"Thanks for the humor guys," Ron said. "We needed that. Now back on task. Take a look at the requirements. Mary wrote them exactly as we had established them. Are you still in favor of these as the requirements?"

"I have a question." Sally asked. "Does a candidate need all five requirements to be considered, or is there some flexibility?"

Susan replied, "All five. A legal requirement says if you have posted requirements, you cannot hire anyone who does not have all the requirements."

"Really?" Bill asked.

"Yes, Bill, all the requirements," Susan said.

"But, no one really follows that, right?" Bill asked.

Susan replied. "There are more companies that do not adhere to this than there are that adhere to it. It might be ignorance of the regulation, or more often, I think, they are just going to do what they want, no matter what the regulation is."

Bill continued to pursue this issue. "In my previous company, I think we must have broken this rule every time we hired. To be honest, I have done the same thing here in hiring for my department."

Ralph jumped into the conversation. "Susan, report Bill to the authorities!"

Once again the room filled with laughter.

"Thanks, Ralph," Bill continued. "Let's assume I have a resume from a candidate and they have almost all the requirements. All they lack is, instead of five years of people management experience, they only have four years of experience. In that case, could we include them? I mean, it's only one year short, and they have or exceed all of the other requirements."

"Like I told Sally earlier, no, Bill," Susan replied. "It is all or nothing. Period."

"Is that your final answer, or can I call a friend, as that one game show used to allow people to do?" Bill responded.

Letting the laughter fade away, Susan replied, "It is my final answer; and no, you cannot call a friend." She smiled.

"Well, I think we are all clear on the requirements, even Bill," Ron said. "Now take a look at the final paragraph. Simply stated, this invites candidates to apply—in other words, send us a current resume along with a narrative letter about themselves. Anyone have any edits?"

"I am okay with it," Linda said. "But can you describe a narrative letter?"

Susan answered, "Linda, I read some of the information Ron has on Spence's Choosing Winners© System, and I found that companies will ask for a cover letter, and some candidates include a cover letter without any request. In Spence's system, they ask for a narrative letter to differentiate it from a cover letter. The concept is that in a narrative letter, a person will write about their accomplishments and/or successes, as well as something unique about him or her. This gives you more insights into the person. Whereas, all a cover letter states is: 'Here is my resume.'"

"I wonder how many people take the time to write a narrative letter. Did you find anything about that, Susan?" Sam asked.

"According to what I found in my research, only about twenty percent of candidates will include a narrative letter," Susan replied.

"Assume a candidate does not include a narrative letter." Sam added, "Is that person eliminated from the search?"

"No," Susan replied. "It is not a requirement. But they have missed an opportunity to really share with us what drives them."

"Any other comments on the final paragraph?" Ron asked. "Hearing none, I assume that we agree. Now, let's talk about what is next."

"Do we need to take one more once-over to make sure there are no typos or words misspelled, and then we can post the job announcement?" Bill said.

"Correct, Bill," Ron replied. "Susan we will put this in your hands. You do all of our other job postings, so it only makes sense for you to do this one, too."

Bill replied. "No problem, Ron, I can do that. Do you want me to place it on any unique sites or just in the ones where I usually post job announcements?"

"Do your usual postings," Ron said. "However, I want us to do something beyond the postings. I am going to send the posting in an email to my contacts, letting them know we are looking for an operations leader and asking them to share the posting with those who they believe might have an interest. Can we all do this?" He noted everyone nodding and exclaimed, "Okay, then, let's get the ball rolling!"

"Susan, before you go, I have a question," Ron said. "Are you still sending an email to everyone who sends us a resume, regardless of their qualifications?"

"I am," she replied. "I think that is respectful of the time a person spends to respond and send a resume. It is the right thing to do. Years ago my mentor told me that the way you conduct a hiring process and respond to candidates tells a lot about your company and your culture. He also added that when you tell someone you will get back to them at a certain date and time, you need to follow through and do it."

"That is one smart mentor," Ron replied. "Please show me what the email will be for this position."

Susan replied, "I thought you might ask that, so I prepared one and have a draft copy with me." She handed Ron a copy.

Thank you for responding to our posting for an Operations Manager and sending us your resume. We are currently receiving resumes for the next few days before beginning our interviews. Here is our hiring process:

We begin with an initial telephone screener interview. This takes about forty-five minutes. Following that, we select candidates for the second, more in-depth telephone interview that takes about an hour. We will then narrow the field to between three and six top candidates and do a one-to-one video interview. We will bring the top three candidates into the company for a series of interviews and assessments.

If you do not hear from us by June _____, 20__, you have not been selected for the initial telephone screener interview.

"Thanks, Susan," Ron said. "This is excellent. Unless someone has any more questions, I believe our work is done for now. Thanks everyone for giving your time to work on this new process to find a new Charlie. Just a side note: Susan and the HR team will work on resume evaluations and will report back to us once this step is completed. Have a good evening everyone."

As everyone started to leave the room, Ron turned to Susan. "Do you have a minute?"

"I do," she said.

"You have been in HR for several years," Ron began. "After going through this exercise, how do you feel about it?"

"Ron, I really like it," she said. "It is thorough, complete, and is totally consistent with our value system. Is it a little tedious? Yes. Will it typically take longer to make a hire? Probably. Is it perfect? No. But, it is so much better than anything else I have seen, and we will have fewer hiring mistakes and lower turnover. I do have a question."

"What is it?"

"We are basically using the Choosing Winners© System. Do we have authorization to use it?"

"That's a good question," he replied. "No, we do not have authorization to use it."

"Is that a concern?" She asked.

"I don't think so," Ron replied. "Brenda at Mid-Town HVAC has given us the information about the system, and they are authorized with a license agreement. I assume it transfers to us. Also, Spence was a speaker at one of our peer group meetings. I missed that meeting, but our chair, Brandon, always has said that when a speaker talks at our group meeting we can use the materials presented without any agreement with the speaker. He claims the honorarium paid to them covers us in using the materials."

"I understand your assumption," Susan said. "It would sure be beneficial for us to get the training on the Choosing Winners© System; then we will know we are authorized. It might be prudent to do some research or even contact the consultant and ask point blank if we can use the materials. Think about it, and we can talk about that later."

"Good point," he said. "I agree the training would be good to do, and it might be wise to check with the consultant and not rely on what others say. I will get the details and get back to you."

Prepare a clear and specific job posting.

Chapter 8

RESUME EVALUATION

After several days, resumes began to arrive. Ron called together the Leadership Team to discuss the scoring method, and the group slowly gathered in the conference room.

"Are these scones store bought, or are we blessed with Mary's homemade scones?" Ron asked.

Mary smiled. "They are my creation, Ron, and there are blueberry, cherry, and apple, so choose what you want and enjoy!"

"I sure will," he said. "I will take a blueberry one."

"Go for it," Mary said. "The coffee is freshly brewed."

"Thank you," Ron replied, as he turned to speak to Susan. "Good morning, how was the quilting last evening?"

"I had a great time," she said. "Sally has a real talent in choosing and matching the colors on a quilt. I am learning so much about quilting, and I thought I knew a lot before I joined this group! It is so gratifying to work with the other ladies, knowing that the quilts we make will be given to someone in need. I really like the fact that the quilts are not quilted, but that we put ties on them and then people at Church tie a knot and say a prayer."

"That's great," Ron said as he turned to speak to Sam. "How is the band?"

"Thanks for asking." Sam said. "We are improving weekly. And Mary keeps giving us opportunities to play at her coffee shop. This weekend we will be at Mary's shop, and we have some new numbers to play."

"Thanks for the information," Ron replied. "My wife and I will be there to listen!"

Noticing that everyone had arrived, Ron began the meeting.

"I called Brenda at Mid-Town HVAC and read more on the Choosing Winners© System. I learned that they actually score resumes," Ron said. "At first I thought, *How on earth would you score a resume?* But after she explained the process it made a lot of sense."

"Score resumes?" Susan asked. "I have been in HR for a long time and have reviewed numerous resumes. I have never heard that you can score them. That has to be a whole lot better than reading page after page. Tell me how that is done."

"Better yet, I can show you," Ron said, and he passed out a copy of a resume scoring format to the Team members (see page 64).

"Well that sort of helps," Sally said. "I could use some explanations."

"I agree," said Susan. "Give us some help here Ron."

Ron picked up the sheet of paper with the sample resume scoring on it and said, "Pick up your copy, and let's walk through the process. I am very new to this, and it will help me to walk through it with you."

"We start with the requirements," Ron continued. "You list all of the requirements and our form will have five lines for our five requirements. Note that if they have the requirement you will give ten points. If not, you give it an NQ, meaning not qualified.

"Now there may be times when you are not sure if the requirement is met. In those cases give a zero and score the rest of the resume. When all the scoring is complete, if even with the zero, this candidate has a high score, call the candidate and get some clarity. If, after the call, you still believe the requirement is not met, mark it NQ, and eliminate the candidate from the search process."

Linda asked, "When do you usually need clarity on a requirement?"

REQUIRED

_____ YES (10)   NO (NQ)_____

_____ YES (10)   NO (NQ)_____

_____ YES (10)   NO (NQ)_____

PREFERRED (30 - 60 POINTS)

_____ YES (10)   NO (NQ)_____

_____ YES (10)   NO (NQ)_____

_____ YES (10)   NO (NQ)_____

DESIRED (20 - 35 POINTS)

_____ YES (10)   NO (NQ)_____

_____ YES (10)   NO (NQ)_____

_____ YES (10)   NO (NQ)_____

_____

TOTAL _____

ACTION: _____Screen _____Hold _____Reject

"Good question, Linda," Ron replied. "Typically, it involves the number of years of experience. If the requirement is five years, and you are not sure the candidate has five years, call and ask a simple question as to how much experience in operations the person has completed. Accept their answer, either way, and record ten points or NQ."

Sally said, "I think we earlier said that if a candidate only has four or five requirements, but has all the preferred and desired items, they are still not qualified?"

"Exactly. They are not qualified," Ron said. "That is why you want to make sure that you really need to have the requirements."

"I am beginning to really like this scoring," Susan said. "With the preferred items, it looks like we need to assign point values."

"Correct," Ron answered. "The point range for preferred is thirty to sixty points. We assign sixty points to the most important preference and then scale down to the last one. In our case, for this search, we only have two preferred items, a bachelor's degree and experience in a family-owned business. In my opinion, I would give sixty points to experience in a family-owned business and fifty points to a bachelor's degree. What do you think?"

Everyone on the Team nodded.

"Now the desired items." said Ron. "We have seven items and the point range for desired is twenty to thirty-five."

"I know it does not affect us with this position, but a desired item could have more points than a preferred item, assuming I understand the scoring?" Susan stated.

"Correct," Ron answered. "As it was explained to me, at times you realize a desired is more important than initially thought. This gives you the latitude to change."

Mary interrupted, "Let's list the desired items in our order of priority and then assign point values."

"Good idea," Sally agreed. "I will get us started. I believe of the seven desired items, the most important to me is experience in sales."

Bill added to the scoring, "I think that experience in marketing is next. I believe an operations leader really needs to understand marketing."

Charlie added, "Let's put EOS next. I know we are just now researching it, but I am sensing that Ron has a high interest in EOS."

Ron smiled at Charlie.

"I think next is a degree major in business," Susan added. "It sure can't hurt."

"This is getting difficult," Sam said. "Of the four remaining, I am not excited at all about any of them and really don't care where they fall on the list."

"I agree," Susan said. "When we set the points we can give them the same, and I think it should be the minimum."

"I agree," Ron said. "Mary please list these three at the bottom, and now I think we can set point totals."

Mary listed them at the end of the list. "All set," she said.

Ron got everyone started. "Of the requirements, which is most important to us?"

"For me, it is all about the people," Susan stated. "We have talked about wanting a people person. I think five years of people management experience is the most important."

"I agree with Susan," Linda said. "Our company culture very much focuses on our people, so we need someone who values all people and knows how to work with them."

"I need just a little clarity," Ralph said. "How do we define people management?"

Ron answered. "It means that this person has at least five years experience with direct reports, responsible for their evaluation and development. It also includes having been responsible for hiring and taking necessary disciplinary actions."

"Thanks," Ralph answered. "I agree with that explanation. How about the rest of you?"

Charlie, Linda, Sam, Bill, and Sally all nodded.

Ron said, "With it as the most important, we can give it ten points."

"I am not sure I understand where the ten points comes from for this item," Bill said, slightly raising his hand.

Ron explained, "According to the system, required items all receive ten points. A candidate either has the requirement or not. On the form, when a resume is evaluated, the evaluator gives ten points if the requirement is clearly evident and a zero if it is not clear. If the candidate clearly does not have a requirement, the evaluator records an NQ for 'not qualified' and stops evaluating the resume. It really does not make a difference what order the requirements are on the form. I just want it clear how they rank in overall importance."

"That makes sense," Bill responded. "Thanks."

"Let's save some time," Ron said. "I think we can list them in this order, operations experience, industry experience, technology, and P&L. Everyone agree with that? How about a show of hands?" All the team members raised their hands.

"Remind me as to the points for preferred items," Sally said.

Ron replied, "There is a range from thirty points to sixty points. I asked Brenda Ross, at Mid-Town HVAC, why thirty to sixty, and she said because that is the way the trainer taught them. She also said that the trainer said the point totals can be whatever the company wants to use. At this time, I would like to stay with the recommended points and we can take a look at it later if we decide to implement this hiring system."

"I agree," Susan said. "This time we only have two items—experience in a family-owned business and a bachelor's degree, so we will not have much of a point spread."

Sam spoke next. "I think family-owned experience should have sixty points and a degree only forty points."

"I am okay with that," Ron said. "Show of hands if you agree." As he noted all the raised hands, he continued, "Now let's deal with the desired items. I had Mary list them in the order I believe reflects our opinions. Mary please read the items."

Mary read the items, and then she asked, "Is everyone okay with the order I just read? If so, again a show of hands."

The team agreed, and all hands were raised.

Ralph spoke first. "I would like to give sales and marketing experience both thirty-five points. I do not see where one is more valuable than the other."

Sally said, "I agree Ralph. What do you think Bill?"

"I agree," Bill said.

Charlie said, "Ron, I know you are really considering EOS. If this is a possibility, I would also give this item thirty points."

"I am really getting interested in EOS," Ron replied. "I agree and would like to give it thirty points. Everyone okay with that?"

All the members nodded.

"I have a suggestion," Susan said. "I would just give the last four items twenty points each. I do not see any significant difference."

Ron replied, "I agree. Mary set the final four at twenty points each. Now we have the score form ready, and Susan will be in charge of resume evaluation. At our meeting next week, I want Susan to spend time going over how to do a telephone-screener interview. You will probably not do the telephone screeners, but it is important that you understand how it works, so when you receive the results you will understand what it all means. Please add about thirty minutes to your calendars for that meeting. Thanks for your work today!"

Resume Score Form: Operations Manager

REQUIRED

5 years people management experience: YES (10)   NO (NQ) _____
5 years of operations experience: YES (10)   NO (NQ) _____
3 years industry experience:
(manufacturing) _____ YES (10)   NO (NQ) _____
Technologically savvy: _____ YES (10)   NO (NQ) _____
Understands P&L and budgeting processes: YES (10) NO (NQ) _____

PREFERRED (30 - 60 POINTS)

Experience in a family-owned business: YES (60)   NO (0) _____
Bachelor's degree: _____ YES (40)   NO (0)   _____

DESIRED (20 - 35 POINTS)

Experience in sales: _____ YES (35)   NO (0)   _____
Experience in marketing Knowledge/
experience with EOS: _____ YES (30)   NO (0)   _____
Degree major in Business: ____ YES (20)   NO (0)   _____
Holds an MBA: _____ YES (20)   NO (0)   _____
Five years senior management experience: YES (20) NO (0) _____
Experience with customer service: YES (20)   NO (0)   _____
                                        TOTAL   _____
ACTION: _____ Screen _____ Hold _____ Reject _____

Score resumes; do not read them.

Chapter 9

TELEPHONE SCREENING

The next week, the Leadership Team convened at 9:30 a.m. on Monday morning for their regular meeting, and they added thirty minutes to learn about telephone screening.

"Hey, Sam," Ralph said. "As a musician, do you ever take time to watch musical talent competitions or other types of talent shows?"

"Sometimes," Sam replied. "Why do you ask?"

"Just curious," Ralph said, "I happened to watch a vocal talent competition last evening, and it was actually interesting."

"I have found that all are excellent." Sam answered. "I really like pure singing and the quality of the performers is really good. I enjoy playing my guitar, but do not ask me to sing. You will regret it if you do."

"And he plays a mean guitar!" Mary chimed in. "His band is a favorite of our customers at the coffee shop."

"Just curious, Sam, but what is your favorite genre?" Bill asked.

"I like most of them, but I guess I really am a country guy," Sam replied.

"Me too," Bill said, "On the way to the office this morning, I was playing the local country station and heard Carrie Underwood singing, 'Jesus Take the Wheel,' and it really helped me change my attitude."

"Great song," Sam said. "It really makes you think."

Ralph joined the conversation. "Will I ever see you and your band on *a talent show*? And, just in case, may I have an autograph now?"

"Sure Ralph," Sam said. "That will be fifty dollars."

"Fifty dollars!" Ralph exclaimed.

Sam quickly came back, "Okay, if you insist, seventy-five dollars."

Bill saw an opportunity to join in. "Ralph you better agree quickly or the price will only be going up!"

"Listen to Bill," Sam said. "The price will increase in five minutes."

Just then Linda joined the men. "What are you doing? Bidding on something?"

Everyone laughed, and Sam said, "Ralph wants to buy my autograph."

"Save your money, Ralph," Linda replied. "I have his signature on several forms and you can copy it from one of them."

The group, seeing Ron standing at the front of the room, realized it was time to stop the chatter and take their seats.

Ron called the meeting to order. "Let's do our round table sharing, give our department reports, and have Ralph review financials. Then we will review the telephone screening process."

The team got to work, and when they completed the agenda, Ron said, "I have asked Susan to lead the discussion about the screening process. She has done more research and met with Brenda, the HR leader at Mid-Town HVAC, who uses the system. It's all yours, Susan."

"Thanks, Ron," Susan replied. "I have learned a lot about this, and I am anxious to share my discoveries with all of you. The screening process consists of a three-part telephone interview. It begins with the interviewer studying the resume of the candidate before the telephone call and preparing specific questions to ask the candidate.

"As they pointed out to me, if you don't prepare, then don't make the telephone call. Also, you make initial contact with the candidate through an email in which you offer a list of dates and times that are available, instructing the candidate to select three times that work.

When you have the replies from all of the candidates, set your interview schedule and email each candidate his or her date and time."

"Susan," Bill asked, "is this the first contact with the candidate, this request for interview dates and times?"

"No," Susan replied. "They told me they send an email to all the people who sent in a resume. Basically, they thank them for applying and give a brief summary of the process.

I like this part of the process a lot. Let me read you the email I am using for our search, which is based on their example.

Initial Candidate Email

"Thank you for sending us your resume in response to our posting

for an Operation Manager. We are currently receiving and evaluating resumes. Our process has several steps. We begin with an initial telephone screener interview followed by a second more intensive telephone interview, and then an online interview. Our goal is to have three top individuals selected for an on-site interview day in our offices. If you do not receive an email inviting you to set an interview time by [fill in the date], you have not been selected to participate in our process. Thank you."

"I think you said you are using this now for our search?" Sally asked.

"I am," Susan replied.

"Good," Sally said. "I like it. I have never seen this done. However, if I were the candidate, I would sure appreciate having an idea of the process. I am sure, for many candidates, this is the first time they have had a response to their resume submission. I think it really enhances our image as a company."

"When they get the email asking for dates and times, they should not be surprised," Charlie said. "Like Sally said, I like it and see many benefits."

Susan replied. "Let me read to you the email asking for dates and times. I will send all of you a copy of each email:

Second Candidate Email

"Recently, you received an email from us acknowledging that we received a copy of your resume in response to our posting for an Operations Manager. Please accept this as your invitation to participate in our process. Below, I have listed several dates and times that are available for interviews. Typically, these average about 45 minutes. Please select at least three dates and times that you can be available for an interview and send your selections back to me by email. I will respond to you within 24 hours after receiving your email. Please note that all times are EDT. You will need to convert the times to your time zone.

"I won't read you all the dates and times since you will have a copy."

Ralph asked, "Did Brenda at Mid-Town give any indication as to how well this is working for them in their hiring?"

Susan answered, "They did, Ralph, and it was totally positive. They have been using this process for about three years, now."

"I think we took you off track with our questions," Ron said. "However, I am glad we took this detour, as it has proved very valuable to us in understanding the system. I continue to be impressed by the thoroughness of this system."

Susan continued. "Back to the task at hand. The three parts of the initial telephone screener are first a resume review or, as they told me they call it, an interrogation."

"Interrogation?" Bill interjected. "Really, they call it an interrogation?"

Susan, laughing, answered. "That's what they told me."

"Anyone here have experience as a detective?" Bill asked facetiously.

"Actually, Bill," Susan replied, laughing, "Not that bad of an idea.

Perhaps a little extreme, but they also stressed to me that they view the hiring process as a discovery process. That really made a lot of sense to me."

"I agree," Sam said. "We need to discover all we can about candidates before they begin to work here. Everyone has strengths, and everyone has weaknesses, or as I learned earlier, vulnerabilities. We must know all we can before we offer a job."

Linda was sitting at the table intently listening to her team members when she commented, "I'm not sure I like the word interrogation, but I fully understand learning all we can about a candidate before the job offer. Susan, how does this interrogation work?"

Bill jumped into the conversation. "That's easy. We tell the candidate we are going to ask a lot of questions about their resume. We tell them, 'It is important that you tell the truth and nothing but the truth. I want you to know that I will be making note of any inconsistencies, and if necessary, bring you into the office for a lie detector test.'"

"Oh, my goodness!" Sally exclaimed. "You can't be serious!" At this point the team broke into laughter as Bill sat with a big grin on his face.

"All joking aside," Ron said, "I think whoever is doing the interview needs to be well prepared, thorough, and firm with the candidate. I had a mentor several years ago who told me that resumes were marketing tools. He said that most resumes do not have blatant lies on them, but nearly all resumes are enhanced, like most marketing pieces for most companies. The resume puts the candidate in the best light possible. Our job is to go past the light and into the dark areas and discover the truth. Susan take us through a resume interrogation."

Susan explained, "Of course you have to prepare before you call the candidate. Go through their resume and cross-check for the requirements, preferred and desired items. Be prepared to ask for clarification and examples as needed."

"Brenda at Mid-Town said that if the resume indicates the person is still in a current employment situation, she will ask if that is correct, and if he or she is still employed. She indicated that many times the person will respond that when they sent the resume they were employed but that things had changed since they emailed the resume."

"If that happens do we disqualify the person?" Ralph asked.

"No," Susan said. "She told me she will ask them what changed. Depending on the response, follow up with appropriate probing questions. However, I need to take a step back. When they answer the call, she will introduce herself and use an icebreaker question. And she stressed that the question cannot be political or religious."

"Oh, but I assume I can ask them a sports-related question and whether or not they are an Ohio State Buckeye fan! We really need more Buckeye fans on this team," Bill added.

"Probably you could get away with that," Susan responded. "But are we really going to ask sports-related questions?"

Bill continued. "I guess not. So then I guess we ask them when they were born and where they go to church."

"You can't be serious!" Susan replied.

"Just trying to test you," Bill said with a big smile on his face. "Seriously, what might be a good ice breaker?"

Susan said. "That is a good question. You could use a weather-related question, a question about where they live, and maybe who their favorite author is and the last book they read. You have a lot of options. Just remember to plan it in advance and not off the cuff."

"I am with you, Susan," Sally said. "What other things do we need to cover during the interrogation?"

"I would like some guidance too," Sam added. "While I understand I probably will not be doing the telephone screeners, I want to understand the whole process."

Susan replied. "I have been training some of my HR team members to not only score resumes, but also how to do the screeners. They are really excited about being involved and are anxious to begin with the first candidate. Once they complete the screeners, they will prepare a report on each candidate screened. You will understand the report better if you are fully aware of how the screeners were done. With that said, I prepared a list for my HR team members to use and here is a copy of it."

Susan distributed the list.

Screener Interrogation Questions

- Ask them why they have applied for this position.
- If the resume does not have the month and year for beginning and ending of each employment, ask the candidate to provide the information.
- If there are gaps in employment, ask why.
  Ask the candidate if the resume is accurate and complete regarding all past employment.
- Whether a degree is required or not, ask candidates their degree status.
- Ask the candidate for the reasons they left their previous positions.
- Ask the candidate what are their expectations for compensation. If their salary is way beyond the position's salary, you need to terminate the interview.
- If the candidate is not from the area where the position is based, ask about relocation issues.
- Inquire about and discuss any claims made on the resume, in relation to goals achieved, sales records, or increased profits for example.

Susan asked the group if they had any questions. Ralph immediately raised a hand.

"I assume," he said. "That you get the months and years of employment in each position to determine if their are any gaps. Why?"

"It is part of the discovery process," Susan explained. "It goes along with asking them the reason they left each employment. Were they looking for a new opportunity? Were they part of a lay-off? Were they dismissed?

"Brenda told me that she reviewed a resume once, and the person had an eight year gap in employment. She learned the candidate had given birth to two children during that time. Obviously, the gap was not a problem. However, she said to me, 'You need to consider when the gap occurred. Was it current? Or one or two positions previously?'

"If the gap is current we may need to include some things about industry changes in the onboarding program for this candidate. Discover, discover and discover some more. Any other questions?

"Not sure about asking about a degree," Charlie said. "For example, in our situation a degree is not required. So why even ask?"

"That is an excellent question, Charlie," Susan responded. "First, if a degree is required, you need to say to the candidate, 'I see you have a degree from State University. Did you graduate?'

"Brenda Ross told me that she asked this of a candidate once. He wanted to know why she was asking. She told him that she just wanted to double-check it with him before calling the university to confirm it.

"'You'll call the university?' He had asked.

"She told him that she would and that they would tell her yes or no about the degree, but nothing else. He told her to save her time because not only did he not graduate, but he hadn't even attended the university.

"'Why is it on your resume?' she had asked him. He told her he wasn't getting any calls to interviews so a friend had said he needed to list a degree and that no one would check. So she told him he would not be considered for the position.

"The bottom line is," Susan explained, "if they have a degree on their resume, ask about it—even if you do not have a degree as required, preferred, or desired. This is an integrity issue. If they will do this on a resume, what else will they lie about?"

"Susan," Sam asked. "Why do they ask salary information?"

Susan thought for a minute and said. "I was trying to remember what she told me. Got it. She said why waste time with a candidate you cannot afford. She also added that when she asks for their salary level, she will divulge the range for the position. Any other questions?"

"Could you explain claims made on the resume?" Linda asked. "I am not clear on what you are getting at and what questions you would need to ask."

"Sure can," Susan said. "Assume a candidate indicates that they have increased sales for the company by 70 percent in one year. This cannot go unchallenged. You might want to ask the dollar total compared to company revenue. Or you might want to ask if anyone helped the person achieve this increase?

"I could go on and on, but this is a good example of preparing before the interview so you know what to ask. Make sense?"

Everyone nodded and Ron said, "You are doing a great job of explaining this to us. Thank you for being so well prepared. And you are training your staff on this, as they will be doing the actual interviews. I am really excited about this process and beginning to see how it would help us hire the right fit and match for our company. Take us to the second part of the screener."

"Again you have to be prepared," Susan said. "You will need to prepare three to five questions pertaining to the duties and responsibilities. We have done this for our operations manager search, and I will share them with you,"

Susan gave everyone a copy of the questions.

"Let's review them and I can explain as needed."

---

1. How many employees have you typically supervised in your previous positions?

Were you responsible for evaluating their performance?* (if yes) Describe the evaluation system you used.*

Tell me about a time when you had an employee not meeting expectations and what you did.*

In this position, you will be expected to be a coach for your employees. Tell me about a time you had to coach an employee and the success you achieved.*

Now tell me about a time when you coached someone, and you did not achieve the results you wanted.*

After everyone had read the questions Susan asked, "Any questions?"

"I have one," Bill said. "What is the deal with the asterisk?"

"Funny you should ask," Susan responded. "Those are stop signs telling the interviewer to stop and listen. Keep in mind that their answers to questions may prompt you to ask a follow-up question not on your list."

Sam spoke up. "You really have five questions here, not one, if I am reading this right."

"Correct," Susan replied. "They all pertain to one area of responsibility."

Ron interjected, "Susan I really like this style of questioning. You don't have to be thinking of your next question and miss what the candidate is saying. You can really focus on their words and how they are saying it. I like the 'Tell me about a time when . . . ' question. That brings it down to reality. If they answer correctly, you get to hear what they have done. Love it! I am anxious review the next question."

"Thanks, Ron," said Susan. "You have the next question in writing, but let me quickly read it for you," Susan read the next question:

---

2. How effective have you been in hiring new employees to join your team?*

When you need to hire a new employee, what process do you use; your own, company mandated or an off the shelf program?*

Assume you are hiring a new employee. Tell me the characteristics, traits, behaviors and values you are seeking in your new hire.*

Mis-hires are expensive, and we have all had at least one. Tell me about one of your mis-hires.*

Now tell me about one of your best hires ever and why this was your best hire.*

"Wow!" Ralph exclaimed. "I like these questions. Where has this been all the years I have been hiring people? I love the question having them describe a mis-hire."

"Susan this is fantastic!" Sally said. "It really brings value to interviewing, and I think it actually makes it fun."

"Fun?" Bill replied. "I admit I like this, but I am really struggling as to how hiring can be fun. Enlighten me."

"That's easy," Susan said. "First, when you are interviewing a person, you want to find the right fit and match to improve the team.

That's fun. When you are interviewing a person, think about how much you can learn about them, yes, but also the ideas they share with you. To me, that's fun!"

"You make a good argument," Bill responded. "Bring on the fun!"

"Just for you, Bill," Susan responded to Bill's humor. "We do appreciate you and your ability to lighten the mood for us. Any more comments or questions? Seeing none I will move to the third and final question."

---

3. Would you describe yourself as a motivator of others?* (if yes) Tell me how you do that.* (if no) Why do you feel that way?*

As a manager do you involve your employees in planning, decision-making and implementing?* (if yes) Tell me about a time when you involved your employees in one of these activities.*

In your opinion does involving others result in any benefits for the individual, team or company?*

Tell me about your overall expectations for those that you supervise.*

"There you have it," Susan stated. "Our three technical job questions. Any questions or comments on the third and final question?"

"I have a question for Ron," Sam said. "How would you like the candidate to answer the section on motivating?"

Ron thought for a minute and said, "I hope they say no, or that they are not a motivator of others, but are a person who creates a motivating environment. If you held a gun to the head of someone or a knife against their throat, in that situation you could legitimately lay claim to being a motivator. In most cases, if not all, the drive to survive would motivate you to do whatever the attacker wanted you to do."

"And there are managers who use fear to—so they think—to motivate others. I want the focus to be on creating that special environment that people thrive and grow within. A fit-and-match candidate will creatively weave the answer to all of these sections together."

"The third part of the screener is a structured, validated interview," Susan said. "We do not have access to it at this time officially. However, Brenda's CEO has allowed her to give us a copy to review."

"Can we have a copy?" Linda asked. "I would love to study it and see how it might help us."

"I made a commitment to Brenda that I would only share it with those trained by Brenda," Susan said. "If, down the road, we buy in to this system we can be trained and certified."

Ralph commented. "I understand and have no problem with it. However, can you at least describe how it works?"

"What do you think, Ron?" Susan asked.

Ron answered. "I see no problem with your explaining to the team the structured screener and how it works."

"Thanks, Ron," Susan replied. "Anticipating that I would be able to explain this structured screener, I made a list describing the interview,"

Susan gave each team member a copy of the list and then read it to them.

- The interview was developed, based on a research study of outstanding managers.

- There are eight questions dealing with purpose, values, communication, responsiveness to others, listening, delegation, demeanor, planning and related activities, and involvement of others.

- The interviewer reads the questions, telling the candidate that questions can be re-read but never explained.

- The process is called content coding. The answer given by the candidate is compared to the validated answer from the research study and a letter symbol is used to denote whether it is consistent or not consistent with the research.

"Question?" Ralph asked. "Are the results on this interview the determinant factor in deciding whether a candidate moves on to the next step or is rejected? Or am I missing something here?"

Ron answered. "No. Susan please explain how the decision-making is done."

"This may be a little complicated, so listen carefully," Susan said. "I will welcome any and all questions, except of course from Bill." She grinned at him.

"Ah shucks," Bill said. "I already had prepared a list!"

"Okay, here we go," Susan said. "First, the structured screener results are not the sole factor in deciding if a candidate advances to the next step. Let me list for you some key items in the decision-making process,"

Susan handed out a one-sheet document with all of the key points listed.

SELECTING CANDIDATES FROM THE SCREENER

- The actual submitted resume.

- The Resume Score Form.

- Results from the Resume Interrogation.

- Results from the three technical questions.

- Results from the Structured Screener.

"As you can see," Susan began her explanation, "we have five decision points. You need to review all of the decision points to determine who advances.

"First, the actual resume. What is your overall opinion? Is it professional? Any punctuation or spelling errors? Is it easy to follow? Any questions?"

"Just one," Sam said. "After I review it, where do I record my observations?"

"Good question," Susan said. "We have a Summary Sheet that the interviewer—or you if you do your own interviews—completes after finishing the screener. I will give each of you a copy. We are in the process of having it produced in a PDF fillable form to save everyone time and give us the ability to email it to the hiring manager in each search."

"Now that is a new one to me," Bill said. "Hiring manager? Oh, and that is not one of my prepared questions, just so you know."

"At any given time one of us may be the hiring manager," Susan said. "For example, Ron is the hiring manager for our operations leader search. Bill, if you were hiring someone for your team, you would be the hiring manager. Whoever the new hire reports to is the hiring manager. Ideally, the hiring manager will involve his or her team in the interview process."

"Thanks," said Bill.

"Now on to the resume score form," Susan said. "The interviewer needs to cross check everything to ensure it is accurate. It is most important to make sure the requirements were judged correctly. Any questions?"

"Does the hiring manager get a copy of the score form?" Ralph asked.

"Absolutely," said Susan. "The hiring manager gets a copy of everything, and my HR team member working on the search will sit down with the hiring manager and go over everything."

"That sounds like a lot of time. In fact this process seems to take a lot of time," Bill said.

"It does," Ron jumped into the conversation. "Compare this time to hiring the wrong person and dealing with a mis-hire on the team, having to go through a termination and then doing the whole process again. I believe this process, while obviously not perfect, provides the best way to hire the right fit and match."

"I could not agree more," Linda said. "This will really be beneficial in hiring people in our manufacturing facility. I am assuming we would use the same process with all hiring."

Ron replied. "Yes, but you do make some adjustments depending upon the position. For example, I understand Brenda told Susan there are three different structured screener interviews: manager, general, and sales."

"Thanks, Ron. "Susan said. "The report the hiring manage receives gives all of the information we acquire in the screening process, including extensive notes on the resume interrogation, technical questions, and the structured screener results. As you leave the meeting you will receive a copy of the Screener Summary Sheet, and if you have any questions, just ask me."

"Sounds good, Susan," Ron said. "We can adjourn for now, and Susan will send out a meeting notice when she is ready to continue taking us through the process. I am assuming she can give us some examples from the hiring process at that time."

"I will make that happen," Susan said. And the meeting adjourned.

Telephone Screeners consist of three parts.

Chapter 10

TRAINING ON SCORING

Susan assigned three HR team members to the search. They were tasked with doing the resume scoring and telephone interviews for the hiring manager, Ron, saving him hours of time and giving him thorough information to use in his decision-making process.

As part of the process, Susan met with her team members: Maria Smith, Cathy Douglas, and Mark Hart.

"Good morning everyone," Susan said. "There is coffee on the counter along with some scones that Mary made."

"You ladies please go first," Mark said. "Once I get close to Mary's scones, I cannot stop eating them."

"Mark, is there anything you do not eat?" Cathy asked.

"Liver." He answered.

"Not even soaked in onions?" Maria asked.

"Not even onions or peppers or special sauce, no liver period." He said.

"Maria, tell us about your interest in quilting," Susan said.

"I wanted a hobby, and Susan and Sally introduced me to quilting and I love it. Cathy is also getting involved in quilting," Maria said.

"How about you, Mark? Are you interested in quilting?" Susan asked.

"Ah, no," he said. "I will stick with golf. And I am considering being part of the golfing tournament Bill is promoting and it is for charity."

"Okay, let's turn our attention to the task at hand. I have had several excellent meetings with the Leadership Team," Susan said. "They agree with this process and are anxious to see what we can provide for them. I assume we have the position posted and emails to our contacts done?"

"Done," said Mark. "The posting is on three Internet sites and we have sent out 100 emails to our contacts."

"And how many resumes have we received?" Susan asked.

"As of this morning, we have seventy resumes," Cathy replied. "We will begin scoring resumes tomorrow."

"We have the resume scoring form that you and the team developed," said Maria. "We would like to go over it with you to make sure we are clear on all the details."

"We will do that in a few minutes," Susan said. "I need to let you know how important the resume scoring is. Brenda at Mid-Town HVAC told me they made a major mistake while implementing the process. They had prepared the score form and then gave it to some team members without doing any training. She said they thought anyone could use a form and record information accurately. They finished all of the scoring and began screening. Out of every ten resumes, nine did not meet all of the requirements because the scorers missed a step. They had to start over. So she said we have to make sure we train our people.

"Can you imagine having to go back to square one because you skipped one step?"

"Oh, I can," Mark replied. "I stand here guilty as charged!"

"Wow!" exclaimed Cathy. "What did you do or not do?"

Mark answered, "We were putting out our first client newsletter, and I was assigned to do the final proofreading. I glanced through it and thought it looked okay, so I did not do a complete proofread. Needless to say, I made a big mistake.

"We sent it to print and when it came back, you know what hit the fan. I have never forgotten this, and I never take short cuts. I learned the hard way."

"Did you lose your job?" Cathy asked.

"No," Mark replied, "I was given a reprimand and informed that should anything like that happen again, I was out the door."

"Well," said Susan, "let's keep you on this side of the door and get busy and review the resume score form. Then we will go through training on doing the telephone screener interview."

"Works for me," Mark responded. "I like this side of the door.'

Susan explained, "You have in front of you the Resume Score Form developed and approved by the Leadership Team. Look first at the 'Required' items. Required means there are no exceptions."

REQUIRED

5 years people management experience:YES (10) NO (NQ)_____

5 years of operations experience: 3 years
industry experience (manufacturing)   YES (10)   NO (NQ)_____

Technologically savvy: YES (10)   NO (NQ)_____

Understands P&L and budgeting
processes: YES (10)   NO (NQ)_____

Susan continued. "They must have five years of people management. That means they have supervised, evaluated, and dealt with, let's say, HR issues for direct reports. If you can confirm that on their resume, award the ten points. If not, and you are confident that they do not have five years, record NQ on the line and stop scoring the resume."

"We actually stop after one item?" Cathy asked.

"Yes," Susan answered. "They must have all the requirements, or they are not eligible to be considered for the position."

Mark spoke up. "I have a question. What if it is obvious they have managed people, but I cannot verify five years. Maybe I can verify four-plus years, but am not sure."

"That is when you record a zero on the line, and you continue scoring the resume," Susan answered. "If they appear to be eligible on the overall resume by the results of the scoring, then you call them to cross check the years of experience. That holds true for any items requiring a number of years of experience. Any other questions on this item?"

When no one responded, she continued.

"Next we need to determine if they have three years of operations experience," Susan directed. "Basically, if they do, they will actually have the word 'operations' on their resume. You are all aware of Charlie's duties in our company. Just refresh yourself with what he does, and you will be able to score this item. Record 10 points if they have it. If not, mark NQ, and stop scoring the resume. Again, if you think the number of years is too close to call, you can make a telephone call."

Susan moved to the next item: three years of industry experience, meaning manufacturing experience.

"Almost all resumes mention their industry," Susan said. "You know what we do, and we are a manufacturing company. Basically, a manufacturing company makes things. Again they must have three years to score a ten; otherwise you record NQ on the line. And the same rule applies if you are unsure of the actual years they have.

"The next requirement is that the person needs to be technologically savvy. Anyone want to guess what this is?"

Maria spoke first, "I think it means they are computer literate and competent with different computer programs and apps."

"That's a good explanation, Maria," Susan said. "It should be easy to find on a resume, as almost all people list their computer skills. If they do not, mark it with an NQ. They should have read the posting and have seen the requirement."

"If in doubt," Mark asked, "should we call them?"

"Mark, that is a judgment call on your part," Susan responded, "if you feel better making a call, then go for it."

Susan moved on to the final requirement.

"The final requirement is they need an understanding of P&L, and also budgeting processes. Anyone want to tell me what they think this is?"

"I will," Cathy responded. "P&L refers to Profit and/or Loss and the budgeting processes mean they understand how budgets work and money is managed."

"Excellent," Susan responded. "Honestly, if they have scored ten on the four previous items, they have this. Plus, more than likely, they will have this on their resume. But, again, if you have any concern, use your judgment and call them. And perchance it is not there, score an NQ and eliminate them from consideration."

Next Susan moved on to the Preferred items.

PREFERRED (30 - 60 POINTS)

Experience in a family-owned business: YES (60)   NO (0) _____

Bachelor's degree: _____ YES (40)   NO (0) _____

Susan said, "As you can see we only have two preferred items. Note that the point totals are higher than requirements. Why do you think the points are higher?"

Mark quickly answered. "Because requirements they must have and are ten points across the board. Preferred items are, if you will, optional and deserve more weighted values."

"Very insightful, Mark," Susan said. "As it was explained to me, those who developed the score form originally were going to use a check mark for 'yes it is there.' Then after using it for a while, they realized at times the information from the resume was not clear, so they chose to use 10 points, O points and NQ."

"I see there are only two preferred items," Maria said. "Why?"

Susan answered, "That is what the team decided. Whatever the brainstorming team decides is what we deal with on a score form. In this case, they only chose to have the two preferred items. I am confident you know our company is a family-owned business, and while they did not make this a requirement, it was important enough to be preferred. There are advantages for us if new hires have family-owned business experience."

"So," Cathy began, "We either give the family-owned item sixty points or zero?"

"Correct,"Susan answered. "You do not need to call and ask if they have this experience. It was listed in the posting, and we will assume they are adults and know how to respond. The same goes for a bachelor's degree, and rest assured, if they have one, it will be on the resume— and sometimes even when they don't have one."

"Wait a minute," Mark said. "Even when they don't have a degree?"

"Yes," Susan said. "Some people out there are not honest. In fact, Brenda told me about a candidate who listed a degree to get more interviews, thinking no one would check."

"That's just plain stupidity," Maria exclaimed. "Do you think this happens often?"

Susan replied, "Not that often. But you would be surprised how few companies do these kind of background checks."

"Yeah," Mark responded. "I remember a few years ago a university hired a man to be their head football coach, and they discovered he had falsified his resume by listing a degree he did not have. The offer was withdrawn."

"I trust it is clear," Susan said. "They get the points, or zero, as they cannot be given an NQ because preferred items are not required." All nodded in agreement.

Susan moved on to the Desired items.

DESIRED (20 - 35 POINTS)

Experience in sales:	YES (35)	NO (0) _____
Experience in marketing knowledge/ experience with EOS:	YES (30)	NO (0) _____
Degree major in business:	YES (20)	NO (0) _____
Holds an MBA:	YES (20)	NO (0) _____
Five years senior management experience:	YES (20)	NO (0) _____
Experience with customer service:	YES (20)	NO (0) _____

"A mentor of mine once told me that preferred items are things you'd like to require, but do not for fear of eliminating good candidates," Susan shared. "Desired items are a wish list. Would you like to have an explanation of any of the desired items?"

Mark replied, "I think we all are okay with sales and marketing experience, but if Maria and Cathy are like me, I have no idea what this EOS item is."

"Want to take a guess?" Susan asked.

"Not me," Mark replied. "How about you Maria, or you Cathy?"

Let me explain EOS in the short form," Susan said. "If they have it, believe me, it will be clearly on their resume. Now, EOS stands for Entrepreneurial Operating System. There are many components to it, and it is designed to help organize companies and their systems to increase effectiveness.

"Ron is studying this and is considering implementing it. If a candidate has the EOS knowledge or experience, he or she would be extremely helpful during implementation."

Maria said, "I only have a question about one of the remaining items. What is senior management?"

"Let me explain that item, and we will be done with the training on the resume score form," Susan said. A person with senior management experience has been part of what some people call the 'C-Suite,' meaning they have been a CEO, CFO, COO, or any related titles. For example, a Vice President in most companies would be senior level."

"That makes it clear," Maria said, as the other two nodded in agreement.

"I believe you are ready to roll!" Susan said. "Go and start scoring the resumes—and do not hesitate to come to me with any questions. Once you are well along in your scoring, I will pull us together to train on the telephone screener. I am confident you will enjoy the scoring."

"Thanks for the training, Susan," Maria said. "I think I can speak for all three of us. We like what we we see and appreciate your confidence in us."

"I am confident in all three of you," Susan replied. "While you get started, I will meet with Ron and give him an update."

Susan went to Ron's office to give him an update on their progress.

After she filled him in on the training, she added, "Ron, I still am a little concerned about using this *Choosing Winners*© System without any approval or authorization from the vendor. Brenda told me they went through a comprehensive training with the organization and have been certified and approved and licensed to use the system. Are you sure we are okay with using this system?"

"I am," He replied. "I spoke with Brenda's CEO, Brian Bradford, at the last peer group meeting, and he assured me we were okay in using speaker materials. I also asked Brandon Wright, the chairman of our peer group, and he confirmed that I could use the materials since the developer, Spence, spoke at a peer group meeting and was paid an honorarium."

"Okay, I just tend to be cautious," Susan said. "As I was reviewing everything from Brenda, I noticed the copyrighted statements, and I was concerned."

"Don't worry about it," he said. "Sally is using some sales materials with her team that I also got from a peer group speaker, and again, Brandon said it was okay."

"Thanks. I feel better about it now." She replied.

"Keep this process moving forward Susan, and make your HR team experts in scoring and screening."

"Gotcha," she replied. "Said and done. I will keep you posted."

People must be trained before they score resumes.

Chapter 11

TRAINING ON THE TELEPHONE SCREENER

The HR Team enjoyed scoring the resumes and were finally ready to conduct telephone screener interviews. Since this would be their first time to use the three-part screening process, they were excited to learn so they could successfully identify potential leaders for the company.

Maria, Cathy, and Mark gathered in the conference room waiting, for Susan to arrive and begin the training.

"How did your scoring go?" Maria asked Mark and Cathy.

Mark spoke first. "It went really well. At last count, I believe we've received about 125 resumes, and we each scored a third of them."

Cathy added, "Susan mentioned that we will telephone screen twenty-five candidates. Is that a good number?"

Mark responded, "I would think that out of the twenty-five, we should be able to identify three excellent finalists."

"I am anxious to learn how to do the screener," Maria said "Never in my career in HR have I seen such a detailed and planned process. I believe Susan has referred to hiring as being a discovery process, and so we will be discovering all we can about the candidates."

"I like that," Cathy said. "A discovery process. Like you, Maria, this is the first time I've had the opportunity to participate in a defined process."

Mark interjected, "Susan should be here momentarily, anyone need more coffee?"

"No thanks," Maria said. "Please keep those donuts away from me!"

"Me too, Mark," Cathy said. "Thanks for offering but I have had too many donuts this morning."

"Well," Mark said. "I am going to get more coffee and have at least one more donut."

He'd barely finished speaking when Susan walked in and asked, "Anyone need more coffee or a donut as we start?"

The three team members snickered.

"Did I say something funny?" Susan asked.

"No," Mark said. "We had just finished talking about whether we needed more coffee and my team members are avoiding the donuts, so I am taking care of the donuts for them."

"You are such a good team member, Mark, eating the donuts to protect your team members," Susan said with a smile. "I am so proud of you,"

Mark bowed.

"Before we dive into learning how to do the telephone screener," Susan began. "I want to thank you for getting the resume scoring completed ahead of schedule. I am not sure if you know yet, but after scoring 125 resumes, we have identified twenty-five for the telephone screener."

"Is twenty-five about what you expected?" Mark asked.

Susan replied. "Yes. Brenda told me to expect about twenty to twenty-five percent of the total field of candidates to make it through the scoring. We are right at twenty percent. Based only on the resumes and your scoring, do you feel like we have a strong field?"

"I do," Maria replied. Cathy and Mark nodded. "Great," Susan responded. "Let's get on with our training," Susan went to the white board and wrote:

The Three-Part Telephone Screener

1. The resume interrogation
2. The "technical" questions
3. The structured screener

"The screener is three parts," Susan said. "Part one sometimes is referred to as the resume review, as we seek clarification from the candidate about his or her resume. Part two consists of three questions pertaining to the responsibilities identified in the brainstorming. Part three is a structured interview based on a study of outstanding managers and leaders. It will take you an average of forty-five minutes with each candidate to complete the screener. Any questions so far?"

"Interrogation?" Cathy asked. "That wording seems a little strong to me. After all, I am not a detective trying to solve a crime or anything."

"Well," Susan replied, "You are not solving a crime, but you are asking questions to clarify points on the person's resume. And like a detective, you are essentially interrogating the person. I think the word 'interrogation' is used to stress to the interviewers how important and critical their role is in finding the right fit and match."

"Okay," Cathy said. "From now on call me Sherlock."

"Well then, Sherlock it is!" Susan said, as the coworkers laughed.

"How do we do this detective work?" Mark asked. "Are there guidelines or specific questions?"

"Both," Susan answered. "Let's begin our training with the resume interrogation, but first, some general information. You will need to send an email inviting the candidate into the process. We have a prepared one for you to use. In the email, you will give them some date and time options," Susan gave each a copy of the prepared email.

"When they have replied and you have selected a date and time for the interview, send them a confirming email specifying the date and time," Susan said. "When you call them, call exactly on time. For example, if you confirmed 1:00 p.m., then you dial the phone at 1:00 p.m. Also, make sure you are aware of time-zone differences."

"That sounds simple enough," Mark said. "I like dialing the phone at the exact time because it shows professionalism and that we do what we say, even with a time to make a telephone call. I guess this also lets them know a little about our culture."

"I agree, Mark," Maria said. I have a question for Susan, and I probably know the answer, but I will ask it anyway. What if the previous interview runs over, and you cannot dial the phone right on time?"

Susan smiled and said, "What do you think I would say?"

Maria answered. "That I did not leave enough time in my schedule and was a poor planner. Right?"

"You know me well," Susan replied. "However, if that happens—and no matter how well you planned, it might—send a text to one of us that you are running late. We will contact your next appointment and tell them you are running late, but will be calling them shortly. Try to give us a good estimate of the time so we can be specific with the candidate."

"Thanks," Maria said. "I just hope it never happens to me."

Susan continued the training.

"You dialed on time and the candidate answered the phone," Susan began. "What do you think comes first?"

Everyone was silent, thinking, and then Cathy said. "I would verify who they are and who I am. I would ask them if this is still a good time to do the interview."

"Excellent," Susan replied. "Most of the time, they will respond that it is still a good time. However, Brenda told me about a time she made the call and asked if it was still a good time. The candidate began to say yes but suddenly shouted, 'Watch out.' Brenda heard the phone drop to the floor and the candidate running."

"What happened?" Mark asked.

"She said she just hung on and waited," Susan answered. "It was about ten minutes until the candidate returned to the phone and told her what happened. She had been looking out the window of her home and saw the neighbor's child get hit by a car. She ran out to help."

"Did she share how the child was?" Cathy asked.

"She did," Susan replied. "The child was conscious and not bleeding, but obviously had been hurt. Someone called 911, and since other neighbors were present, she returned to the phone."

"That has to be difficult to continue the interview," Mark said.

"She did not continue," Susan said. "She asked to reschedule since she was shaken. Brenda set a new date and time with her. You may experience many different situations as you do your interviews. In fact, Brenda told me about another example. The candidate answered the phone softly saying 'hello.' She asked if he was John, and he said yes. She identified herself and asked if this was still a good time for the interview. He asked who she was and what she wanted. Then he said he had just hung up from another call, learning his mother had died. She expressed sympathy and told him she would get back to him later."

"What was the end result?" Cathy asked.

"When she called back a week later, he withdrew his resume and declined to continue." Susan said. "The key is to be sensitive and responsive to others."

The team sat quietly, thinking about the stories Susan had shared with them. Then Susan broke the silence.

"You need to have a planned icebreaker to use in the interview. Do not mention politics or religion. You can refer to the weather, any non-controversial national news item, or their university. For example, if they graduated from Ohio State you could ask about the Buckeyes or ask what a buckeye is. Or maybe if they're from the University of Florida, you could ask if their mascot is a live gator. Just keep it neutral and not controversial. Make sense?"

All nodded.

"Okay, let's work on the interrogation piece," Susan said. "You have a copy of the recommended questions to verify resume information. The first question on the list, is asking why they applied for the position. It's not a major deal, but we do like to keep track of what attracts people to our company. You could follow up with how they learned about the position, what web sites or networks."

"Next, ask the recommended questions regarding previous employments, making sure they provide the month and year of each so you can see any gaps that you'll want to ask about. Gaps are not necessarily bad. We just need to know why the gap exists. Next, I would ask them if their resume is accurate and complete regarding all past employment. Any questions so far?"

"Typically, what reasons would we expect to hear for gaps?" Maria asked.

Susan thought for a moment. "I have had the following over the years: caregiving for a family member, personal illness, a surgery following an accident, having a baby, taking time off between jobs, and going back to college, to name a few."

"What if they say they were terminated and had to take time to find a new job," Maria asked. "Is that a disqualification?"

"It could be, but probably not likely until you discover more information," Susan responded. "Brenda told me about a time she asked a candidate if he was still employed at the job he listed as current. He said he was not, but that at the time he submitted his resume he was. She asked why he left, and he replied that he was terminated. She asked him the reason for the termination, and he replied that he could not talk about it right then, due to some legal issues. He asked to be able to continue in the process, feeling he would have closure on the issue soon.

Brenda decided to keep him in the process. In the end, he was exonerated, and she hired him as their new CFO; he was with them for twelve years.

"Wow!" Mark said. "That was some story."

"Now look at the next recommended question," Susan said. "Ask them about their degree status, even if nothing is listed on the resume and even if a degree is not required.

"I may have shared this story with you previously, but one candidate I talked with had listed a bachelor's degree on the resume. I asked him if he had completed the degree, and he asked me why I asked, since it was on his resume. I told him I often called the university to verify a candidate's degree. He admitted that he did not have a degree, and I informed him he was not qualified."

"It takes all kinds, doesn't it?" Mark said.

"Next, make sure you ask about compensation," Susan said. "We do not want to get to the end and have a candidate we cannot afford. Also, if they are not from our area, or the commute appears to be too long, ask about relocation issues for them. In fact, ask them if an offer is made, can they accept and relocate to our area. This position is not open to anyone who wants to be remote. They need to be in the office daily.

You can share with them that we have a very good relocation package for the right person."

"How big an issue is this relocation item?" Maria asked. "Have you ever had any major problem with it?"

"We have not," Susan replied "However, I remember when a local school district hired a new superintendent of schools. In the first month of his employment, he resigned because his wife refused to move to the new area. So, let's make sure we are clear about relocation."

"I would hate to have that happen to us," Cathy said.

"Now, on to the tough part of the interrogation section of the screener," Susan said. "You need to inquire about and discuss with them any claims they make on the resume."

"Claims made?" Mark asked. "Help me understand that."

"Sure," Susan responded. "It can be a variety of things. Perhaps they claim they reduced employee turnover by fifty percent. Or maybe they claim that they increased sales by a high number. Or they had zero mis-hires. Or personally implemented a new program. Or just about anything else that they take credit for doing."

Maria said, "Give me a little help here. What are examples of questions we could use to pull this information from the candidate?"

"Let's say they claimed to increase sales by a high percentage," Susan said. "Ask them what percent that was of total sales, and how long did it take. Did they do it alone, or did others help. What were the key components of their success? Looking back would they make any changes? That's just a few, and some of the questions will apply to just about any claim they make on their resume. Is that helpful?"

"It is for me," Mark replied. "I think we just need to really study the resume so we are prepared to discover this from them. And, we need to be creative in writing our questions."

"I agree, Mark," Susan said. "Now we need to look at the three questions we will use for the identified areas of responsibility. But first, let's take a twenty-minute break."

Following the break, the HR team returned to the conference room for part two of their training on the telephone screener interview.

"I am enjoying this training," Maria said, as she and Cathy entered the conference room. "It really makes sense to me now, although I was skeptical at first."

Cathy said, "I never realized something like this was available to help us interview."

"I'm back, you lucky people," Mark announced as he plopped into a chair. "Did you miss me?"

Both looked at Mark and Cathy said, "Yes we really missed you, just like we miss a bad headache!" They laughed together.

"Are you ready to get on with part two?" Susan asked, as she entered the conference room. "In part two, you will ask questions pertaining to the responsibilities of the position. The questions have been prepared, and I want to review them with you, so you know how to ask them and what to listen for from the candidate."

"These all pertain to the responsibilities?" Mark asked.

"Correct," Susan replied.

Cathy then asked. "We only have three questions to master?"

"Not exactly," Susan responded. "The first question actually consists of five separate questions, one flowing from the previous. And, depending upon the answers, you might ask some follow-up questions."

"Somehow this appears to be more than just asking three questions," Cathy said.

"It is," Susan replied. "It gets easier as you master the skill."

Susan wrote the first question on the white board:

How many employees have you typically supervised in your previous positions?*

"There is no specific number to listen for," Susan said. "We just want to confirm that the person has supervised others. It is also an easy question to begin the process. Note the number they give you."

"What if their answer is zero?" Maria asked.

"I doubt very much that would happen," Susan replied. "But if it did, the interview is over. You would need to clarify their answer, but then explain that the position requires prior supervision responsibilities."

Susan wrote the second question on the white board:

Were you responsible for evaluating performance?*
(If yes) Describe the evaluation system you used.*

"I would hope that they answer yes to the first part," Susan said. "After all, they are applying for a key leadership position."

"I have a question," Mark said. "The first part is an obvious yes or no. Why even ask the second part? Is it really necessary?"

"That's a good question, Mark," Susan responded "I asked that myself when I first experienced this style of interviewing. It is a closed-ended question and serves only one purpose. To frame the mind of the candidate into the topic, you want to learn more about his or her thinking and experience. In other words, it sets the stage, or as people working in television would call it—a segue. It helps you and the candidate transition."

"Obviously if they reply no," Cathy said, "we move on to another question. For the second part, specifically what are we listening for in their response?"

"You want to hear a specific example of an evaluation system," Susan replied. "Listen for the key parts of their system and how often they do evaluations. You might find you need to ask them if the system was provided by the company, something they designed, or something they bought off the shelf. It would be okay to also ask them what they like and don't like about the system and how successful it has been with their employees."

"I never realized how deep you go into a topic to learn more about a candidate," Maria said. "This really confirms for me that we are using a discovery process."

"Great observation, Maria," Susan responded. "I think we have covered this topic, so let's move on to the next,"

Susan went to the white board and wrote:

Tell me about a time when an employee did not meet expectations and what you did.

"This question is also a good example of using what is called Descriptive Situational Interviewing," Susan shared with the team. "It is different from purely situational questioning since in situational questioning, you are in the hypothetical tone, asking them what would you do, not what *did* you do."

Mark said, "I cannot believe how much I did not know about interviewing."

"Too many companies and managers do not value or understand the need to teach their managers who interview and how to interview," Susan said. "To make it even worse, most companies do not have a specific hiring system. And if they do have one, it is usually not part of company policy, and there are no consequences for managers who violate the system."

Hearing a sound at the door they all turned to see Ron in the doorway.

"Hi, Ron," Susan said. "How long have you been listening to us?"

"Oh, just a few moments," he replied. "Susan, I agree with your observations about training and hiring systems. Honestly, I find it pathetic, but in doing so I am condemning our company and specifically me as president. The good news is that we are now training and are implementing a hiring system."

"Would you like to join us," Susan asked.

"Thanks for the invitation, but I have to decline," Ron said. "I just wanted to see how it was going on my way to meet with our accountants."

"Thanks for stopping in, Ron," Susan said. "I know the team appreciates your interest in what we are doing."

"Carry on!" Ron said, as he left.

Susan directed the team back to the task at hand.

"With this question, you are listening for a real example of a time when an employee was not meeting expectations," Susan said. "This could be job performance issues or some behavioral issues. You want to hear a real-life example and what the candidate did to correct the issue with the employee."

"Should we be listening for some sensitivity while also a strong focus on accountability?" Cathy asked.

"Excellent observation, Cathy," Susan replied. "We want to hear what the results were in this situation. I think we have this covered. Let's move on to the next item."

Susan returned to the white board and wrote:

In this position you will be expected to be a coach for your employees. Tell me about a time you had to coach an employee and the success you achieved.

Mark said proudly, "That is a descriptive situational question!"

"You are right!" Susan said, smiling. "For this question, we want to hear about a specific time when the candidate successfully coached an employee. Now, as you listen, the example can be helping an employee learn something new, helping the employee improve performance, or working on a negative behavior. Depending on the answer, you might need some follow-up questions, or you can use the phrase, 'Tell me more.'"

"What if I get a generic answer?" Maria asked.

"Then you need to come back at them," Susan replied "Say to them, 'I appreciate your example, but I did ask for a time when you did the coaching. Please tell me about a real time you coached someone and achieved success.'"

"That seems a little harsh," Mark said. "Can you give us a softer way to say it?"

"No," Susan answered. "We have to hold the candidate accountable, and they are top managers, so they can take it. Our president, Ron, is a very caring and sensitive leader. He told me once that as the interviewer, it is not your job to be the public relations department for the candidate. Be kind, but be firm. He said some candidates are trying to play a game with you. Do not allow that to happen."

"I can see what you are saying," Maria said. "I appreciate what Ron told you. It makes a lot of sense, and I will do my best to be kind but firm."

"Any other questions?"

Susan went to the white board and wrote the next question:

Now tell me about a time when you coached someone and you did not achieve the results you wanted.*

"What if they did not have an example for successful coaching?" Mark asked. "Do I still ask this question?"

"Well Mark," Susan asked. "What do you think?"

"I think it would be a waste of time," Mark answered.

Susan responded. "You are correct. If they did not have a success story, I am sure they will not have an example of not achieving results."

"I am beginning to really understand this," Cathy said. "Tell me if I am right. We want to hear a real-life example of a time when they coached someone and did not achieve the results desired. It might be a performance issue, a training on something new, or attempts to change negative behavior, for example."

"Excellent, Cathy," Susan praised her. "Again, you might need to use some follow-up questions or the phrase, 'Tell me more.' Now, let's take fifteen minutes to refill our drinks and absorb what we've learned so far."

When it was time for the team to gather again, on her way back to the conference room, Susan stopped to chat with Ralph.

"How is the training?" Ralph inquired. "Making progress?"

"We sure are. I am really proud of my team and how quickly they are learning the skills. All three are inquisitive, too," Susan said.

Just then, Bill came down the hallway. "Susan, how is the training?"

"I was just telling Ralph how well it is going and how quickly my team is catching on to the skills," Susan told him.

"I saw Mark yesterday, and he told me how much he was enjoying it, and how much he is learning," Bill said. "He was so excited he could not stand still. It would have been a good time to take him golfing; he would have been so hyper that I could have easily won."

"You know," Susan said, "I began this to prepare my team for screening in our search for an operations manager. It has evolved into a full-scale training on interviewing. I believe we are planting seeds to implement a new hiring system."

"That's exciting," Bill replied.

Susan continued to the conference room, where she found the three team members waiting for her.

"Everyone ready to learn more?" Susan asked. "Okay then let's look at question two,"

Susan wrote on the white board:

How effective have you been in hiring new employees to join your team?*

"This is an open-ended question," she told the team. "You might get responses all over the board. You might have to ask some follow-up questions or, as we have said previously, use 'Tell me more.'"

"Mark, what do you think we are listening for from the candidate?"

"Well, obviously, that they believe they have been successful," Mark answered, "but I guess we need to define success in respect to our culture."

"Cathy, what do you think?" Susan asked.

Cathy paused and then replied, "Maybe something like they say on a scale of one to ten that they rate themself as an eight."

"And Maria, what do you think?" Susan asked.

Maria thought for a minute and said, "I would think someone might say they believe they have been very effective."

"I agree with all of you," Susan told them. "Remember this is a closed-ended question, and you will most likely get a short answer, perhaps an answer like one of you just gave. That is not enough. After they respond, ask them to provide an example of their hiring success. Also, you could follow up with 'Tell me about your rate of employee turnover.'"

"I never would have thought about turnover," Mark said. "We have so much to learn."

"That is why we are doing this training," Susan said. "Once we finish you will feel very comfortable as an interviewer. Let's move to the next question,"

Susan wrote the question on the white board:

When you need to hire a new employee, what process do you use: your own, company mandated, or an off-the-shelf program.

"Susan, can I take the lead on this question?" Maria asked.

"Go for it!" Susan said.

"I don't think it matters which of the three they choose, or if they give something else," Maria said. "Basically, it is, in effect, a closed-ended question with a straight-forward answer. I think this will require some follow up questions, like 'Tell me how that process works.' And probably, we will need to use, 'Tell me more.'"

"Good job, Maria," Susan praised her. "I could not have said it better. The intent of this question is to determine if they have used a system, and if they did, can they describe the process in detail. Let's move on to the next question."

Susan wrote on the white board:

Assume you are hiring a new employee. Tell me the characteristics, traits, behaviors and values you are seeking in your new hire.*

"Why do you think we are asking this question?" Susan asked.

"Let me take a swing at it," Mark replied. "I think this will help us understand what this candidate believes are the things most important in an employee. Also, if they ignore the question and answer by giving skills and experience, it indicates that the behaviors and values are not all that important to them."

"Excellent, Mark," Susan said. "I like how you picked up the idea of a person giving skills and experiences, avoiding the *who*. If a candidate gives a short reply—maybe saying, 'high energy and driven,' then use,

'Tell me more.' Also, we can see if their answer matches with what we look for in new employees."

Susan wrote the next question on the board:

Mis-hires are expensive, and we have all had at least one. Tell me about one of your mis-hires.*

"Again we have a descriptive situational question," Susan said. "We need to be prepared to go beyond the actual question and the candidate's initial answer. Depending on their answer here are some possible follow up questions,"

Susan wrote them on the board:

Specifically, what were the issues with the mis-hire?

How long did it take to realize you had a mis-hire?

Did you provide help to the employee or consider a PIP?
How did the mis-hire impact your team members?

Did you research what went wrong in the hiring process?
Did this cause you to evaluate your hiring process?

Did you do a good job of documentation?

"Are these questions helpful?" Susan asked.

"Is the sky blue?" Mark asked. "These are really helpful."

"Let's move on to the last question," She said, and wrote it on the white board.

Now tell me about one of your best hires ever and why this was your best hire.*

"Again we have an open-ended question," Susan said. "There is not a right or wrong answer. In fact, you will want to compare these descriptors with the candidate's answer to the characteristics they seek in a new hire. There should be some correlation."

"Their answer also provides more insights into the candidate's beliefs and values. Also, listen for excitement in their tone as they talk about this person. The only follow up question might be, 'Tell me more.' Any questions?"

"Before you move on to the next set of questions," Mark said. "Can we take a short break?"

"Yes, let's take a twenty-minute break," Susan said.

As the team left the conference room, Charlie entered and spoke to Susan.

"I am just curious," he said. "How is it going?"

"Charlie," she said, "I am really excited about how quickly my team is learning, and it is fun getting to know them better. I hate to admit it, but I have been neglecting this team over the past three months, and that is not fair to them."

"I was doing some reading last evening," Charlie said. "What you just said reminds me about what I read regarding building and maintaining positive relationships with employees. The author stressed that in successful companies, the people like each other. In his research, he had discovered that when people like each other, the work environment is safe, productive, and bring the desired results. It sounds like you and the team are bonding, and based on what I read, you will find a lot of positive results."

"Thanks for sharing, Charlie," Susan replied. "I agree. Working with the team on the training has some really beneficial side effects. I've enjoyed learning their unique personalities."

"Keep up the good work," he replied.

As Charlie left, Susan went to the white board and wrote the next question, finishing it just as the team returned to the room.

Would you describe yourself as a motivator of others?*
(If yes) Tell me how you do that."
(If no) Why do you feel that way?"

"Everyone ready to get to it?" Susan asked. "The next question is on the board for discussion."

Mark said, "This is different with the 'if yes' or 'if no' responses. And won't every candidate say they are a motivator of others?"

"Well, Ron said he hopes they say no," Susan responded.

"Seriously?" Maria asked.

"Yes," Susan replied. "He told us that he thinks no one can motivate others. A leader creates a motivating environment in which people want to achieve. At first I did not agree with him, but after thinking about it, I agree. The candidate's answer will tell you a lot about him or her."

"This interview training is turning into a class on leadership and management!" Cathy said. "I am learning so much about leaders."

"That's great, Cathy," Susan said. "By focusing on the traits of leaders you will be even more effective in interviewing leaders. I have been thinking about something recently and let me ask you what you think about it. I am not mandating this, but I would like you to consider it. I would like for us to read a book a month and discuss it."

"What type of books?" Maria asked.

"This is not in concrete," Susan said. "I imagine leadership books, HR-topic books, and books about processes."

"I like this idea," Mark said.

"Me too," Cathy and Maria said in unison.

"Great," Susan told them. "I will put a proposal in writing, and we can review it at our next meeting. I think we can move on to the next question," Susan wrote:

As a manager, do you involve your employees in planning, decision-making and implementing?*
(If yes) Tell me about a time when you involved your employees in one of these activities.*

Mark immediately said, "what if someone says no?"

"Good question," Cathy said. "I noticed there is not a follow up for 'no.'"

"I guarantee that everyone will say yes," Susan replied to them. "That is just fine. This is a closed-ended question designed to get them thinking about planning and the other two topics. The key is the open-ended question, where they have to give you an example of actually involving others. I can also guarantee that you will have several candidates who say yes and then cannot give an example."

"What would be an answer that does not show involving others?" Cathy asked.

"Here is one I heard," Susan said. "'Involving others? I do it all the time. If I need a new project manager, I call HR. If I need to prepare a budget, I call accounting and tell them I need a budget.'"

"Does the person involve others?" Susan asked. "What does he or she do?"

Mark answered, "I think that is abdication. There is no involvement, and the person is passing off his or her responsibilities to others."

"Excellent observation," Susan said. "Absolutely no involvement. Let's move to the next question, which ties to this one."

In your opinion, does involving others result in any benefits for the individual, team, or company?*

"You want to hear 'yes,'" Susan told the team. "Then listen for specific benefits. They might talk about individuals, the team, or the company. It really makes no difference. Some will talk about all three."

"Do you have some follow up questions for us?" Cathy asked.

"I do," Susan explained. "Here are a couple." She wrote them on the white board.

How would an individual benefit from being involved?* How does involving the employees benefit the company?*
How will involving employees help a team?*

Susan continued. "Listen carefully to the responses and specifically listen for a reference to involving employees, as it will help them make a commitment to the company. People leave companies for several reasons, such as working for an incompetent manager. Not getting involved in planning, decision-making, and implementing is another top reason for leaving the company. Compensation seldom figures in to a decision to leave the company. Let's look at the last question,"

Susan again wrote the question on the white board.

Tell me about your overall expectations for those that you supervise.

"I am beginning to get used to these open-ended questions," Maria said. "While I like them in the process, it makes it harder on the interviewer when it comes to listening and being on your toes with follow up questions."

Cathy said, "I agree with Maria. But though it's more challenging, I do see the value of using open-ended questions. And I really like it when we ask a closed-ended question before the open-ended question."

"Excellent observations," Susan said. "What do you think we are wanting to hear from the candidate with this question?"

"I think the key word is 'expectations,'" Mark offered. "I would think these would be appropriate for all team members. I guess I would hope to hear willingness to learn, timely in completing projects, open to suggestions, open communication, objective in problem-solving, and showing empathy towards others. That's all I can think of right now. I am sure you will give us some more."

"How about you, Cathy?" Susan inquired.

"I don't disagree with Mark's ideas," she said. "But I am trying to come to grips with the word 'expectations.' I think I want to keep overall expectations separate from specific evaluative criteria based on job-description metrics. I guess what I am thinking is that expectations could be behavioral guidelines. If that is true, most of Mark's ideas would be expectations."

Susan said, "I believe you are both right in your responses. Maria, what are you thinking?"

"This might not be what you are asking for in this question," Maria said. "In my previous position, the company had general operating principles, and when I was there, I accepted them as our overall expectations."

"Excellent, Maria," Susan replied. "With this question we are hoping the candidate knows operating principles and has experienced them."

"Can you give us more information about operating principles?" Mark asked.

Susan responded, "Operating principles are how a company puts their core values into practice and gets things done. They can define your culture and your overall organization.

"Without going in to too much detail right now, basically, operating principles detail how to communicate, how to problem solve, how to relate to each other, how to make decisions, and how to plan. I believe they fall under an umbrella of core values. So for this question, the key is to listen and see if the candidate understands the concept of overall expectations and is clear on some specific details."

"What's next?" Mark asked.

"Well, I believe you are competent on resume scoring and also resume interrogation and questions related to the job responsibilities. That brings us to the Structured Manager Screener Interview," Susan said. "This is entirely different from what we have done so far, and the skill set is also very different. Let's reconvene tomorrow morning at 10:00 a.m."

The team packed up their materials and filed out of the conference room.

Susan felt good about the team's progress. However, she was deeply concerned about using the Structured Manager Screener without direct authorization. She understood Ron's perspective, but she was not at all comfortable about using the materials. She decided she would need to meet with Ron and, again, directly share her concerns.

Preparation is the key to success in screening candidates.

Chapter 12

MANAGER SCREENER

The next day, Susan met with Ron in his office to discuss the training and develop a plan for a hiring system for the company.

"The training still going well?" He asked.

"I am really pleased at how well all three of them have done and how quickly they have learned," she replied. "They are fully trained on scoring resumes and the first two parts of the initial telephone screener interview. We are now ready to train on the Manager Screener. Do we have access to it yet?"

Ron raised his eyes to the ceiling and said, "We do not."

"She won't even let us use it, just this one time?" She asked.

"They use it under a license agreement. She thought since we are in a peer group together she could let us use it," He answered. "Rather than risk losing the agreement, she contacted the provider and asked if she could let us use it. They refused. They told her we were welcome to take their training and get licensed if we wanted to use it."

"Do they have a one-time user fee?" She asked.

"I had the same thought and asked her to check with the provider. She did, and the answer again was no," he replied. "I really counted on getting to use it. In our peer group, we tend to let fellow members use things like this all the time, regardless of agreements in place. We do it quite often, and Brandon Wright, the chair of our group encourages us to share. His attitude is that if they don't know about it, so what. Oh, he always adds, 'No harm no foul.'"

"Can we schedule training with the provider?" She asked.

Ron replied. "We can, but they cannot fit us into their schedule for about six weeks. We really can't wait that long since Charlie will be leaving in about two weeks."

"I feel like we're between a rock and a hard place," Susan said. "How about asking the provider if we can use this now if we go ahead and sign up for the training."

"I like the way you think," he responded. "I had the same thought. I called the provider and asked if we could do that."

"And?" she asked.

"In one word, no," he replied.

"That doesn't make sense," Susan argued. "If we sign an agreement for the training, and put a large deposit down, why would they say no?"

"I don't have an answer for you," he replied. "I suggested that and offered to pay the whole fee in advance. Again, no."

"But why?" She asked heatedly. "Why not?"

Ron waited, giving her a chance to calm down. "The provider asked me how we could use it without training. Honestly, I did not have a good answer."

Holding her head in her hands, Susan asked in a frustrated voice. "Now what?"

"Let's pull the team into this discussion," he said. "I will have Mary check and see if we can meet sometime today,"

"Tell Mary that I am available any time today," she said. "This is important."

Mary reached all the team members and scheduled the meeting for 3:00 p.m. in the conference room. That afternoon, promptly at 3:00 p.m., the meeting convened in the conference room. Once all were in the room, Ron explained the purpose of the meeting and asked Mary to keep notes.

"Susan and I have hit a roadblock on the training of our folks on tele-phone screening," Ron began. "We had planned to use the structured Manager Screener from Mid-Town HVAC. Now we have discovered we cannot use it unless we are trained and licensed to use it. The provider does not have any openings for six weeks. We would like to discuss what do we do next."

Bill spoke first. "Why can't we use the screener from your peer group member? Many times over the past few years, you have shared materials with us from various speakers who spoke to the group, and we have used the materials. What changed?"

"That's right." Sally spoke up. "Remember when that speaker talked about having a sales plan, and you gave me the materials to use? Why is this different?"

"We have a copy of their Manager Screener," Ralph said "Just like in the past, use it and keep the process going."

"Another thing we could do," Sam said. "Although I am not recom-mending it, we could just change a word here and there, and we would not violate any copyright."

"What if we signed an agreement to do the training in six weeks?" Charlie asked, "Paid them in full and they let us use the interview while we wait for the training?"

"I am getting confused." Linda said. "Can we define the real issue, which I believe is: Do we have integrity or not."

The room fell into a deep silence. Everyone's eyes turned to Ron.

"That is really convicting, Linda," Ron said, "It is something we must discuss," Ron went to the white board and wrote:

Operate from integrity, doing what we say.

"That," he said, "is one of our key core values. Please keep that in mind as we work through this issue. I am not singling anyone out, but think back to what was just said about using the materials. It seems like we, and I am most guilty, forgot about integrity. We thought about several ways to get around reality. We thought about several ways that violate our value system. I stand in front of you as the one who is most guilty. Now the good news. We have not given into temptation. We can now correct what we have done in violating our integrity."

"Well, Ron, that takes care of using the materials without approval," Ralph said.

Charlie said. "I remember my mentor telling me to always have personal core values and only work for a company that has clear and communicated core values. That is why I have been here for ten years.

"I agree with Ralph; we absolutely cannot use the materials without the provider's approval. That may create some issues for you, Susan, but we cannot knowingly violate our core values. It sounds like we may have unwittingly been violating our core values in the past by using materials from peer group companies and using copyrighted materials."

"So where are we?" Susan asked. "I am not sure what to do. Do we stop the search and wait until we are trained, or do we forge ahead without using the Manager Screener tool? Or we could—and I know we won't—use the materials and hope we never get caught, although most of us would not be able to sleep at night."

"How about another option?" Linda asked.

"Go for it," Susan replied. "I am all ears and open to any ethical options."

"Would Mid-Town HVAC be willing to do the Manager Screeners for us and give us the results?"

"That's a good thought, Linda," Ron replied. "I called Brenda at Mid-Town and asked. She said no—that if she did that, she would violate her license agreement. Her license is for use only in her company."

"But she gave you a copy of the Screener and said you could use it." Sam said.

"She did," Ron said. "In fact, all the peer group companies have a copy of it. That is the culture the chair has fostered. If I had not started asking questions about getting our team certified and trained, and just used the interview, probably no one would know the difference."

Ralph rose and went to the white board. "Here is what I believe to be our two options." And he wrote the on the board:

Halt the search and get trained and then restart the search.
OR
Forge ahead and do the search in the way we always have done searches.

"Ron are you still committed to having us develop comprehensive hiring process?" Bill asked.

"Without question," Ron replied. "Now more than ever. And the materials from this provider are excellent and offer us a lot for our process."

"I have maybe a dumb question," Sally said. "Isn't the brainstorming with the *who*, *what* and *ticket*, the resume scoring form, and the three part telephone screener all from this provider? And don't they have a couple of more steps?"

"That's right, Sally," Susan said.

"Does that mean." Sally continued. "We have been using a lot of their copyrighted materials already?"

You could have heard a pin drop in the room.

"Oh my gosh!" Susan exclaimed. "Sally you are right. Guilty as charged."

"How did this happen?" Ralph asked. All eyes turned to Ron.

"Like Susan said," Ron replied. "Guilty as charged. I used the provider's materials because I had them from Brenda at Mid-Town and because of the group's culture. I just started to use them without giving a thought to right or wrong. Last year we did the same thing with the sales plan I gave Sally and she implemented. And, Sally, you need to contact the provider and find out what we owe them."

"Wow, Ron!" Sally said. "I never thought about that. I will call them first thing tomorrow morning. I don't want to stop using the materials. They really work!"

Charlie then said. "Ron when we are done here and decide what we are going to do, I strongly encourage you to confront Brandon Wright about the culture and his own abuses, and then drop your membership."

Ralph jumped in next. "Ron with your value system, you have no choice but to leave that peer group. Plus it saves us $2,500.00 a month in membership fees."

Ron looked around the table. "Charlie and Ralph are right. I want to stay focused on our issue here, but I commit to this team that I will confront Brandon, and I will resign from the group. But, right now let's decide how we will handle the search and implement our new hiring process. And I need a few minutes to get my thoughts together, so let's break for fifteen minutes."

"This really presents us with a challenge." Sam said to Linda, as they left the conference room "We have to stand tall for our core values, no matter what the cost."

Linda replied, "I agree. I really feel for Ron. He has been in this peer group for several years and has trusted what he was told. I do agree with Ron resigning from the group and confronting Brandon, though."

"So do I," Sam said, "I know Ron will follow through."

After the fifteen-minute break, the Leadership Team reconvened.

"Before you get us started," Charlie said. "We are all with you, and if you are guilty, we stand with you also as guilty. Let's set that aside for now and get focused."

"Thanks, Charlie," Ron said. "Let's get back to our two options." With that, he went to the white board and pointed at the questions Ralph written previously.

Halt the search and get trained and then restart the search.
OR
Forge ahead and do the search in the way we always have done searches.

"Any ideas?" Ron asked the team.

Susan spoke first. "I hesitate to stop the search. After the resume scoring, we appear to have some solid candidates. We would not only lose valuable time, but we probably would lose some good candidates. Here is what I have been thinking."

She went to the white board and continued.

"Let's contact the provider and get the training scheduled," she said. "Ask them what we owe for using their materials outside of an agreement. I have trained Maria, Cathy, and Mark on the scoring and the three part telephone screener, except for the Structured Manager Screener.

"They have learned how to do the resume interrogation, and they have learned the 'what' questions—the questions pertaining to the responsibilities. I can prepare questions for them to use to assess the personal side of the candidate, just like the manager screener does, but without their research base and content coding process. Are you with me so far?"

"That sounds good, Susan," Ralph said. "What's next?"

"The next step is what the provider calls the Probe," Susan said. "It is again a telephone interview and is based on their research of outstanding leaders and managers. Recently, I learned that they will conduct these interviews for a fee if you do not have an agreement or even if you have an agreement. Following the interviews, they provide you with in-depth behavioral assessments of the candidates. Are you still with me?"

Ron said, "We are and I like what I am hearing."

"Once the probe interviews are done," Susan said, "we can use their behavioral assessments and the results of our screeners to narrow the candidate field for our one-to-one video-sessions. I can prepare the questions for the online interviews. Following that, we can select the top three to bring into the company for an interview day."

"Help me understand something," Sam said. "Are you using their five-step hiring process without a license?"

"Good question, Sam," Susan replied. "I cleared all of this with the company and a license agreement is being prepared as we speak. And we will have a short consulting agreement back-dated, and a fee paid, leading up to the training so I can ask questions of them, and they can be fairly compensated for our use of the five-step process. Let me list the steps we will take now on the white board for you to review."

We do not halt the search.

The training is scheduled.

Susan will prepare interview questions for part three of the screener interview process.

We will sign a consulting agreement to fill the gap between now and the completion of the training.

The provider will conduct the probe interviews and give us behavioral assessments of the candidates.

Susan will write the questions for the online interviews and questions for the interview day.

Susan completed listing the six points on the white board. "Anyone have a question or some observations?"

"Great save, Susan," Ralph said. "I not sure how you did this, but you did."

"Susan," Ron chimed in. "Thank you! We do not have to violate our core values and our integrity. I have learned a lot, thanks to all of you. I told you I would drop out of the peer group, and I will first thing tomorrow. I want to meet with Brandon and share my feelings with him. I doubt that I can change his behavior, but I will always know I did what was right. Now, what is next for us Susan?"

"First, thanks to everyone for your support," she said. "I know you will be there if I need you. Next, I am going to prepare the interview questions for the screener and then prepare my team on how to use them. I will also make sure the consulting agreement and training dates are set, and I will work with the provider to get our license agreement. I will reschedule my meeting with Maria, Cathy, and Mark so they will begin their training tomorrow afternoon."

The next morning, Susan devoted most of her time to preparing the interview questions for the screener. She met with Ron over lunch to confirm where she was headed with the search and to give him support for his exiting from the peer group.

After lunch, she gathered her materials and headed for the meeting with her team. As she turned the corner on her way to the conference room, she encountered Charlie.

"Susan," he said, "I want you to know how proud I am of you and the way you put this plan together. Everyone else feels the same way."

"Thank you, Charlie," she said. "I am really going to miss you. I know it is a great opportunity, but your leadership has been invaluable for our company."

"I will miss all of the team and my own team," he said. "But I will just be down the street!" He gave Susan a big smile. "Have a good training," he said.

Susan entered the conference room, and the three team members stopped their conversation.

"I sent you a long email detailing where we are with the search and training," she said as she sat at the conference table. "Did you get to read it?" All nodded their heads.

"Good. I want to first talk about the Manager Screener we will not be using and then share the interview questions you will use in its place."

Mark said. "While we are not training on the Manager Screener, can we at least see a copy of it?"

"Not now," Susan answered. "Until we have our training, the one copy in my possession stays under lock and key. No offense, but it has to be that way." Leaving her chair she moved to the white board. "I am going to write down some key points about the Manage Screener. I think this will help you understand the questions I have written."

She wrote the following on the white board.

Screener has eight questions.

There is a response guide for each question.

The interviewer compares responses to the guide. The interview is based on research.

The process is called content coding.

"If we were using the Manager Screener," Susan said, "you would tell the candidate that you are going to read a series of questions to them and that all the questions are open-ended. You would then tell them that you can repeat a question any time they ask, but that you cannot explain anything.

"I want to go ahead and use this even though we are not using the Manager Screener. Any questions so far?"

Seeing none, she continued.

"The Manager Screener is based on a study of outstanding managers. You ask the question and compare the candidate's answer to the response guide. You then use a letter symbol designating whether the response is consistent with the study results or not. This is called content coding. With the questions I have prepared, we do not have a study so we will not have a validated response guide. However, we will discuss listening for what we would want to hear from a new team member in our company. We will refer to them as 'listen-for.'"

"The concept of content coding sounds interesting," Maria said. "I am anxious to get the training."

"Me too," Cathy responded. "Have you lined up the training for us?"

Susan responded. "Yes. We are a go! And based on what I am learning about the provider, you will thoroughly enjoy the training. Once we are trained on all parts of the five-step process, we will have a hiring system for our company. It is long overdue.

"Now, here are the questions we will use in this search. I will write the questions on the white board and then go back over them in detail,"

Susan wrote:

1. What is your driving purpose?*

2. Have you identified your core values?* (if yes) Tell me about them.*

3. Describe your experience in developing a strategic business plan.*

4. How much do you want to know about your individual team members? Why?*

5. Tell me how you prefer to communicate with your team members. Why?*

6. Tell me about a time when you encountered a tense situation and how you responded to the situation.

7. Describe a time when you avoided a problem do to anticipating the outcome.*

8. Are you a good problem-solver?* (if yes) Tell me about a problem you have solved in your work and how you solved the problem.*

"I believe with the other questions we are asking, these complete the circle. What do you think?"

Mark answered. "I agree. I like these questions."

"Remember," Susan said, "these focus more on the personal side of the person, if you will, their emotional quotient or EQ. These are not really skill-based questions. That is the same for the Manager Screener when we finally are trained and get to use it."

"Susan you mentioned earlier we would have a listen-for for each of these. Is that next on our schedule?" Cathy asked.

"It is, and let's look at the first one," Susan replied. She read the first question to the team: "What is your driving purpose?*"

"Obviously," Susan began, "a question like this does not have a right or wrong answer. We do not have study data to create a response guide. But based on our culture, our beliefs, and core values, what do you think would be a listen-for?"

Maria spoke first. "I would hope their purpose is helping others, as that is totally consistent with who we are."

"I agree with you, Maria," Mark said. "I was just thinking, what if a person answered, 'I have no idea. Never thought about it.' How would you respond?"

"If that happens, and it very well could, then tell them to take a couple of minutes and think about it," Susan directed.

"I am thinking about how people would respond," Cathy said,. "I would think we would hear something like achieving success, getting results and helping build a company."

"Good insights, Cathy," Susan replied. "Let's make helping others our listen-for, and be sure you take good notes on how they respond. Now the second question."

Have you identified your core values?* (If yes) Tell me about them.*

"Your turn Mark," Susan told him.

"Well I assume we want to hear yes, Mark said, "and then hear some values."

"How many values do you think you will hear?" Susan asked.

"Good question," Mark responded. "I would think most people can list at least three values. Do we judge what they say? In other words, do we decide if a word they give is really a value?"

Cathy spoke next. "We can't judge their values. Words have different meanings to different people. However, I think we need to listen for at least three values. I also think it would be better if one of their values is integrity. That is in our company core values, and I know it is one of mine."

"I think three values works for us," Susan said. "Make sure you write down all the values they list. Now question three: Describe your experience in developing a strategic business plan."

"Do they have to have been the leader in developing the plan, or could they have been a participant?" Mark asked.

"I am okay with either," Susan said. "I think the key here is that we want to hear they were actually in a process. You might hear them describe the SWOT Analysis, which many companies use in strategic planning."

Mark quickly interrupted and said, "SWOT analysis. I have heard of SWAT teams in law enforcement, but SWOT in business planning?"

Maria jumped in. "Mark, SWOT stands for strengths, weaknesses, opportunities, and threats. In my job before I came here, the company used SWOT and included all of us department heads in the analysis. I know it is old school, but it really works."

"Thanks, Maria," Susan replied. "We are listening for a description of their involvement in strategic plan development. As you listen to them, focus on any processes or strategies you hear them describe. Now let's look at question four: How much do you want to know about your individual team members? Why?*"

"I would love to hear a simple answer: a lot!" Susan said. "And they say they want to know so they can help them. What do you think?"

Maria spoke first. "I agree. That would be totally consistent with our values, and that is what our managers do. However, I wonder how many will feel that way. I expect we will hear from a lot of arm's-length managers. Ugh."

Cathy interjected, "what is an arm's-length manager?"

"Let me answer that," Mark said. "I have worked for some of them before coming here. These are the managers who do not want to get too close to you. I often hear them say you have to keep an arm's length because you might have to fire the employee some day, and you don't want friendship to get in the way. Is that close, Susan?"

She nodded.

"Is there anything to that idea that if you are too close it impacts your decision-making?" Maria asked. "An attitude like that has to have a negative impact on the culture."

"It definitely has a negative impact on the culture," Susan responded. "In my opinion it is more than negative—it can be toxic."

"I think the only answer that fits our culture is what Susan said initially," Mark said. "They want to know a lot so that they can help others. Otherwise you end up with a lot of high egos that only care about themselves."

"We agree. Leave the ego at the door. Now, question five: Tell me how you prefer to communicate with your team members. Why?"*

"Anyone want to take a stab at this one?" Susan asked.

"I will," Maria answered. "I really want to hear them say they prefer one-to-one interaction. We have allowed the technology gurus to push us into email and text instead of talking to each other.

"Don't get me wrong. I appreciate the value of email and texting if it is used for the right purposes, but a few weeks ago Ron sent me to one of our clients to help them with some implementation issues. I stood next to the general manager in a room filled with cubicles. In front of me were two adjacent cubicles with an employee at each desk. I noticed the one employee sent an email to the one in the adjacent cubicle.

"I assumed it was probably a meeting summary or technical information, but I asked the employee about it. I got a strange look, but he answered that he was just answering a question.

"I said, 'Why don't you just stand up and talk over the half-wall instead of sending an email.' He looked at me like I was nuts and turned back to his computer. Emails, I believe, should be to confirm information and send large files. Talk to each other for the simple communications!"

"How do you really feel, Maria?" Mark asked with a grin.

"I am curious," Susan asked. "How would you describe communication in our company?"

"Multi-faceted," Maria responded. "I think we do an excellent job of choosing how to communicate based on the person and the situation. I think if you asked anyone in the company they would say they prefer to communicate one-to-one. But, they would also say email, text, and video meetings, as needed and appropriate."

"I think we know what to listen for," said Susan. "Now question six: Tell me about a time when you encountered a tense situation and how you responded to the situation.

"What do you think we want to hear with this question?" Susan asked.

Mark spoke first. "I think we want to hear that the candidate, even in a tense situation, remained calm and achieved results."

"I agree," Cathy responded. "It has to be a real example, not hypothetical. I suspect we might hear them describe a customer confrontation, difficulty with a vendor, or an angry employee."

"I have a question," chimed in Maria. "What if they give a hypothetical answer. Do we just go on to the next question, or do we follow up?"

"Go on to the next question," Susan replied. "This is a screener. If this were at the one-to-one step in a video meeting, I would probably follow up like this, 'I am beginning to understand how you respond in tense situations. Can you be more specific?' What we really want from this question is to get a sense of their overall demeanor."

"Let's move on to question seven: Describe a time when you avoided a problem do to anticipating the outcome."

"Ron told me when I began here as HR Director that in interviewing candidates for supervisory or management positions, he wanted me to do my best to determine if the candidate understood anticipation," Susan said. "I think he called it an 'anticipatory focus,' meaning they are always planning for the unexpected. He said, half laughing, 'If you find it in a candidate, jump up and down, and do a happy dance.'"

Maria responded, "I don't think I have ever really thought about the concept of having an anticipatory focus. Now that I really think about it, a manager who really anticipates the unexpected is very valuable to a company. I believe Ron has that focus."

"He does," Mark replied. "Several times I have heard members of the

Leadership Team say that Ron told them to always consider what might happen down the road that would create issues. Now I know that there is a name for it."

"The key here is," Susan said, "listen carefully to their response and determine if their example is truly one of anticipation. I have used this question in interviews several times and I must say less than fifty percent actually give an example of anticipation."

Cathy then asked, "If they do not give an example of anticipation, are they ruled out for the operations role?"

"As much as I would like to say, 'yes,'" Susan replied, "the answer to your question is 'no.' They get ruled out, or ruled in, on the totality of the information we gather from them during the screening process. Let's move on to question eight.

"Are you a good problem-solver?* (If yes) Tell me about a problem you have solved in your work and how you solved the problem."

"I can assure you that everyone will say yes," Susan said. "All managers view themselves as great problem solvers."

"What are we to listen for in their description of a work-related problem?" Cathy asked.

Susan replied, "First make sure it is a work-related problem. Many managers will give an example of a problem that is not work related. Listen for how, or if, they involved others in coming to a solution and if they considered several options.

"So, listen for a process. Do they have a real problem-solving process or do they fly by the seat of their pants? And of course, listen for anticipation. Any questions?"

"I think we are ready," Cathy said.

"Great!" Susan exclaimed. "You have done an excellent job during the training, and I look forward to the results. Keep me posted as you work through the resumes and do not hesitate to ask questions or ask for help."

On her way back to her office, Susan saw Ron walking in her direction. "Hey, Ron, do you have a minute?"

"I need to take some time to prepare for a meeting, but I can take a minute."

Susan said to Ron, "The training is done, and I am really proud of the team. I know they will do a good job for us."

"Fantastic!" Ron exclaimed. "I am anxious to see the results."

"What meeting are you prepping for?" She asked.

"Remember my issue with the peer group and the chair, Brandon?" Susan nodded.

"Well, before I leave today, I want to prepare what I'm going to say to resign from the peer group. I could probably send an email, but I want to confront him in person," Ron said.

"This is not easy," Susan replied. "I know how much you enjoyed the meetings and several members of the group."

"That's true," Ron responded. "But it hit me hard as we dealt with using materials that we were not entitled to use. Our value on integrity means so much more than my membership in a group. If I had been more vigilant, or even asked specific questions about using materials from speakers, we would not have this issue."

"Don't be so hard on yourself." she said. "You all trusted each other. I don't think you or the members were the problem. Brandon promoted using speaker materials with no regard for copyrights or authorization. In peer groups the chair is a critical component and in my opinion he violated the members' trust. You are doing what needs to be done."

"Thanks for your support," Ron said, "I will let you know how it goes with Brandon. We have lunch scheduled for tomorrow."

Always act with integrity!

Chapter 13

RON TAKES ACTION

Ron's meeting with his peer group chair, Brandon Wright, was set for noon at an Italian restaurant. During his thirty-minute drive, he went over his thoughts again. He knew what he needed to do, but he knew he would miss the members and their sharing ideas with each other. However, he was totally committed to leaving the group to keep his commitment to the core values of the company—which were also his values, and the team's values.

Actually, at times here and there, for the past couple of years in the group, he had struggled with the way all of them used materials from previous speakers. But he had rationalized that since Brandon said it was okay, and all of the others were doing it, then why not take advantage of the free information. He regretted never bringing the topic up in a meeting.

Ron kept going over in his mind what he would say to Brandon and how he would say it. He had been in the group for several years, and Brandon had been the chair all that time. While he generally got along with Brandon, he was not fond of Brandon's personality and attitudes. Brandon was very opinionated. He usually said how he felt without any filters. He was a master manipulator. He had a loud, booming voice, and he never learned how to speak softly.

Pulling into the parking lot he noticed that Brandon's sports car was parked next to the door. He drove and parked five spaces away from

Brandon's car, then walked to the front doors of the restaurant. He had made a reservation, so he assumed Brandon was seated.

Brandon always made it a point to arrive first and be there to welcome you to the meeting. One of the speakers years ago had pointed out that by being first, you control the environment. And Brandon liked control.

Ron stopped at the welcome desk and gave the associate his name.

"Thank you, Mr. Howell," she said. "Your guest has arrived and is seated at the table. Please follow me."

Ron followed her to the table.

The minute he saw Ron, Brandon rose and stuck his hand out.

"Good to see you, Ron. We missed you at the last meeting. The speaker was fantastic and he shared a lot with the group. I saved you a copy of everything so you can use his ideas."

"How kind of you," Ron responded. The men sat at the table.

"Well, how's business?" Brandon asked.

Ron replied, "We are actually doing great. We have a lot of orders in progress and our backlog is about six months, so things are good."

"Hey," Brandon said, "I heard a rumor that Charlie has taken a position as president of one of your customers. Is that true?" It never takes long for Brandon to pry into your business and see what he can learn that just might be helpful to him. He was always on the lookout for ways to manipulate the other person.

"That's true," Ron answered. "I will really miss him, but I am happy for him and this opportunity."

"He won't be easy to replace." Brandon said. "I know you value his input, as he has saved your butt more than once." Brandon always got his digs in quickly and liked to put down others any way he could.

Ignoring the digs, Ron said, "Yes, Charlie is super. He has been with us for ten years and we have become very good friends and Christian brothers."

Brandon jumped back into the discussion. "Gosh, Ron, do you have to always bring up the Christian thing? This is business, not church. Anyway, you need to find someone to replace Charlie."

"I know the perfect guy to be your operations manager. He is in my good buddy's peer group, and I can get you and him together early next week. Saves you a lot of time and you get a great guy."

Ron sat still and quiet, thinking, *No way will I miss Brandon. He's always there, being the great manipulator.*

"Thanks, Brandon." he replied. "Have him send me a resume, and I will put him in our process. We have spent a lot of time putting our search together and training our HR team on interview skills."

"Ron, Ron, Ron," Brandon said, "you need to listen to me very carefully. This guy is only available for a short time. He recently parted ways with his employer do to cultural differences. He won't be in the job market long. "

"Ron, when you hire at this level, the candidates you want will not apply. They expect to be invited and not have to go through the meaningless interview stuff. I am recommending him to you, so you don't have to check references. Above all, do not offend this guy by asking for his resume. He, like all top executives, expects and deserves special treatment."

"Brandon we have our standards and processes. He is welcome to apply. Regardless, I am curious," Ron said. "What were the cultural differences?"

"Just some minor disagreements with the CEO," Brandon said. "He has been with that company about six months and the CEO would not listen to his suggestions. He finally said enough is enough and resigned. And with Charlie gone, you need a strong-handed operations person to keep you in line. According to my buddy, this guy is perfect for you."

"Well," Ron replied, "like I said, we have a process and if you want to let him know about our opening he can send us his resume."

Ron sensed that Brandon was getting irritated. "Ron, I told him about this opening the minute I heard Charlie was leaving. I told him I would talk to you and set up a meeting for him with you. I guaranteed him that you would meet with him. I owe my buddy a favor, and he knows I am connecting you with this great candidate."

Why have I put up with this behavior for so long, Ron thought. It was becoming easier and easier to leave.

"Sorry about that Brandon," he replied, "but everyone goes through our application process."

"Sorry you feel that way." Brandon said. "I will stay in touch with him, and when you can't find a candidate to hire, he might still be available. But, I doubt it. Ron, you need to listen and act on good advice."

Ron was saved responding by the server. "What can I bring you gentlemen to drink?"

As usual Brandon ordered a glass of chardonnay. Ron ordered coffee. "Are you ready to order or do you need more time," the server asked.

Ron told the server, "Please give us a few minutes."

"I haven't seen you for almost two months," Brandon said, "since you missed the last peer group meeting. How is the family?"

"All is good," he replied. "Cindy enjoys her quilting with the church group, and the four children are all doing well in school."

"Speaking of church—you aren't still wasting time on that board at your church, are you?" Brandon asked. "I know that a few meetings ago, the group told you to jettison it so you would have less distractions and could focus more on your business. I think you are the only one in the peer group that spends time on church. Not sure what you could ever gain by being in a church group."

Ron's frustration was building. "It's not just a typical board. I am an elder in my church and, Brandon, my faith is important to me."

"Well, I just find that guys who get active in church stuff lose their focus at work, and before long, profits drop," Brandon said. "I would never give time to that. I don't understand how or why you spend time reading a Bible. It is just an old book."

"As long as we are talking about my faith," Ron said. "I am also on the board of directors for iWork4Him, a not-for-profit organization focused on faith in the market place. I believe in and support their mission of bringing Jesus into the marketplace."

Brandon shook his head. "Whatever. I didn't know that, and I've never heard of this group. More religious malarkey. But, it's your life, Ron. I have tried to help you. If you keep being involved in church stuff, you will surely lose your company."

The server returned, "Are you ready to order?"

"We are. I would like the baked lasagna and a salad," Brandon said.

Ron ordered Caesar salad with grilled salmon, and as the server left, Brandon picked up the conversation again. "Do you remember Scott Clay who left our group about a year and a half ago?"

I do," Ron said. "Nice guy, and I always enjoyed talking with hm. I don't know if you knew it, but he is also an elder in his church."

"He's dead," Brandon announced. "Died in his sleep last week."

"He died? What happened?" Ron asked.

Brandon replied. "I always knew he would not live long since he was Mr. Five-by-Five. A real fatty. The group was always trying to get him to diet. In my monthly one-on-one, I also pushed him about his weight, but even making fun of him didn't help. Well, now he is gone."

"How are his wife and family doing?" Ron asked.

Brandon replied, "I have no idea. Once he left the group, I wrote him off. I have absolutely no use for anyone who leaves the group. I just never have understood how anyone can leave the group, particularly with me as the chair."

"Do you mind if I say a prayer and bless our meals?" Ron asked as the food arrived.

"You go right ahead." Brandon said. "I am digging into this lasagna!" Ron bowed his head and said a silent prayer while Brandon started eating.

The men sat quietly eating for several minutes when Brandon asked, "Well, Ron, why did you want to meet today? Got some big problems other than losing your top leader, Charlie? And remember I have the guy for you."

Brandon took a bite of his salad.

"No problems," Ron replied. "I just wanted to tell you that I am resigning from the peer group, effective immediately."

Brandon spat out his bite of salad and exclaimed, "What the hell?"

Sputtering, he managed to get some words out, "You can't just resign. You have a commitment to the group. You still have to pay the dues for the next three months. And why the hell would you resign?"

"Brandon," Ron said, "I don't think you really want to know why."

Brandon sat in silence. He set his fork down on the table and picked up his glass of chardonnay, downing at least half of it. He stared at Ron with anger and disgust.

"After all I have done for you," he began, "and all the help you have gotten from the group, how can you just resign. Without me and the group, you would be a total failure and your company that your daddy founded would be bankrupt.

"And the thanks I get is you sitting here telling me you are resigning from the group. And I even have the guy to replace Charlie, who could save your sorry butt. This is bullshit."

"Do you want to know why or not?" Ron asked.

Brandon just stared at him angrily. "Who do you think you are that you can just resign from my group. Do I want to know why? Not really. I was close to throwing you out of the group anyway. Keep your reasons to your damn self. I would appreciate it if you would just leave."

Ron stood and said, "That's fine. I will keep my reasons to myself, and I doubt if I told you it would do any good any way."

"Just move your sorry ass out of here," Brandon said. "and stop at the hostess desk and pay for the lunches. Oh, leave a big tip for the server."

Ron looked at Brandon, and without another word, left and took care of the bill.

Unlocking the car with his remote, Ron got in and sat still. He felt disgusted, dirty, and cheated. He really wanted to tell Brandon how he felt. He wanted to tell him about the lack of integrity in the group and the lack of integrity in Brandon.

But he needed to put this behind him and focus on his company and its people. He started the car and headed back to the office. He had the next thirty minutes to process what had just happened and try to reach his own closure, since he did not have that with Brandon. He called the office and asked Mary to see if Charlie and Susan could meet with him on his return. His only regret was that he hadn't confronted Brandon about the wrongful use of the speakers' materials.

Ron made good time getting back to the office. He went straight to Mary's office.

"Hi, Mary. Are Susan and Charlie available?"

"They are in your office," she said. "Need anything?"

He shook his head no and mouthed, "Thank you."

He walked into his office and greeted Susan and Charlie. "Thanks for taking time to meet with me. I just need to talk."

"I take it you left the peer group?" Susan asked.

"I did. At least verbally. I think I need to send something in writing," He said.

"You look a little frazzled," Charlie said.

"I guess I am. I should have expected this from Brandon."

Susan asked, "Expected what from Brandon?"

"Manipulation. Taunting. Berating. To name a few," Ron said.

"By the way," Charlie said, "about fifteen minutes ago Brandon called. I was not able to pick up, but he left a voice mail. Want to hear it?"

"Do I have a choice?" Ron asked.

"Yes you do," Charlie said. "It is up to you."

"Play it." replied Ron.

The team leaned in toward Charlie's cell phone as he put his voice mail on the speaker mode.

"Hey Charlie, this is Brandon. Sorry I missed you, but we can talk later. I heard that you have resigned and have accepted a new position as president of another company. As president, you need to get into a peer group. I have an unexpected opening in one of my groups. Had a member, a real jerk, resign from the group today. Would love to have you in the group. Call me and we can discuss the details. Oh, and if you need an operations manager in your new role, let me know. I have the guy for you."

"Are you kidding me?" Ron exclaimed. "Just a few minutes ago he described me as a sorry ass. Now I am a jerk. And now he is pushing his operations guy on you, Charlie."

Susan said. "Consider the source."

"What happened in your meeting?" Charlie asked. "Did you lay it on him about the ethical issues with the group—and with him?"

"No," Ron answered.

"Nothing at all?" Susan asked.

"Not one point," Ron replied. "I told him I was resigning and he said, 'What the hell' and proceeded to berate me. Oh, and he said that he has the guy for our operations manager position who will save my butt and my company. It was pathetic."

"Makes you feel good about your decision?" Susan asked.

"Totally," Ron replied. "I keep thinking how could I have positioned the discussion so that I could tell him my reasons. I really wanted to lay out for him how unethical the group is, but I never got a chance. How did I put up with his behavior for so long! And why did I allow myself to violate my integrity."

"Let's step back a minute," Charlie said. "What is this about having the guy for me if I need an operations manager in my new role?"

"I forgot that part," Ron said "He began by saying he heard a rumor that you had resigned to take a position in another company. He said that I would miss you because you have saved my butt many times. He then said he had the perfect guy for our operations role. It seems this guy recently resigned from a job he had only six months, over disagreements with the CEO. Brandon then said that a good buddy of his, a peer group chair, recommended him."

"I declined to meet the guy, which angered Brandon because he had assured the candidate and his buddy that I would meet with the guy. I told him to have the guy send a resume, and we would put him in the process. He also said that people at top positions do not go through processes. They get referred and hired without any extensive interviewing."

"I really don't know Brandon," Charlie said, "other than you introduced him to me a couple of years ago. Based on what you just shared, the guy is not worth your time. I am glad you didn't waste time telling him about the integrity issues. Time would have been better spent if you talked to the wall."

Susan added, "Ron, put this behind you. You, and we, do not need that negativity."

"I agree," he said. "Done."

"I am so excited about our search and the use of a process," Susan said. "My team is really well prepared and doing a good job. Ron, focus on this, and don't think about Brandon. He is now history."

Charlie and Susan left for their offices, leaving Ron alone so he could put his thoughts together. Looking back into Ron's office, Susan noted he had his head bowed and was obviously praying. It was going to be a long night for Ron.

Never, never compromise your integrity.

Chapter 14

MAKING PROGRESS

After several days of diligent work, the HR Team had finished scoring and was getting close to completing the screener interviews. Susan decided it was time to check in on her team and see how their interviews were going. Mark and Cathy were on their telephones, obviously conducting telephone interviews, so she stopped to talk to Maria who had just ended an interview.

"Hi Maria. How are the interviews progressing?"

"We are making excellent progress," Maria told her. "We are finding some good potential candidates. I know I can speak for Cathy and Mark that we are thoroughly enjoying doing the screeners. And the reaction of the candidates has been excellent."

"That sounds great," Susan replied. "By the way I never heard the final count on resumes received."

"Mark, Cathy and I had a huddle this morning and Mark told us the final resume count was 145."

"Wow! I did not realize we received that many," Susan exclaimed, "When do you think the screeners will be completed?"

"Actually, our last screener will be finished this afternoon about 3:00 p.m.," Maria said. "That is Mark's last one and Cathy and I finish about 1:30 p.m."

"Do you think we could meet tomorrow morning and review the results?" Susan asked.

Maria said, "I don't see why we can't, but just to be sure I will check with Cathy and Mark and make sure they can be ready."

"Let's do this," Susan responded. "I will set a meeting for 9:00 a.m. tomorrow in the conference room, and if it doesn't work for Mark and Cathy, we can adjust it."

"Okay," Maria said. "I really think we will all be ready in time for the meeting."

"Thank you," Susan said. "I am really anxious to see the results. See you tomorrow. I have a few things to wrap up before the end of the day."

On her way to the parking lot, Susan stopped at Ron's office.

"Busy?" She said softly through Ron's open door.

Ron looked up and said. "Oh Susan, come on in for a minute and tell me how your team is doing. I am starting to get somewhat anxious about our search."

"I just met briefly with Maria," she said. "We have received 145 resumes and my team will complete the screeners, probably as we speak. I am going to meet with them in the morning to review the results. If you have time, you are more than welcome to join us."

"I would love to sit in on your meeting," he replied. "However, I have a meeting with Ralph and the bank."

"Are you okay after the meeting you had with Brandon a few days ago?" Susan asked. "Pardon me if it's none of my business."

Ron was quiet for a moment and then said, "I am okay. It was something I should have done a couple of years ago. And, honestly, his behavior in the meeting made it easy for me. I have a feeling the peer group will be told something entirely different than reality."

"Does that bother you?" She asked.

Ron paused. "Yes and no." he said. "I had some excellent relation-ships with some of the members, and I will miss our discussions. If I ever even see Brandon again, it will be too soon. To think I tolerated his behavior for years and never spoke up or challenged him. . . . It will be hard to forgive myself for not acting sooner."

"Do you think the members are fearful of him?" She asked.

"If you had asked me that several months ago, I probably would have said no," Ron replied. "I think we were all under his thumb, his manipulation. To be honest I feel like I have been set free."

Just then Charlie walked into the office. "Can I join in with you?"

Ron nodded and said. "Susan updated me on the progress of the search. We have received 145 resumes and her team is finishing the screener interviews. Now I am getting anxious. So, why have you blessed us with your presence?"

"Wow! I am a blessing? Who knew?" Charlie said and the three laughed. Charlie continued, "I had an interesting telephone call a few minutes ago."

"Let me guess," Ron said, "Brandon."

"Bingo!" Charlie responded. "Would you like to hear about it, or would you rather not?"

"If I say no," Ron said, "something tells me you will tell me anyway."

Susan piped in, "Of course he will. You know Charlie."

"Go ahead, Charlie," Ron said. "Let's hear the gory details."

"First," Charlie began, "he congratulated me on my new position. Oh, before I go any further, I will be brief and to the point. I have to summarize a twenty-minute call during which I probably spoke three minutes."

"Okay, so after he congratulated you, what did he say?" Ron asked.

"He said he did not like to tell tales out of school, but he had to ask you to leave the peer group. He said he felt your weaknesses as a leader were not healthy for the other members and that they didn't like you anyway. Then he talked about how many good things he has heard about me over the years and how without me, you, Ron, would have run the company into the ground."

"He then told me your seat with the group was mine. Finally, he told me about this guy I needed to hire if I need an operations manager."

"I almost feel sorry for him," Ron said. "Almost. Brandon is now history."

"I'm glad to hear you put Brandon in history," Charlie said. "He is not worth one minute of your time or my time. Anyway, I need to head out. I am meeting with two of my mentees this evening. I absolutely love Christian mentoring!"

Susan added, "Tonight is quilting night at the church. We have requests for two quilts for next Sunday in church. I am going to pick up my three children and take them to dinner before I get out my needle and thread!"

"Thanks to both of you for your support," Ron said. "I needed that, and I know I can always count on you. I have an elders' meeting at the church this evening so I also need to get going. See you tomorrow."

With that, they all headed their different directions.

As Ron pulled out of the parking lot, his cell phone rang. He saw it was Mary's number.

"Hi, Mary. What's up?"

"Ron," she said, "I just heard that Sam was involved in an auto accident this afternoon."

"Is he okay," Ron asked anxiously.

"Thank the Lord, yes," she said. "He was t-boned when another driver ran a red light. All I know is that he is bruised, has a broken arm, and is home. I am not aware of any other injuries."

"Thanks for calling me." He said. "I will call Sam right now."

Ron pushed the button for Sam's cell phone, and on the fourth ring, Sam picked up.

"Hi, Ron," he said. "Before you ask, I am doing fine. It could have been worse. The other driver, an elderly man, is in the hospital. He needs our prayers."

"I will pray for him. Do you want some company?" Ron asked.

"No. I am okay. I know you have an elders' meeting this evening and are probably on your way right now. And my mom and dad are here, and you know my mom."

"I do," Ron said. "I know she will take good care of you, so I won't worry."

"Mom is a true Nurse-Nancy," Sam said.

"Mary said you have a broken arm. How bad is it?"

Sam replied, "I do. I have some bruises and I am stiff all over and my right leg has severe contusions making walking a little difficult. The Lord must have had an angel riding with me. My truck is really damage and not sure how well it can be repaired.."

"Feel free to stay home tomorrow and heal. You do not need to come into the office. Take time and let your body heal," Ron said.

"Thanks, but I am all right," he said. "I am not one to sit at home. However, I just might be a little late for work in the morning."

Ron laughed and said, "I will have a tardy slip filled out for you."

"Thanks, Ron." Sam replied. "Mom is telling me to hang up. See you tomorrow."

"Take care, Sam," Ron replied, "You are in my prayers."

Focus on the positive and push the negative away.

Chapter 15

INITIAL RESULTS

Susan got into the office a little early with some fresh donuts, apple fritters, coffee, and orange juice. She could barely contain her excitement, waiting to hear the report from her team. She poured herself some coffee just as her team entered the conference room.

"Donuts!" Mark exclaimed. "Apple fritters! It's like heaven on earth." He put one of each on a plate. "Maria and Cathy get some treats!" Mark invited them, but both of them just gave him a harsh look and went and poured some coffee.

"Let's hear about your progress and your results," Susan said. "I am really anxious to hear everything. Who can get us started?"

"I was elected by default to give the report," Maria said.

Susan, with humor in mind, replied, "Who's fault was it?" Everyone laughed.

"It was my own fault," Maria said, "I did not speak soon enough."

"Well, Maria, the floor is yours," Susan said.

"I know we gave you a resume count earlier, but the final count is 185. Of these, using resume scoring, we discovered that thirty-five lacked at least one of the five requirements. That left us with 150 who had all the requirements and most of the preferred and desired items.

"Based on earlier discussions we then met and reviewed each resume to select twenty percent for the telephone screener. We actually completed thirty telephone screeners, and we have identified our top twelve for the next step."

"Excellent summary, Maria," Susan said. "Thank you to you, Mark and Cathy for a job well done."

"I have a list of the top twelve, and their resumes, ready for you—as well as the results of the screener interviews," Maria said. "How do you want to proceed?"

"My first reaction was to just forward your top twelve to the next step," Susan said, "because I trust you and you were fully trained on the process. However, after thinking about it, I would like for us to have a discussion and have you summarize each candidate for me. This also provides me with a knowledge base when we get the results from the next step. Does that work for you?"

Maria responded. "Yes. We can start with the first one on the list," Maria handed Susan a copy of the top twelve.

"I see we have three women on the list," Susan said. "I am a little surprised, because we typically do not have many female applicants since we are a manufacturing company. Maybe things are changing!"

Maria started the report, "The first one is Sarah Matthews. She has a resume score of 200, all of the requirements, a bachelor's degree, both sales and marketing experience, a major in business, and customer service experience. The interrogation was perfect. On the three technical questions, she clearly has supervised, and she gave an excellent coaching example. She has had responsibility for hiring, and she purports to use a system similar to what we are doing with this search. She sees herself as a motivator, but was not clear on understanding a motivating environment. She was consistent with five of the eight structured screener questions."

"Did you do her interview?" Susan asked.

"No, Cathy did," Maria said.

"Cathy," Susan said, "since you did her interview, would like to add anything?"

Cathy shared, "She is very articulate. She took time to think before answering a question. I could tell she was listening intently. Even over the phone you could sense her sensitivity level. She asked good questions during my icebreaker time. Strong value system. She is definitely a calm and patient leader. Her primary focus and purpose is helping others. The only area I was not clear on was her strategic business planning."

"That was very good, Cathy," Susan said. "I like the way you organized it, and then I liked your personal comments and observations. Let's move on to the next candidate."

The team took turns reporting on the twelve candidates for Susan's benefit. Each team member took a turn reviewing the candidates and sharing their personal observations.

"Job well done, team!" Susan congratulated them. "That was really helpful. Now we move our top twelve on to the next step. I did finalize our consulting agreement with the Choosing Winners© group, and I have signed us up for the training and to use their system."

Mark asked. "Do you have the dates for the training and where it will be held?"

Susan replied, "I will finalize the dates tomorrow. They will come here for the training."

"I don't remember how long the training lasts," Cathy said. "I think two days?"

"That's right," Susan replied. "I will send an email with the dates as soon as they are set."

As the four picked up materials and prepared to leave the conference room, Maria said, "I heard that Sam was in an auto accident. Is he okay?"

Just then the conference room door opened and in walked Sam, arm in a sling.

"How is the search going?" He asked.

"That's not important," Cathy said. "How are you?"

"I'm really okay, and I appreciate the angel the Lord sent to protect me," He replied. "I heard a news report on the radio on my ride to the office and learned that the other driver passed away during the night. The reporter said that he probably was driving over the speed limit and hit the other vehicle, a large pickup truck on the driver's side. The reporter added that the other driver sustained minor injuries. I remember when I got out of my truck that his car actually ended up under my truck and the windshield was smashed. By the way, I can't drive with my arm in a sling so my mother drove me to work. You can draw straws to see who takes me home."

"Well, we are so thankful that you are okay, and we will pray for the other driver's family," Susan said.

Sam replied, "Thank you. How is the search going?"

Susan answered. "Search is going well, thanks to this super team. We have twelve candidates we are sending to the Choosing Winners© organization to do phone interviews for us."

"Sounds like congratulations are in order! Good job!" Sam said to the whole team. "I knew Susan had a great team behind her."

Smiling and thanking Sam, and wishing him quick healing, the team members left the conference room.

"Thanks for stopping in," Susan said. "I know the team really appreciated your congratulations. They have done a great job."

"We are lucky to have them." he said. "I went to see Ron, and he is out of the office. I understand he left his peer group, but that Brandon gave him a hard time. Is he handling it okay?"

"I talked with him yesterday afternoon," Susan said. "He was handling the whole deal very well. Any doubts he had were wiped away by Brandon's behavior. It seems like Ron's only regret is taking so long to see the lack of integrity."

"I have known Ron for a long time." Sam said. "He will be just fine."

Susan said good-bye to Sam and turned her attention to the next step. She would send the twelve candidate names and email addresses to the Choosing Winners© organization and schedule a meeting with the Leadership Team and her three team members to go over the basis for the telephone interviews being done by the consultants.

Preparation and focused work produces positive results.

Chapter 16

PROBE INTERVIEW

That afternoon, the Leadership Team and the HR Team gathered in the conference room so Susan could explain the product that the consultants would provide—assessments of the top twelve candidates. She also invited Ron's assistant, Mary, to the meeting, asking her to take notes. As the teams gathered, several saw Sam with his arm in a sling and asked questions.

After Sam explained what had happened to him, Ron turned the floor over to Susan.

"Thanks, Ron." she said. "Our consultants will interview our twelve candidates who were selected following the screener process. The team, Mark, Maria, and Cathy, went through each candidate's information in detail, and they have done an excellent job of narrowing the field to the top twelve."

"Pardon me," Ralph said, "I just have a quick question. Did we have any internal candidates?"

Susan turned to the team. "Did you have any internal candidates?"

Maria answered. "We did not have any internal candidates.

"Thanks," Ralph said. "But let's assume we did. How would they have been handled? If they were already an employee here, would there have been special treatment?"

"Ron do you want to answer that?" Susan asked.

"Our policy is that internal candidates enter the process with a resume and go through each step, the same as external candidates."

"I don't disagree," Ralph said. "But, what is the rationale?"

"We believe an internal candidate needs to compete for the position and not have it handled to them or be given special treatment," Ron said. "In the end, they will feel much better about themselves, as they competed and succeeded."

"That makes a lot of sense," Ralph replied.

"I was speaking to the consultant at the Choosing Winners© organization and I asked him about internal candidates," Susan shared with the team. "He basically agrees with what Ron just explained. He told me that their organization also conducts full searches for some clients, using all the tools they are teaching us. He told me about a time they were doing a search for a director of manufacturing for a client, and there were five internal candidates."

"When it was time to select the top three to six candidates for the one-to-one interview, none of them were selected. He shared that he was concerned about giving this news to his client."

"When he told the client," the client said, 'Obviously your process works. I would have been stunned if even one had made it.'"

"He told me that if an internal candidate is not selected, one of the consultants will meet with that person and offer suggestions for growth and development."

Bill continued the discussion down the same path. "There is one person in this room who I thought might apply. Why not Linda?"

Linda looked startled. "Only you, Bill, would ask this question. To be honest, it never even crossed my mind. There is a big difference between the operations role and my role in manufacturing. I love what I am doing and am not interested in changing. My manufacturing team has made so much progress, and we have great plans for the future. I want to be part of that future."

"Thanks for sharing," Bill said, "I look forward to what you and your team will do in the years to come."

"Unless there are other questions," Susan said, "we need to focus on the task at hand, the basis for this interview the consultants will conduct for us and the product they will produce for us."

Hearing no questions, Susan began her presentation.

"The interview they use is based on the twelve areas of Proficiency of Outstanding Leaders and Managers. I am going to go through all twelve proficiencies so when we get the reports, you will be prepared to understand them. These proficiencies are based on a study of outstanding leaders and managers.

The interview consists of thirty-six questions—three questions on each of the proficiency areas. Each question has a response guide, based on their research and the candidate's response is compared to the guide and it is determined whether the candidate is consistent or not consistent with the research. Mary please distribute a copy of the proficiencies to everyone. I will go through each one of the proficiencies, explaining it, and of course answering your questions. We begin with Purpose."

PURPOSE

This leader/manager strives to make a long-lasting, positive impact on the organization and its people. This individual has an appreciation for the significance of the role and a realistic view of the influence of the position for promoting team member growth, customer satisfaction, and organizational direction. Believing others want to do their very best is characteristic of this person. This leader or manager's greatest satisfaction comes from the growth of team members and improving the "bottom line." Considerable time and energy is devoted to improving the work environment, customer satisfaction and overall credibility of the organization.

Susan stated, "This describes what drives the best leaders and managers. It is what gets them out of bed each day to do their job. These leaders spend time and energy coaching, working on the overall environment, and building credibility. Any questions or observations?"

"I am impressed," Charlie said. "that really matches up with our *who* description of our new operations leader and our core values."

"I like the focus on being positive—believing that others do want to do their very best," Sally said. "And Charlie, that is what you have preached for years."

Ralph spoke up next. "I trust you all noticed the focus on improving the bottom line. That is my kind of person!"

"I am not surprised that you picked up on that, Ralph. Now, anyone else have anything to share?" Susan asked looking around the room. She moved on to the next proficiency.

OPERATIONAL FOCUS

This leader/manager is effective and efficient at managing situations, events, and people. This individual has a thorough working knowledge of specific management and leadership values and behaviors. This person operates from a base of anticipation and prevention in order to minimize and manage crisis and conflict in the organization. This leader/manager understands financial procedures and practices and is financially astute. It is typical for this person to set short- and long-range goals for personnel, facilities, equipment, and the budgeting process. This person is prepared and prevention-oriented. This leader/manager has an excellent balance in leadership style and management behavior.

"I like the emphasis on anticipation and prevention," Susan said. "And even though goals are important, there is still concern for the finance side. I have seen too many operations leaders who think the finance is up to the accounting team and that they do not have to worry about the finances. And that commercial is sponsored by Ralph."

Ralph stood up and took a bow.

"Susan, I think this supports our *who* that we put together in our brainstorming," Ron said. "I know we have several more proficiencies to cover, but do you have an example of what an assessment report might be like for a person who was interviewed?"

"I thought this might be of interest," Susan said. "Maria, please give everyone a copy of an assessment written about operational focus. This is a real assessment, and the person is referred to as 'candidate' instead of he or she, it has been substituted to make this totally confidential."

It is very clear that *Candidate* will seek the reasons for the poor performance of an organization and will focus on the people in their efforts to make improvements, and it is evident that they will work from clear and specific priorities. *Candidate* indicates that the person's top leadership qualities are passion for leadership, high standards for self and others, ability to follow up, and a focus on self accountability and accountability for others. *Candidate* states that managers need to have specific areas of expertise and states that they are most expert in people and team development, hiring, driving customer service and a strong business acumen.

"Do you see how this reflects the proficiency statement?" Susan asked the group.

"I think so," Sam said. "I do like the use of 'very clear,' 'evident,' and 'states.' I assume they actually include the words used by a candidate. And I like that they obviously asked about the candidate's leadership qualities, as it gives us an opportunity to compare them, based on their own words, to our *who* criteria."

"That was impressive, Sam," Bill said. "I agree with you."

"I'm not sure what the specific question used was," Ron said, "but I like hearing that the candidate, when faced with a problem, takes time to study it, speak with the people, and then works from set priorities, knowing they cannot do everything at once."

"Excellent analysis guys," Susan said. "Anyone else? Let's move on to Value Base. Also, keep in mind that the interviewer is asking three questions on each of the twelve proficiencies. They are comparing the answer to a response guide to determine consistency with the research. Now Value Base."

VALUE BASE

Possessing a clear and strong value system, this individual behaves in ways consistent with stated beliefs and behaviors. This strength in a clear and strong value system is based on a commitment to valuing the human worth and dignity of all people. This leader/manager believes it is important to be seen as a positive person and understands that positive behavior generates a positive work environment. This person expects leaders /managers to be consistently open and honest and expects that the organization must have a clear set of behavioral rules and operating principles. This individual is aware of the significance of the role of leader/ manager and exercises care to bring high credibility to the organization.

"Any thoughts or observations?" Susan asked.

"This sounds a whole lot like not only our *who* criteria," Linda said, "but also our core values."

"I agree," Ralph said. "I like the inclusion of operating principles."

"Susan," Ron asked, "do you happen to have a sample assessment of a candidate on Value Base?"

"I think so," she said, turning towards Maria. "Please look through my stuff and see if there is one on Value Base."

It did not take long for Maria to respond. "I have one. I will give everyone a copy."

Candidate believes that a manager must have a strong value system and states that he or she values integrity, honesty, people with honest opinions, smart people, and inclusivity. It is evident that they share their values with others through direct communication and their actions. It is difficult to ascertain if they will help their employees to be accepting and positive regarding their differences, and it is not clear if they clearly focus on the worth and dignity of others in resolving conflicts. It appears that they believe unethical and immoral behavior, on the part of managers, creates a negative environment. It seems like they expect managers to be open and honest at all times.

"This sample gives me an opportunity to tell you about how certain words or phrases are used in the written assessment," Susan said, "and to point out that this candidate's ability to actually apply his or her values is questionable. When you read that the candidate believes, or 'it is clear' or 'evident,' that tells you the candidate is consistent with the response guide. When you read 'it is difficult to ascertain, or not clear,' the candidate is not consistent with the criteria. And when you read it 'appears or seems like,' it indicates that the candidate might be consistent and more information is needed. I hope that is helpful."

"Reading this description of the candidate's value base makes me very uncomfortable," Charlie said. "It is not consistent at all with our values. I would think this is at least a red flag."

"What is a red flag?" Bill asked, "My Buckeye flag has a lot of scarlet on it, which is like red." This got everyone's attention.

"Nice try Bill," Charlie said. "A red flag means 'watch out,' 'danger,' or to a lesser degree 'concerns are present, seek more information.'"

"Good description, Charlie," Bill replied. "This response clearly has some red flag issues. If indeed this is part of this person, the candidate is not a fit for our team."

"I will provide you with a written list of the descriptors and what they mean when we get the reports," Susan said. "Any other comments? Seeing none, let's move on to Visionary."

VISIONARY

Living in the reality of the present, this leader/manager is also able to see its impact on the future. This person is seen as innovative, imaginative, and creative. This person recognizes the importance of proven practices, but is always open to new ideas and change when necessary. This individual recognizes that the organization will grow if the right people are hired and then coached and developed. This manager has the ability to identify talent and find the right fit and match for the organization. This person stays up to date about new practices and trends through research, reading and networking.

"My first reaction," Sally said, "this sounds like Charlie. He has always maintained that proven practices are important, but he is open to hearing new ideas and changes. And the key word as applied to Charlie is necessary."

"I like the opening," Ralph said. "Too often we do not accept our realities and how they impact our decision-making."

"This matches with our core value of not being satisfied with the status quo and looking for a better way," Sam said. "In my field of technology, change is just part of our life."

"I like the focus on hiring the right people," Linda said. "I think our work on this search, getting trained, and implementing a new process are all consistent with this statement. We want all our leaders to value hiring the right people."

"Any other observations?" Susan asked. "Let's move on to the next one."

"How about a break?" Bill asked. "I am about to float away."

"I hear you," Susan said. "Let's take a fifteen minute break."

When the team regathered, Susan introduced the next proficiency.

RELATIONSHIP BUILDER

This leader/manager has excellent human relations skills and values positive and productive relationships with all audiences. Using many and varied strategies to develop and maintain these positive relationships with team members and customers is characteristic of this person. This individual sees the positive and good in situations and freely and openly communicates these insights to others. In addition to being positive, this person believes that knowing people well and interacting on a one-to-one basis are key to favorable relationships. This leader/manager likes people and wants to be liked by them and is highly valued by customers.

Susan asked, "Any reactions to this proficiency?'

"I have to admit the last sentence confuses me," Ralph said. "I am not sure how this liking fits into the operations position."

"Hmm," Sam jumped into the conversation. "That means you would rather that we not like you? I do get frustrated with you some times, but I still like you."

Susan smiled at the humor and stepped into the conversation. "I asked the consultant about this, as I was a little surprised by it. He said that in their control group of 350 managers, over seventy-five percent of them stated they like people and want to be liked. In their research they then asked why it was important to be liked and the responses focused on better and more productive relationships. He also added that those who do not want to be liked tend to be what is referred to as an 'arms length' leader."

"That really makes a lot of sense," Bill said. "In marketing and sales, we have forever said that customers buy from those they like."

"What is this 'arm's length' belief and why do people want to keep an 'arm's length' from their employees?" Sally asked.

"Keeping an 'arm's length'," Susan answered, "means they keep their distance. They do not want to be close to their employees for fear that they might have to some day discipline them, or even terminate their employment. In my opinion, a competent manager need not fear knowing their employees. Anything else you have questions about?"

"I am identifying with the many and varied strategies for developing and maintaining positive relationships," Sally said. "I have been watching Ron for several years now. He is an excellent example."

"I agree," Susan said. "Let's take a look at Growth Activator."

GROWTH ACTIVATOR

This person is a catalyst in a growth environment. This coach/mentor facilitates growth opportunities for others: arranging, directing, implementing and teaching. This person utilizes the talents and strengths of team members to help and teach other team members. This manager is aware of the behaviors and attitudes of successful team members and uses this knowledge when selecting new team members. This excellent delegator considers a team members strengths and interests, as well as job responsibilities in delegating responsibilities to others. This person uses delegation to give team members an opportunity to grow beyond their current responsibilities.

"The first time I read this, I loved it," Susan said. "Reading it again, I am falling in love all over again. Does this sound like who we want as our operations leader?"

"It sounds like what we want from every leader in the company," Sally said. "I believe we have this quality in most of our leaders, if not all."

"I like the delegation piece," Sam said. "I am not a good delegator, and reading that, I am beginning to understand why I am not a good delegator. However, I am a little vague on the interests piece."

Ron said, "Those who understand delegation are also excellent Situational Leaders. They do consider strengths, job responsibilities, time issues and importance to the company. They also know if you delegate to someone with the strength, but he or she does not really want to do it, it will get done, but not at the quality level we want. Interests can also apply to using it to help an associate to grow."

"I need to keep us moving. The next section is Communicator," Susan said.

COMMUNICATOR

This leader/manager is a direct, open and honest communicator. This person uses many and varied ways to communicate with team members and customers—verbal, non-verbal, and written. One-to-one interaction is of great importance to this individual, and consistent effort is made to maximize the use of one-to-one interaction. This person is a highly skilled presenter and discussion leader. An excellent listener, this person is constantly seeking to gain insights to help team members and customers. This individual is one whom others seek out in order to be heard. Responding to inquiries in an adult logical manner is typical of this leader/manager.

"What is the meaning behind, 'others seek out in order to be heard?" Bill asked.

"It is that person who is most open and welcoming to others," Susan said. "In our company who do you think this is?"

Bill thought for a moment. "Charlie. He is always willing to listen to you no matter what he is doing. I am going to miss that, so this new operations leader better be someone we can go to and just talk."

"I agree with Bill," Sally offered. "Charlie is a great listener."

"What else did you see that is important in our new team member?" Susan asked.

"The ideal leader uses a variety of communication techniques depending on the person and the situation," Ron said. "This communicator has not forgotten the value and importance of one-to-one communication."

"Well, since no one will ask, I will," Sally said. "What is an adult logical manner?"

"Think about it for a minute," Ron said. "It says that this person responds to inquiries in an adult logical manner. This means when asked a question, this person will listen, using active listening skills, be patient, be sensitive and caring, and would never make fun of someone asking a question."

"Thanks, Ron," Susan said. "I'd like to say that you took the words right out of my mouth, but that would be a lie. I also was trying to figure it out. Let's move on to Accord."

ACCORD

This person consciously works to establish open and honest working partnerships with various groups within the organization. It is of the utmost importance for this leader to involve others in decision-making, planning, and implementing activities. This person understands that team members have a stronger sense of commitment to the organization when they feel a sense of ownership. Desiring overall harmony between and among all of the groups in the organization, this person also wants team members to have an appreciation for the ideas and opinions of each other. This person believes that by knowing as much as possible about individual team members provides for more helping opportunities.

"What is this section saying to you?" Susan asked.

Ralph answered, "This is powerful. Not that the others have not been, but this is loaded with truth, and specifics regarding leadership and commitment. It reminds me of the time when my manager asked me how I planned to get my people to make a commitment to the company. I don't remember exactly what I said, but it was along the lines of make a commitment to them first, give bonuses, and tell them the mission and goals of the company. I will never forget the expression on his face and him saying to me, 'Ralph you have so much to learn.'"

"Did he ever tell you what answer he had expected?" Sam asked.

"He did," Ralph answered. "Only after I was knee deep in alligators and the water in the swamp was rising. He proceeded to explain that you, as the manager, if you want to build commitment, you will involve your team in decisions, planning, and then implementing programs and processes.

"I was not involving anyone. I was telling people what to do without any involvement or explanations. Then, he said to me that people do not typically leave a company for more money. Most of the time it is because of a weak, poor, incompetent manager. And he told me if I didn't change, I would soon lose my team."

"That had to hurt." Linda said.

"It did," Ralph replied. "The good news is he got my attention, and then he began intensely coaching me. Now you lucky people have the exceptional end product." He looked around at the team members who were all smiling at his words.

"We certainly are thankful for you, Ralph," Bill said. "And in looking through this, I think this section also implies team leading and team building."

"Good observation, Bill," Susan said. "I agree. Let's go to Sensitivity."

> ### *SENSITIVITY*
>
> This leader/manager is sensitive and responsive to the thoughts and feelings of team members and customers. Using a variety of methods, this person actively strives to discover others' thoughts and feelings. While focusing quickly on the individual and his or her needs, this person will not lose sight of the task to be accomplished.
>
> This manager is open, approachable, caring, concerned, and shows a genuine interest in others. Having a clear mission of helping others grow, this person automatically moves to assess team member, customer and organizational needs. This person responds immediately to the obvious and critical needs of others.

"I believe that everyone in this room would love to work with this person," Susan said. Not only is it describing a sensitive person, but also one who is responsive to the needs of others. Remember we said we need a servant leader? Here it is."

"And notice that it is similar to communication." Sam said. "This person is using a variety of ways to discover the thoughts and feelings of others. I worked in a company several years ago that would not tolerate this kind of behavior."

"In fact, I remember my manager telling me that all he wanted from us was for us to come to work on time, walk past his office without saying good morning, get to work, take a proper lunch break, and then go home without stopping to say good night. He also stressed that if he noticed any drama in the office, heads would roll. Nice guy."

"You can't be serious, Sam," Linda said. "You are pulling our legs."

"I wish I were," Sam said. "This was my reality. It was a totally negative environment in which no one cared about anyone. The turnover was way above average, and people were so frustrated they often ended up yelling at each other. This would cause him to come running out of his office and yell at us to shut up and get to work. The good news is that I learned a lot from this guy about what not to do."

"Sam that is quite a story. Sorry you had to live in that environment," Susan said. "Let's move on to the next point."

STABILITY/OBJECTIVITY

This leader/manager is calm and patient. Thorough data collection and input from others affected by decisions helps this person make good decisions. Possessing a commitment to prevention and anticipation, this individual is seldom caught off-guard or taken by surprise. Logical in approach, patient in behavior, and confident in direction, are characteristic of this leader/manager. This person does not over-react or use poor judgment in conflict or crisis situations. This individual is highly objective and fair, and believes that equal treatment could mean the same for all regardless of individual uniqueness.

"How about that final sentence?" Ron asked. "What does that say to you?"

"I'm glad you brought that up," Charlie said. "That is a difficult concept for people to understand, and I have found most beginning managers have no idea what it means, or how to react to it. So many times over the years, I have heard managers say that they always, absolutely treat everyone equally. They are good liars."

"I worked for a manager once who treated us all always equal, and at all times," Linda said. "I remember I once asked her to spend more time with one of my associates who had difficulties and several performance issues. The manager told me she could not give more time to her than she gave to other employees. She added that she always treats people equally."

"No apology," Bill said, "but that is just pathetic. How do people like that keep their positions?"

"How many of you have worked in a company where managers involve people in decisions, planning and implementing?" Ron asked. "Or are sensitive and responsive to needs? How many have known all they can about their employees in order to be able to help them? Or how many were prevention-oriented and took care to anticipate the unexpected? How about a show of hands?" Not a hand was raised.

"Let's move on to Performance Expectations," Susan said.

PERFORMANCE EXPECTATION

This manager has high expectations for self and others. This person has a clear understanding of the relationship between team member performance evaluation and their growth and development. This manager expects each job to be described with clearly stated responsibilities. This manager wants a specific system of evaluation with clearly spelled-out assessment criteria. This person wants to be held accountable for performance and will hold others accountable. This leader/manager has an appreciation for the balance between the performer and performance. This manager clearly defines areas for growth and expects the same from others.

"The consultant shared with me that another way to look at this is by using the word accountability," Susan said. "Does that help with your understanding?"

"Yes, that helps," Ralph said. "I do like the fact they used the word expectation. This is the only company I have worked in that actually sets expectations for the employees and then follows up with clear and specific evaluations."

"I am excited about the plan Ron has set out for us to change the performance evaluation system for the employees," Susan said. "Eliminating the annual review and having twelve monthly evaluations as part of a program, based on specific metrics for all responsibilities on all job descriptions, makes so much sense, and I find it totally consistent with this section."

"I think, Susan," Ron said, "we can move on to the last section."

"I agree," she said. "Let's look at Organization/Preparation."

ORGANIZATION/PREPARATION

This manager is highly organized and well prepared, and expects the same from others. Working from specific goals and priorities is standard practice for this person. This manager maintains a well-defined order and structure to both personal and professional activities. This manager devotes considerable time planning and anticipating in order to reduce and even prevent crisis and conflict in the organization and believes that prevention is the key to reducing conflict and crisis. This individual has a keen anticipatory focus. A commitment to high level organization and preparation for the benefit of others is typical of this manager.

"I like how anticipation is again part of a section," Sam said. "It is so important to anticipate the unexpected."

"You are right, Sam," Ron said. "We need to stress this in our hiring process, and we need to find ways to help everyone be effective at anticipating. I told Susan that if she interviewed a manager who fully understood anticipating, she could film me doing a happy dance and put it on the Internet."

"Oh, I would pay to see that," Bill said. "How about a preview?"

"Dance Ron, dance!" several people chanted.

"Thanks everyone, but it will have to wait," Ron said.

"I find that working from goals and priorities is so important," Charlie said. "Goals are one thing, but having someone who understands the need to prioritize is critical. The old joke about how to eat an elephant—one bite at a time—is so true. Too many managers, when faced with difficult situations, will try to resolve everything at once. Ridiculous."

"I like the focus on prevention." Linda chimed in. "In the manufacturing area, we have to focus on prevention, or we would cause undo harm to a person and probably to the whole organization. Of course, prevention requires a sense of anticipation, too."

"Notice the reference to the benefit of others?" Sam asked. "I have always maintained that planning and organizing is not just for you, but for all the lives that you touch every day."

"I think we have covered everything," Susan said. "When we get the reports back from the consultant, you will have a better understanding of them. The reports will have twelve sections, one for each of the proficiency areas. They will also have a summary paragraph as well as what they call a Predictability Index. This number tells you what percent of the responses were consistent with the researched criteria."

"What's next?" Ralph asked.

"The consultants will send us all twelve reports at the same time. I will then review them with my HR team and then meet with all of you to let you know the status and how many of the twelve will move on to the one-to-one online interview. Ideally we will have no less than three nor more than six move on to the video meeting. Following that, we will invite the top three to come to our company for an interview day."

"Who is doing the one-to-one interviews?" Sally asked.

"I am," Susan said. "Then on interview day the Leadership Team will do a team interview, and Ron will have a a one-to-one interview with each candidate. We will also have the direct reports do a team interview. Any questions?" Hearing none, Susan ended the meeting.

Make sure you know what you want from your leaders.

Chapter 17

WAITING

Susan was meeting with her HR team, waiting to receive the reports from the consultant regarding the probe interview results.

"Susan I made a chart of the top twelve candidates. Would you like to take a look at it?" Maria asked.

Susan replied, "I sure would like to see it,"

Maria gave everyone a copy of the chart.

The Top 12 Candidates

Candidate Current Title R-Score Screen Location Probe

Candidate	Current Title	R-Score	Screen	Location	Probe
Sarah Matthews	Director of Marketing	200	5	Local	
Joseph Martin	Operations Manager	145	6	Local	
Frank Reynolds	Manufacturing Manager	165	4	Relo	
William Brown	EOS Integrator	160	5	Relo	
Rose Marie Jones	Corporate Controller	185	5	Relo	
Mark Livingston	Manufacturing Manager	225	4	Local	
John Paul Allen	EOS Integrator	235	6	Relo	
Richard Anthony	Quality Manager	145	6	Local	
Laura Clark	COO	185	4	Relo	
Peter French	Operations Manager	205	6	Local	
Gregg Johnson	Manufacturing Manager	160	5	Local	
Christopher Reed	Manufacturing Manager	185	4	Local	

Maximum Resume Score: 330

"Please tell us about the chart, Maria," Susan requested.

"I thought it would be important to list their current position title and their resume score. Then I thought, *I wonder who is local and who will need to have a relocation.* Neither determines whom we hire, of course. I then decided to put the screen score on the chart. Of course this chart does not have all the data about the resume interrogation or the results of the technical questions. However, we selected the twelve for the probe interview based on all of the data, not any single item."

"Let's talk about it," Susan said. "For example, we have three women and nine men going through the probe. We did not select anyone on the basis of gender, but it is interesting that we do have three female candidates in a manufacturing world."

"Well, we do have Linda as our manufacturing manager," Cathy reminded the team. "She has been super successful."

"Good observation," Susan said. "What about having a candidate that is currently a COO or a senior management role. During the brainstorming, we made senior management experience a low desired."

"During the brainstorming," Mark said, "as I understood it, the concern about a senior manager was the question of having worked in a really large company. Sarah holds the title of COO, but the company is actually about $20 million in revenue, which is smaller than us. I think you need to be wary of titles."

"Ron would agree with you, Mark," Susan said. "He hates titles. Notice the only senior manager title we have is Ralph, our CFO, and he has the title only because the bank likes CFOs. If she is recommended for the interview, we need to ask questions regarding her role and how she envisions not being a COO in our company."

"We do have salary data for each candidate," Cathy said. "And we did explore relocation. All of them stated that they had no problem relocating for this position."

"Once we have the results of the probe from the consultant," Mark said, "I assume we will add that to our current information and then select three to six for the video interview based on everything we have about them."

"Are you doing the online interviews?" Cathy asked.

"I am," Susan replied. "I am working on the general questions. I will also have unique questions for each candidate."

"Correct me if I am wrong," Maria asked. "I always was of the opinion that you had to ask the candidates the same questions."

Susan replied, "We have done that through the screening process, and even in the probe interview, we will ask each candidate the same questions. However, with a process like this, you have a lot of information, but there are still unique things about candidates that we can only determine by asking unique questions. For example, if the COO candidate makes it to the online interview, I will definitely explore issues related to her title and what the expectations were for her in her current role. Make sense?"

"Yes," Maria replied.

"Do we have any candidates coming from a company at least twice our size?" Susan asked.

"Let me quickly check," Mark said as he shuffled through his papers. "None." He reported.

"You might wonder why I asked," Susan said. "Over my many years in HR, I have noticed something interesting. It is not something I've researched or validated, but I've observed that candidates moving from a small company to a larger company are more successful than candidates moving from a large company to a smaller company. Any opinions as to why this happens?"

"I'll take a guess at it," Mark replied. "The person from the larger company moving to a smaller company quickly finds there are a whole lot less people to delegate to and they have to do work they previously delegated."

"Good guess, Mark," Susan said. "A good friend of mine told me that one time he took a position in a much smaller company as the general manager. Within the first month he was frustrated. One day his accounting manager asked him to join him in the men's room. He was surprised by this request, but followed him to the men's room. The accounting manager had him stand in front of the mirror above the sink and asked him what he saw. He answered that he saw his own image. The accounting manager then told him that was who he needed to begin delegating to, since he and the other team members were overwhelmed by all the tasks he delegated to them."

"What happened next?" Cathy asked.

"He asked the accounting manager to join him for lunch, and they had what he called a real heart-to-heart discussion, "Susan explained. "He told me that he probably owes his career to the accounting manager. Working in a small company is a lot different than a large company and its larger staffs. He went on to be highly successful."

"That makes a whole lot of sense," Mark said. "But is it 100 percent?"

"No," Susan answered. "It is something you must explore, in depth, when you are considering someone from a large company for a role in a much smaller company."

"I would think it would be similar to our situation of being family-owned," Mark said. "That would be something you would explore in the one-to-one interview. A candidate does not need to have worked in a family organization, but one who better understands that there are some differences."

"Exactly," Susan agreed. "Rest assured that I am prepared to deal with that in my one-to- one interviews. Actually, the key is finding someone who values people and wants to know all they can about their employees.

"A family-owned company, as you all are fully aware, has unique dynamics. And sometimes things can get messy. I would like to get your input on the one-to-one questions. What are some areas that you think I should cover that we have not covered in our other questioning?"

"In the screener, we asked questions about supervision and evaluation, hiring and mis- hires, and motivation and involving others," Maria said. "Then our eight-question screener covered their driving purpose, core values, knowing team members, communication with team members, tense situations, anticipation, and problem-solving. Gosh, we sure have covered a lot of ground!"

"How about a values question where they have to describe application of their values?" Mark asked. "You could have them describe a time when they were pressured to compromise their integrity."

"I like that," Maria said. "Or something where they had to deal with illegal or immoral behavior in the company."

"It is always important to keep probing into a person's values during the interview process," Susan said, "and I like both of your ideas. In fact I can see a two-part question. Let's keep rolling!"

"We have not really gotten into the concept of leading-edge leadership," Cathy said. "How about a question asking them to describe how they have dealt with best practices?"

"Good idea," Mark said. "Could we include something on life long learning?"

"Fantastic!" Susan exclaimed. "These are great suggestions. Let's keep going."

"I would like to hear how they handle crisis and conflict within their team," Cathy said. "What I mean is, what would they do if their direct reports were struggling with daily conflicts and crises. Specifically, what would they do to correct the behavior."

"I was just thinking," Maria said. "Their duties include initially reviewing our existing systems and processes and then offering recommendations. You could ask first if they have ever done this, and then ask how they would approach this, if hired."

"That is an excellent idea," Susan said. "This is a benefit from having a new leader join the team. I have never understood why companies do not do this with a new leader. My guess is that their focus is to hire someone who will hit the ground running, and then this review never happens. And, even though this is a key leadership position, they will still not have a specific and planned onboarding program. I can't get over how many companies skip this with top leaders."

"Susan, have you ever disagreed with Ron?" Mark asked.

"I have." She answered. "And there have been a couple of times when I disagreed, even knowing he was strongly devoted to his idea."

"That's my point," Mark said. "We need to ask what they would do if they felt strongly about an issue and Ron disagreed."

"That's really a great idea," Susan said. "I will include this for sure."

"In our screener questions we really did not deal with project management," Maria said. "I think we need to ask a question dealing with what they do to get a new project launched and how they include specific scheduling, goals, and if they allow for some future unforeseen events."

"That is a great question!" Susan said. "You guys are great!"

"We have said we want a servant leader," Cathy said. "What if we asked them to define servant leadership and then describe something they have done that confirms they are a servant leader?"

"I like that," Maria said. "How about probing if they have a sense of humor? You could ask if others would describe them as having a sense of humor, and then have them comment on the value of a sense of humor to a team, and finally have them describe a time they purposely used their sense of humor to have a positive impact."

"Well at least we know how Bill would answer that!" Mark said. "Think how many times he has used it to take the pressure off!"

"I think we need something on budgeting or achieving profitability," Maria said. "I am not sure how to word it, Susan."

"No problem," Susan answered. "I appreciate your bringing this up, and I will prepare an appropriate question."

"We need something on teams," Cathy said. "Our company is all about teams. You could ask if they've ever built a new team or took an existing team that was not functioning well and changed it. Or have them describe how to get a team to be a well-oiled machine that sees results."

"Let's see, we have right now eleven questioning areas. With a one-hour session, I have found that twelve areas is just about right," Susan said. "I have to give them time to ask me questions, and I usually allow—plus or minus—ten minutes. Can we come up with one more question area?"

"It is probably not a big deal," Maria said. "But how about asking them about any experience with contracts and attorneys?"

"Bingo!" Susan said. "We have our twelve. That is important since they will review all contract documents and meet with the attorney as necessary. Thanks, Maria."

"What's next for us Susan," Mark asked.

Susan replied, "First, review my one-to-one questions and let me know what you think. I should have them to you tomorrow. Second, we should have the profiles of our twelve candidates from our consultant, also tomorrow morning.

"Once I have them, I will schedule a meeting so we can review the profiles together and decide which three to six we will move forward to the one-to-one. Once we finish the online interviews, I will schedule a meeting and go over the results with you. I hope the Leadership Team will come to our meeting so they get a snapshot of whom they will be interviewing.

"Oh, by the way, on the interview day, I want the three of you to be guides. You will each have an assigned candidate to host. Thanks for your time today. I want to catch Ron before he leaves this afternoon."

As the team dispersed, Susan gathered her materials and walked to Ron's office. She tapped on Ron's open door. "Got a minute?" She asked.

"I do," He said. "Come on in."

"I thought you might like an update on the search." She told him, as she sat down.

"We are in what I call the waiting period. It will end tomorrow when we receive the profiles of the twelve candidates from the consultant. I am really anxious to get the reports and dig into them."

"Will the results of this profile tell you who to move to the video interview?" He asked.

"Not exclusively." she responded. "It is one more piece of the puzzle. I don't think you should ever make a hiring decision on one piece of information."

"Have you seen the new assessment program, Working Genius," he asked. "I have been researching it, and I like what I have found. Patrick Lencioni has a new book about it and I have a copy of the book."

He picked the book up off of his desk and handed it to her. "Take some time and read it. I am considering having our leadership team take the assessment as part of our team building. And we might want to have the top three candidates complete it also."

Thumbing through the pages, she said, "It does look interesting. We need to discuss it more before having it as part of the hiring system, but I am always open to new ideas."

"Good." he replied. "I think this can help our team. Are you still using the Kolbe in your hiring of new employees?"

"I use it with the department manager level and up the chain," she replied. "I guess I assumed I would have the top three complete it. It does give us some good information, but again, I never use one thing to make the hiring decision."

Mary tapped on the door and said, "Excuse me, but Ron, a gentleman is here who says he has an interview with you for the operations position."

Susan and Ron looked at each other and in unison said, "What?"

"I sense this is a surprise?"

Mary said.

"Absolutely, since I do not have an appointment with anyone," Ron said. Mary asked, "What should I tell him?"

"Tell him I am in a meeting, but will be with him shortly," he said. "Did he give you his name?"

"He did. Said his name is Don Meyer."

"Please tell Charlie to come to my office," he said. She nodded and left the office.

"Do you know him?" Susan asked.

"No, but I have an idea who he is and why he is here."

Charlie tapped on the open door. "I am here," he said.

"Thanks for getting here so quickly," Ron said. "A man in the lobby claims he has an interview with me for the operations position. When Brandon told you he had an operations candidate, did he give you a name?"

"Let me think," he replied. "I think his last name began with an M. Marks, Miller, McClain, Martin. I am not sure."

"Could it be Don Meyer?"

Charlie thought for a second. "It could be. I did not really listen, but that name sounds familiar."

"Thanks. I am going to meet with him. It might be fun. Charlie, tomorrow we need to go over final details on your departure, and Susan, please let me know tomorrow morning when you have the profiles. Charlie, please ask Mary to bring Mr. Meyer to my office," Charlie and Susan left the office.

Shortly, Mary appeared with Don Meyer. "Mr. Howell, this is Mr. Meyer, and he said he has an interview with you for the operations position."

"Thanks, Mary," He said. "Please have a seat Mr. Meyer." As Meyer sat, Ron said, "I do not have you on my calendar and neither does my assistant. Can you tell me anything to enlighten that?"

"Sure. Your peer group chair, Brandon Wright, told me you were hiring a new operations leader, said he had met with you about me, and assured me that you were highly interested in meeting me. He said he had set an appointment for the interview today, and that is why I am here."

"First, I am not in Mr. Wright's peer group. Second, I absolutely do not have an appointment with you to discuss the position."

Seeming bewildered, Meyer said. "Mr. Wright told me to be here and that he recommended me highly to you. He said that basically the position was mine if I wanted it. I have turned down two other interviews because of his assurance that the job was mine."

"I am curious as to why you turned down other opportunities without having met with me," Ron said

"I thought you were in Mr. Wright's peer group, and he was very clear that he has covered this with you."

"I am sorry you have turned down other interviews," Ron said, "but you have been mislead by Mr. Wright. I did not know your name until my assistant told me. The job is not yours."

"But Mr. Wright assured me that he had told you all about me and that you would hire me after the interview," he replied.

"I have a question," Ron said. "Didn't you find it a little unusual that the appointment was set by Mr. Wright and you were guaranteed a position?"

"No." He replied. "This happens a lot at this level in a company. I am an executive, and I do not need to go through regular interview processes. I have been hired in my past three positions in this same manner."

"You do know that Mr. Wright does not work for our company," Ron continued.

"I guess," Mr. Meyer answered. "But as a member of Mr. Wright's peer group, you do answer to him. Correct?"

"Well, that is not correct," Ron responded. "I am not in his peer group. I do not now nor have I ever answered to him. You will not be offered this position."

"Like I said, I was guaranteed this position," Meyer insisted. "As I said, I have turned down other opportunities. Now I understand why Brandon told me you were an incompetent manager, and I needed to be here to straighten you out and save this company."

"Again," Ron said, "you are not a candidate for this position, and you will not receive an offer. You need to get back to Mr. Wright and tell him that you are not getting this position."

"Mr. Wright clearly stated that I would be hired after the interview," Meyer said. "If you do not hire me as promised, you will hear from my attorney."

"Our meeting is done, Mr. Meyer. Have your attorney contact me. Please close the door on your way out."

Don Meyer stood, turned, and headed to the door. "You will regret this," he said, as he slammed the door.

Charlie, who had been standing outside the office, opened the door and said, "I heard a bit of what was going on in here. What the hell was that all about?"

"That is textbook Brandon. He always gets even," Ron said. "I think he may have crossed the line this time."

Charlie walked towards the desk and sat down. "Is he nuts?"

Ron laughed. "I have heard some refer to him in such terms."

"And this Don Meyer," Charlie said. "Why would you ever assume you'd get a job based on comments from a person not even in the company? That says a lot about him as a manager and leader. Now what?"

"I will make our attorney aware of this. I will also prepare a letter to Brandon, and after you and the attorney review it, I will send it to him. Notice how he quickly moved to hiring an attorney. That is exactly what Brandon wanted—to get me involved in a lawsuit. Enough is enough."

"Agreed," Charlie said. "Let me know when your letter is ready. Until then, I'll get back to work."

"Will do," Ron said. He picked up his car keys off his desk and headed home for the evening.

Have a team prepare the interview questions.

Chapter 18

PROBE RESULTS

Susan arrived at the office very early the next morning. She was anxious to see the results of the probe interviews the consultant had done. She was also looking forward to the training so she and the Leadership Team would be able to do their own interviews. She also wanted to write the teleconference interview questions on the white board so the team could see and review them. Setting her coffee down, she picked up a marker and started to write the questions on the white board.

INTERVIEW QUESTIONS

1. Would you be described as a leading edge leader?*

   (If yes) Tell me how you have copied, created or applied best practices.*

   Would those who know you best describe you as a life-long learner?*

   Why do you think so?*

2. We are a family-owned company. Describe what you believe to be unique about a family-owned company.*

   What do you believe are some positives about family-owned companies?*

3. As the new manager you discover that your team members are daily dealing with conflict and crisis.

   What do you think some of the causes might be?*

   What would you do to correct their behavior?*

4. Please describe a time when you were pressured to compromise your integrity.*

   Tell me about a time when you had to deal with illegal or immoral behavior in a company.*

5. If you are selected for this position, you will be responsible to take time to review our processes and systems and then make some recommendations to keep as is, change, or discard. Tell me how you would approach this task.*

6. You will report to our President, Ron Howell. Let's assume you feel strongly about an issue. You know that Ron does not agree with you. In fact, you are aware of how strongly he feels about the issue. What would you do?*

   Tell me how you would respond when Ron challenges your ideas or suggestions.*

(continued on the next page)

7. You are beginning a new project. Describe what you would do to launch the project, and please address goals and scheduling.*

8. We want all our managers and leaders to be servant leaders. Please define servant leadership for me.*

   Tell me about something you have done as a leader that clearly demonstrates that you are a servant leader.*

9. Would you be described as having a sense of humor?*

   What do you believe is the value of a sense of humor to a team.*

   Describe a time when you used your sense of humor to have a positive impact on others.*

10. This position is key to our company's continued growth. Tell me how you will contribute to our growth and profitability.*

    We believe strongly in establishing and keeping to budgets. Describe in detail your involvement in budget planning, and how you monitor the budget during the year.*

11. Our company is all about teams. Have you ever built a new team, that is, selected team members and set goals and responsibilities?*

    Have you ever taken an existing team that was not functioning well and changed it?*

    Tell me what you did.*

    What are the keys in having a well-oiled team that gets results?*

    In your previous roles, have you worked with attorneys on behalf of your company?*

12. Tell me about how you worked with them.*

    Also, in your previous roles, have you ever been responsible for reviewing contracts?* (If yes) Describe what you did.*

After writing the last questions on the white board, Susan stepped back and carefully reviewed what she had written. As she was processing her thoughts, the HR Team came into the conference room.

"Are those your interview questions?" Mark asked.

"They are," Susan replied. "Before we get going in our meeting, why don't the three of you read through them and tell me what you think."

After several minutes, Cathy said. "You have hit all the areas we discussed. This is a great interview."

"I agree," Mark said. "I am glad I do not have to answer them."

"Thank you," Susan said. "Your suggestions yesterday made this possible."

"Do you have the probe results?" Maria asked.

"Not yet," Susan replied. "I expect them to pop up in my email any time now. I, like you, am really anxious to read the profiles."

Just then Sam entered the conference room.

"How is your arm?" Mark asked.

"Slowly healing, I think. At least the pain has stopped," Sam answered.

Bill and Sally walked in at the same time.

"I am here, Susan, so you can start the meeting now," Bill said.

"And what about those not here yet?" Susan asked. "We still have ten minutes until the set time for the meeting."

Bill laughed. "Can't blame a guy for trying."

Ralph and Linda arrived, both with their coffee cups firmly in their grasp.

"I really need my coffee for these early meetings," Ralph said. "Are there any donuts to go with the coffee?"

"No," Susan said. "There is fresh fruit and juice on the counter. Fruit would really be good for you."

Mary entered the room followed by Ron and Charlie.

"All present and accounted for," Ralph announced. "Let's get the ball rolling!"

"Thanks for your help, Ralph," Susan said. "I just now received, in my email, the results of the probe interviews. Bear with me a few minutes while I access the results."

"What are the questions on the white board?" Charlie asked.

Maria answered, "Those are for the one-on-one interviews."

"Those are great questions," Ron said. "They cover a lot of areas. Coupled with your screener results, we are discovering a lot about the candidates. This system is truly a discovery process. So far, so good."

"How long is each interview?" Sally asked.

Maria answered. "One hour. And that includes giving them time at the end to ask their questions."

"What is the purpose of letting them ask questions?" Sally asked.

Cathy answered, "One, they deserve a chance to seek information, and as Susan told us, we need to note the questions they ask. What they choose to ask gives us more information as part of the discovery process."

While walking to the white board, Susan said. "I am going to list the candidates from high score to low score. Do not make any judgments until I finish the list, and then I will give you the details," Susan began writing the names and scores on the board.

Sarah Matthews	70.08		Rose Marie Jones	55.16
Joseph Martin	66.16		Mark Livingston	54.83
Laura Clark	62.25		Peter French	52.58
William Brown	59.58		Richard Anthony	44.66
Gregg Johnson	58.33		Christopher Reed	42.33
Frank Reynolds	58.16		John Paul Allen	32.17

"Interesting," Bill said. "This looks easy. You said we wanted to have three to six advance to the next interview. All we have to do is lop off the top six, and we are ready to go. This will be a short meeting."

Susan, returning to her seat, said. "It is not so easy, Bill. The score is only one dimension. Let me explain this information. The score simply indicates the percentage of their answers that were consistent with the research. The consultants do recommend that scores less than fifty should be eliminated."

"I spoke with them about this and agree with them. So, with that in mind, I am eliminating Anthony, Reed, and Allen. We now have nine to review."

"Educate me," Charlie said. "Does 70.08, for example, mean they were seventy percent consistent with the research? Don't we want people who score over ninety percent?"

"If we only want people over ninety percent, we would not have any candidates left for this search and any searches in the future," Susan said. "The consultant told me the highest score ever on the probe was 79.00."

"I am still confused," Charlie said. "How can that be?"

"I asked the consultant the same question, Charlie." she said. "The tight window for scoring, anything over fifty, indicates a candidate who is generally consistent with the researched criteria."

"I am learning," Charlie said. "Now another left curve, tight window?"

"The consultants' interview teams are known as 'tough coders,' meaning that if the response is off just a little, no credit is given," she answered.

"Okay, now you threw another curve ball," Charlie responded. "What is a coder? Are we doing software now?" That got the whole team laughing.

"Funny, Charlie, are you catching the humor disease from Bill!" Susan laughingly said. "They use a process called content coding, and we will use it following the training. Basically, they compare the candidate's response to a set response guide to determine if it is consistent with the research, and they use a letter symbol. I will not go into all of the details right now, but I hope that answers your question."

Smiling, Charlie said, "Good answer, Susan."

Charlie then asked, "How many questions are on the probe interview?"

Susan replied, "The consultant told me that with thirty-six questions, plus the follow up questions, that makes the total question count over eighty."

Ron took the floor. "Good job, Susan. You and your team have done an outstanding job using a new system. Let's have Mark, Maria, Cathy, and you, too, Susan stand. Let's give them an ovation to show our appreciation."

Charlie added, "Everyone stand with them, and make this a standing ovation!"

"Thank you!" Susan exclaimed. "That was great! Now let's look at the candidates. We have a written profile of each that Mary has copied for you to read as we talk about the candidates."

The team proceeded to talk about the twelve candidates. As Susan had mentioned earlier, she had eliminated Anthony, Reed, and Allen. She told the group that if it made sense, she wanted to have six candidates for the one-to-one since it made better odds in finding the top three from six candidates, not from four or five.

The team studied and talked about each profile and selected the top six:

William Brown	Gregg Johnson
Laura Clark	Joseph Martin
Peter French	Sarah Matthews

Use multiple sources to make hiring decisions.

Chapter 19

ONE-TO-ONE (OTO) INTERVIEWS

Susan had Maria call each of the top six to let them know they had been selected for the one-to-one interview with Susan, and to tell them that they would receive an email with some available dates and times. She also had Maria call Anthony and Reed, two she had interviewed, and had Cathy call Allen, whom she had interviewed, to let them know the company was moving on with other candidates who were deemed a better fit and match. She stressed to each of them to not get into any discussion about why they were eliminated, but to stick to the fit and match explanation. She explained that any details beyond that could open the company to potential problems in the future.

While preparing for the interviews, Susan decided to train her team on conducting one-to-one interviews while she waited for the schedule to be confirmed. She sent an invitation to her HR Team, and all three responded immediately.

Susan walked into the conference room and found her HR team ready to learn about one-to-one interviewing.

"Wow!" Susan said. "I think you are ready to learn, so let's start. The first step is preparation. That means reviewing all the information available about the candidate and write your interview questions. Unfortunately, most managers do not take a written script of questions into an interview with them. They claim they do not need a list of questions because they are managers, and they know what they are looking for in the new hire. Most of them have, at best, a limited idea as to who they want. Then they wonder why they are not successful in hiring new employees. So, I expect you to always be prepared."

Mark said, "That makes total sense. I worked for a manager a few years ago who told us a competent manager did not need to prepare for an interview. He maintained that asking questions 'off the cuff,' was more spontaneous and would keep the candidate at ease and more open."

"That is so sad," Maria said. "Did he also tell you not to take notes so that you would not offend the candidate?"

"How did you know?" Mark asked.

"I worked for a manager like that, Mark," she answered. "Not only was his hiring weak and inconsistent, he had very high turnover. Think about all the harm he caused by having his mangers follow his example."

"I had a similar experience," Cathy shared. "My manager was like that, and he walked them to their car after the interview to see what they drove and if the interior was neat and clean."

"What did vehicle model, neat, and clean have to do with it?" Maria asked.

"A clean car, he told us, made a good hire. He added that it showed a strong sense of maturity and accountability," Cathy added. "A more luxurious vehicle indicated a confident leader."

"Unfortunately, that is reality. If a manager is selecting new computer equipment or software, a lot of time will be devoted to planning and researching. The manager will even take time to see demonstrations. He or she will devote hours to making the final decision. However, when it comes to hiring a new employee, so many manages invest no preparation time and use every shortcut available. We could spend all day talking about these managers," Susan said. "The good news is they do not work here."

"Susan, is there a set way to conduct a one-to-one interview?" Mark asked.

"I believe there is," she said, and handed them a half sheet of paper. "You will find on this paper how I begin a one-to-one. Mark please read it to us," Mark read the one-to-one introduction to the team.

"First, let me tell you how I will conduct my interview. I will begin by having you give a personal introduction, after which I will ask the questions I have prepared for you. I will then give you time to ask me some questions. To begin, I would like for you to take two to three minutes and tell me what you most want me to know about you."

"What stands out to you with this introduction?" Susan asked.

"I was surprised with the statement on how you conduct your interview," Maria said. "That seems a little harsh."

"I understand why you felt that way, but it is a very important statement," Susan replied. "You need to let the candidate know who is in charge, and that it is your interview—not theirs. One of the keys to a successful one-to-one is keeping control. Without control, you will not discover what you need to know about the candidate. This is even more important when you are interviewing sales professionals."

"Thanks, Susan," Maria responded. "I had not considered it that way, but it makes a lot of sense."

Next, Cathy said, "I like the way you tell them you have prepared questions for them and the order of your interview. But, why do you have them tell you about themselves?"

"It helps them to relax," Susan replied. "I want them to be relaxed because they tend to be more open and speak more freely than in a typical interview."

"How about the two to three minutes?" Mark asked. "Does that work?"

"Yes, with most candidates," she answered. "A good friend who is a school principal asked me for some interview tips so I worked with her on one-to-one interviewing. She used my introduction with educators and told me the two to three minutes failed most of the time."

"Failed? How?" Maria asked.

"No one stopped talking at two or three minutes," Susan said. "Most, if not all, of them exceeded five minutes. She told me the education vocabulary was even too much for her to listen to for that long. She stopped asking the question. The good news is that business leaders are concise and to the point. If you ever get one who goes beyond the three minutes, you have to politely interrupt the person, telling him or her that you have limited time for the interview, and you would appreciate it if they would be more concise."

"That's crazy," Mark said. "Honestly I am not surprised. I have a good friend who is a school teacher and he talks forever and ever."

"Let's continue," Susan said. "When you prepare your questions, make sure you use closed-ended questions only to set the stage. I like to use Descriptive Situational interviewing. Here is an example. Susan read this to the team:

"Would you be described as a good communicator?* Are you stronger verbally or in writing?*

"Tell me about a time when a break-down in communication created a difficult situation for you."*

"And here is one of the video interview questions:

"Please describe a time when you were pressured to compromise your integrity.*

"Tell me about a time when you had to deal with illegal or immoral behavior in a company.*

Susan said, "I like to tell people if you only ask closed-ended questions, everyone will be a great communicator, problem-solver, decision-maker, and planner. A closed-ended question is only for setting the stage. Are you okay with that?" They all nodded.

"Just a few more general points," Susan said. "Remember the 90/10 rule. The interviewer talks only ten percent of the time, the candidate ninety percent. Always, no exceptions, have prepared written questions. Always take notes. Set up a comfortable environment. Never answer the telephone or check email. Do not spend time talking about the company. Direct candidates to your website. Got those?" Again all nodded.

Susan continued, "In the interview you need to keep eye contact. Make sure you are listening carefully to their answers to your questions. Be sure to observe their nonverbal behaviors. If they give a generic answer to a question, come back at them, asking them to be more specific or give a real example.

"Some interviewees will try to control the interview by asking you questions. These questions might be about the position, the company, or the relationships in the company. Do not get mired down in these attempts to keep control. These interviewees want to keep you from asking questions so they can keep their vulnerabilities hidden.

"The consultant gave me a copy of Spence's Interview Tool-belt," Susan told them, "and I think it can be helpful to you. I will write it on the white board and explain each of the eight tools as we go through them."

SPENCE'S INTERVIEW TOOL BELT

1. **Use situational questions** ("What would you do if . . . ") and convert them into descriptive situational questions when possible.

2. **The "Here I Am" tool.** (Do not ask for weaknesses. Instead say, "We all have areas in which we can improve. I am working on (insert your area).

   In what areas are you striving to improve?")

3. **Apples and Oranges.** (Have the candidate do a comparison or contrasting to something specific to the job.)

4. **Silence Is Golden.** (Take your time and wait for the candidate to give an answer, or plan your silence in advance, if you have reasons to believe they are hiding something.)

5. **Prove it to me.** (Any time a candidate claims something, such as being the most creative in the company, just say, "Give me an example of your creativity.")

6. **Pete Repeat.** (Take the last word or phrase from their response and feed it back to them. "That was a real challenge," the candidate says. Just say, "A real challenge?" and sit back and listen.)

7. **Two-Step Waltz.** (Always follow up how with why.)

8. **Left-Right Jab.** (Follow a closed-ended question with an open-ended question.)

After walking through each of the eight tools, Susan said, "I think you will find that helpful," Susan continued. "Here are some examples of good question format or style."

- How important is it for you to set and work from specific goals?* (if important)
- Tell me about a time when you set a specific goal for yourself and what you did to achieve it.*
- Would those who have worked for you call you a coach or mentor?*
- (If yes) Tell me about a time when you did a one-to-one coaching to help an employee improve performance or learn something new.*
- Would you describe yourself as a team player and team leader?*
- (If yes) Tell me about a time when you were the team leader and you and your team set, and then achieved a specific goal.*

"I believe these examples will be very helpful as you prepare interview questions for a one-to-one," Susan concluded.

Maria responded, "This is fantastic."

Cathy said, "I never realized so much went into it."

"You are a great team," Susan said, "and quick learners. Thank you! I will begin the one-to-one interviews soon and I would like each of you to sit in the office and watch two interviews each. That way you can see interviews in action."

Use specific interview tools to discover information.

Chapter 20

REVIEW OF CANDIDATES

Susan completed all of her interviews and met with the HR team to select the top three for the interview day. Each of the team members had sat in on two of the interviews as part of their training. Susan met with her team in the conference room to make the decision.

"How did the interviews go, overall?" Mark asked. "I know we each got to observe two, but that left four we did not see or hear."

"All six are quality candidates and we probably would be okay with any of them," Susan reported. "However, they are not all a strong fit and match. We might end up canceling one or two due to something really significant from the Probe interview. Right now I just want to go over the Probe data, and then we will pull all the data from the resume and screener interviews to select our top three. We will then compare the data to what I have learned in my interviews.

"Remember, we do not, as a rule, reject a candidate from one source unless we have conclusive data of that candidate not being a fit or match. Let me review the six from the one-to-one."

Susan began the review. "First, Peter French. He says all the right things, but his ego kept creeping into his answers. His driving purpose is to get stuff done. Based on his answers, here is how I would describe him:

- "He is a leading-edge leader and a lifelong learner. Would not be comfortable in a family-owned company.

- Has high integrity.
- Would not really resolve conflicts—becomes a dictator. Would be very good at reviewing our processes and systems. Definitely would clash with Ron.
- "Excellent at managing a project.
- Not a servant leader; not even close.
- Zero sense of humor.
- Strong with profitability and budgeting.
- Not a team builder at all.
- Good at contracts and working with attorneys.

"Maria, you sat in on this one. What is your opinion?" Susan asked.

"I would not want to work for or with him," she answered. "Your comments about his ego . . . I heard that throughout the session. I don't know how he could work here with his high ego and need to be absolutely in charge. He would not be seeking input from others."

"We agree," Susan said. "Mr. French is out. This is an example of ruling a candidate out without even reviewing the other information. Why? He is great on tasks, but very weak when it comes to people. Not our *who*."

Mark asked, "How did he get this far in the process?"

Susan answered, "That is why we do a series of interviews. If a candidate has a major non-fit issue, we will discover it ninety percent of the time due to our diligence in conducting our series of interviews. Also, I believe if we looked back at the other data about Mr. French, we will find the same issues.

"Next let's talk about William Brown."

Susan began her review of William Brown. "Nice guy. Soft spoken. Super calm and patient. His driving purpose is helping others. Here is how I would describe him:

- "Strong, lifelong learner, not sure about leading edge. Would be comfortable in a family-owned business. Seems to understand how to resolve conflicts. Strong integrity.
- "Would be okay at reviewing processes and systems.
- I think he would get along well with Ron, but need more information. Can effectively manage projects.
- Shows some inclination to servant leadership.
- Has a quiet sense of humor.
- Okay with profitability and budgets.
- Has skill to build a team, but not sure he has ever done it.
- Okay with contracts and working with attorneys.

"You were in the room, Mark, what did you think?" Susan asked.

"I agree, Susan," he replied. "Personally, I like him. Very personable; maybe a little too laid back for our culture. I do like that he has EOS experience. Can we hold a decision until we review the others?"

"Of course," she said. "I had intended to do that with all of them, but in the case of Mr. French, I did not see how he would fit. Let's talk about Laura Clark."

Susan began the review of Laura Clark. "First, I want to comment on our concern about her being a senior manager. Her company is about half our size and everyone on their leadership team has a senior manager title. I really don't see this as an issue. I was impressed with her driving purpose of coaching and developing people. Here is how I would describe her:

- "Excellent leading-edge leader, shared great ideas. Is a lifelong learner.
- Not sure about family-owned, but she is high in responsiveness to others.

- I like her description of handling conflicts and changing behaviors.
- No question about her integrity.
- I think she would be able to review processes and systems.
- She matches well with Ron; respects authority but will question, if needed.
- "I think she is a good project manager.
- She really has an excellent understanding of servant leadership.
- Pleasant sense of humor and knows how to use it in a positive manner.
- She has done budgets for years. and she understands profitability.
- She actually built her team in her current position. Strong.
- No problem with contracts and attorneys—she has been doing that.

"Cathy you sat in on this one. What do you think?" Susan asked.

"She is a strong candidate," Cathy replied. "She never really hesitated to answer your questions, and she was very disciplined in answering them. She gave a lot of detail, which I happen to like. I thought she also handled the question about being a senior manager very well. She is not a big corporate person. She appears to be a good fit. What do you think?"

Susan responded, "Cathy, I also believe she is a good fit. I have three more to summarize for our discussion, so I will keep her on hold for now. Let's talk about Gregg Johnson."

Susan began the review of Gregg Johnson.

- "He has not been in operations, but he has a strong background in manufacturing and would be a strong partner with Linda. He said that his driving purpose is to mentor others and help them achieve their goals.
- "Is a lifelong learner, not sure about leading edge.

- Has previously worked in a family-owned business and seems to know the dynamics. Excellent answer about crisis and conflict. Good skills.
- No doubt about his integrity.
- Has done process and system reviews several times.
- Ron would like him. Personality matches.
- Has actually been a project manager. Strong example. Understands servant leadership and strives to be one.
- Nice sense of humor—quiet, not up front like Bill. More like Linda. Had done budgets for years and understands profitability.
- Has never built a team but clearly has the skills to do it.
- Does contracts and meets with attorneys in current position.

"What do you think Cathy?" Susan asked.

"I believe he would fit in here really well," Cathy shared. "His personality is really a lot like Charlie's. His background in manufacturing would be beneficial to us, and he would be an excellent match with Linda. He is very articulate, and I think he would be very effective in sharing ideas with the team.

"Thanks, Cathy," Susan said. "He appears to be a good fit and match. Let's talk about Sarah Matthews."

"Susan, may I say something before you begin?" Mark asked. "I listened to your interview with Sarah," Mark said. "I heard a lot of positives in relationship to people. But her whole career has been in marketing. She only has two direct reports, and she has never been in operations. How quickly could she learn enough to take Charlie's place?"

"Excellent observation, Mark," Susan said. "I am right there with you. When a candidate is clearly strong with the *who* and you are concerned about skill sets, you need to ask if they can learn quickly or if the road is too long."

"I am also concerned about her only having two direct reports," Mark said. "And previous to that, she did not manage anyone."

"I don't think we want to take her to our interview day," Susan said. "Thanks for your input, Mark. Let's talk about Joseph Martin."

Before Susan could begin, Mary interrupted the meeting.

"Susan, I just spoke with Mr. Martin," Mary said. "He is dropping out of the process. He was just offered another position and has accepted it."

Not what I like to hear," Susan said. "But that happens more than people would ever believe."

"I was not aware that it was somewhat common," Maria said. "Did we know he was close to an offer?"

Mark replied, "No. In fact, during the screener I asked him if he was close to an offer with any other companies, and he said we were his only active search. He lied."

"Here we are with our three finalists, without even doing our total review," Susan said. "We have William Brown, Laura Clark, and Gregg Johnson. We have three excellent candidates. However, I still want to go back to all the data about them and do a full review. It may provide us with some areas we still need to discover, and may help us find out if there are any key issues with them."

Susan continued, "Before we adjourn, I have some thoughts to share with you. It is possible a candidate will tell you an offer is pending for them with another company, and they want you to step up the pace on their behalf."

"Be nice, but firmly tell them we have a process, and we will not adjust it. Many times this pending offer is fictional. And always remember, it is a mis-hire only if you hire the wrong person. If you finish your interview day and decide you do not have a fit and match, be happy. Yes, you have to begin anew, but you have not hired the wrong person."

Susan concluded the meeting. "Well we are done for now, but we need to prepare for our interview day."

Take time to thoroughly evaluate each candidate
to select the top three.

Chapter 21

PREPARING FOR INTERVIEW DAY

After Susan and her HR team met for about two hours, reviewed all of the information about the three top candidates, and agreed they definitely had the correct top three. Susan told the team to reconvene in the conference room right after lunch.

Susan decided to put together a checklist to prepare for and conduct the interview day. She wanted to show her team how much preparation and planning goes into Interview Day.

Interview Day Checklist

☐ Call Peter French and Sarah Matthews with rejections.

☐ Call Laura Clark, William Brown, and Gregg Johnson to invite them to the interview day, and ask candidates about any dietary restrictions.

☐ Send email to Leadership Team with the top three candidates. Contact Charlie to arrange meeting with his direct reports.

☐ Set the date for the interview day. Confirm with candidates and set interview preparation times with Ron, Leadership Team, and Direct Report Team.

☐ Select three separate locations for the three interviews. Prepare the interview day schedule.

☐ Prepare the one-to-one interview for Ron to use.

☐ Prepare the leadership team interview.

☐ Prepare the direct report team interview.

☐ Prepare Maria, Cathy, and Mark to be the three hosts.

☐ Prepare the situational activity.

☐ Ask Mary to plan food and beverages for the breaks.

☐ Ask Mary to set location for three lunches.

☐ Have Mary make travel arrangements for Willam and Laura who both live out of state.

The three team members arrived together. They found Susan already in the conference room, writing on the white board.

"That's quite a long list," Mark said half in jest. "Is that for us?"

Susan turned and said, "Yes. You have a lot of work to do."

"Before we get started," Maria said, "why do we have an interview day with all three finalists here at the same time? What if they see or meet each other?"

"Good question, Maria," Susan replied. "Doing all three on the same day means we can legitimately compare them for fit and match at the end of the day."

"In some companies, if they have three finalists, they might interview one on Tuesday, another on Friday, and the other on the following Monday. Why? Because they put their schedules ahead of the need to have a proper interview plan. What happens is when the interviewers meet to review the candidates, the last one interviewed is usually hired. The interviewers cannot even remember the first candidate they interviewed."

"That makes sense," Maria replied, "and I like it. However, do the candidates actually meet each other?"

"Not intentionally," she said. "If it happens that they are in an area at the same time, the hosts need to introduce them to each other. It happens. And it has never been a problem."

"When you schedule the candidates, you let them know that the other two candidates will be here at the same time and they might be introduced, but at no time will they be 'pitted against' each other."

"That knowledge ahead of time makes all the difference. And as long as I am talking about information for the candidates, on the initial call, tell them they will have three interview sessions. A one-to-one with the president, a team interview the the Leadership Team, and a team interview with the operations direct reports."

"Thanks Susan," Maria said. "The key is to keep people informed and eliminate all surprises."

"Let's take a look at the checklist," Susan said. "We can make some decisions now. For example, Mark, could you call Peter French and Sarah Matthews, and let them know they are no longer being considered?"

"Sure," Mark said.

"Now make sure you do not get involved in a discussion with them," Susan cautioned. "Just tell them the team met and carefully reviewed all of the information about each candidate and selected those judged to be the best fit and match for our team. Tell them the purpose for your call is to let them know they were not selected. Be sure to thank them for participating in our process, and wish them the best. They might pressure you to tell them what they lacked. Do not do that. Stick to fit and match."

"Why not give them some information as to why they were eliminated?" Mark asked.

"Bottom line, it opens the door to potential litigation," Susan said. "As much as you would like to be helpful to them, the risk is far too great."

"Never thought about it that way," he said, "but I do now."

"Cathy, I would like you to please call Laura Clark. Mark, please call William Brown, and Maria, please call Gregg Johnson. Your task is to tell them they are invited to our on-site interview day, and get them to confirm they will participate. Tell them you will be back to them shortly with the date and time, and we will email the interview day schedule to them. Okay?"

All nodded.

"I will reach out to Charlie and Mary and get them lined up to do their parts," Susan said. "I will email the Leadership Team the names of the top three. I will write the three interviews and then ask you to review and edit as necessary. I will also send you a draft of the situational activity. Any questions?*

"Not to sound stupid," Mark said, "but what is a situational activity?"

"That's not a stupid question," she said. "I have often had to explain what it is to team members. Basically, think of it as a test, an assessment. In some situations, it is a skill test, and in other situations, it is what I like to call story problems. For managers it is almost always story problems. And that is what we are using for our search. Any other questions?"

"You are preparing three sets of questions?" Cathy asked.

"Yes," Susan answered. "An interview for Ron, an interview for the Leadership Team, and an interview for the direct report team. All interview sessions are for ninety minutes. We have the team members asking questions for seventy-five minutes and then they give the last fifteen minutes to the candidate to ask questions. I will get the questions to you first thing tomorrow, and please review them, and offer suggestions as necessary. Now let's talk about being a host."

"I will be the host with the most!" Mark said with a laugh.

"I hope all three of you are!" Susan responded with a smile. "As the host, you will meet your candidates in the lobby and do introductions. They are all arriving at the same time, so do not feel awkward introducing everyone. Your first task is to take them on a tour of our facilities. The three of you need to plan your routes.

"After the tour take them to their first interview and come back when it is over and spend the break with them. In addition to the break time you will take them to lunch. Mary will have three separate locations planned.

"At the end of the day you will meet with them in a debrief session, asking how their day went and if they have any questions. Thank them for participating. Finally, walk them to the door.

"You will be part of the meeting of all interviewers, and you will need to report your discoveries about your candidate. And the reality is that you will know your candidate better than anyone else, so be prepared to openly share what you saw and heard.

"The consultant told me about a time with a search where the host helped confirm the team's reservations. The host shared that during the tour, she introduced the candidate to several people. If they were a manager, the candidate was very friendly. The candidate hardly acknowledged those who were of perceived less-important status. This confirmed their concerns.

"Now, here is a draft of the schedule." She distributed a copy to each of them. "Any thoughts or opinions?"

Time Slots

	William Brown (Mark)	Laura Clark (Maria)	Gregg Johnson (Cathy)
8:00 a.m. to 9:00 a.m.	Arrival and Tour	Arrival and Tour	Arrival and Tour
9:15 a.m. to 10:45 a.m.	OTO WITH RON	LEADERSHIP TEAM	REPORT TEAM
10:45 a.m. to 11:00 a.m.	BREAK	BREAK	BREAK
11:00 a.m. to 12:30 p.m.	REPORT TEAM	OTO WITH RON	LEADERHIP TEAM
12:30 p.m. to 1:45 p.m.	LUNCH	LUNCH	LUNCH
2:00 p.m. to 3:30 p.m.	LEADERSHIP TEAM	REPORT TEAM	OTO WITH RON
3:30 p.m. to 3:45 p.m.	BREAK	BREAK	BREAK
3:45 p.m. to 4:45 p.m.	SITUATIONAL	SITUATIONAL	SITUATIONAL
4:45 p.m. to 5:00 p.m.	DEBRIEF	DEBRIEF	DEBRIEF

"That is a full day!" Maria said. "I would think by the end of the day, coupled with all the discoveries from screen and probe, we should know who is the best fit and match."

"I agree," Susan replied. "Ron and the Leadership Team should be able to agree on which candidate they see as the best fit and match and then bring that person back to spend an informal day in the company, along with lunch and dinner with key people.

"While that is happening, at least one of you will do reference and background checks. An offer should then follow. Let's meet again this afternoon to fine-tune all of the details. Like the consultant told me, the way the search is handled from beginning to end tells the candidate all about your company.

"So far we have done an excellent job of letting the candidates know who we are. We kept them informed. We were always on time for every interview and contact with them. We have given them extensive information about our company. So, I don't want to let anything slip up in the final stretch."

"What do we have left to do?" Cathy asked.

"Good question," Susan said. "I need to finish the interview questions so we can review them tomorrow morning. We need to send the date and schedule to each candidate. We need to prep the direct report team, and I want the three of you sitting in on that as well as the prep for the Leadership Team. That is a little of what needs to be done."

"I know that Mary has the three lunch locations identified." said Cathy. "Once we set the date for interview day, she will make reservations. I worked with her, and we have the food all picked for the break times. Mary said she will also have coffee, tea, and some soft drinks. What about the rooms for the interviews?"

"I worked with Mary on that," Mark said. "The Leadership Team will use this conference room that we are sitting in right now, and the direct report team will use the conference room in their area. Ron will interview in his office."

"What about when they do the situational?" Susan asked. "They will need access to a computer. I am sure we do not want to read their answers in their writing style."

"We will use three offices," Maria said. "Bill's, Sally's and Linda's. It is only one hour, and we can adjust."

"Thank you everyone," Susan said. "We are close to being totally ready. Tomorrow we will go over all the details and make sure everything and everyone is ready."

Prepare and then prepare some more.

Chapter 22

FINAL DETAILS

Susan was in a good mood when she arrived at work the next morning. As she entered the building, she encountered Sally.

"Good morning, Sally," Susan told Sally.

"Good morning to you, too," Sally replied. "You look happy today."

Susan replied, "I am happy. Last night was great. The kids behaved and did their homework. We even had a peaceful dinner. And, I had a wonderful discussion with one of my fellow quilters—she gave me great ideas for the quilt I am working on. How are you doing?"

"Really great," Sally replied. "My husband told me about a trip he has planned for our tenth anniversary next month. And I had a great meeting last evening with the leadership team of our women's ministries. We are growing stronger as a group and are beginning to really be open with each other. We are planning a Saturday seminar and are working to bring in a speaker from iWork4Him, a not-for-profit group that brings faith into the marketplace. Ron is on their board of directors. I would love to have you attend the seminar."

"I would like that," Susan said. "Let me know the date."

"Wonderful," Sally said. "You will be my guest."

"Thank you," Susan replied. "And this morning I am working with my HR team planning for the interview day. We will wrap up the final details this morning. We have narrowed the candidate field to three outstanding candidates. I am anxious to see how they respond to everyone."

"Charlie will be hard to follow," Sally said. "It will take just the right person to walk in his shoes. We will all miss him."

"Speaking of Charlie," Susan said, "look behind you. The one, the only—Charlie!"

"Good morning Susan and Sally," Charlie said. "Can I join this meeting of the top minds in town?"

Both Susan and Sally laughed. "Thanks for the compliment," Sally said, "but we are mere mortals struggling to exist in this world!"

"Oh, you are too modest," Charlie replied. "I understand your humility."

"I try to be humble like Jesus." Sally said.

"Amen to that." he replied. "By the way, Sally, I hear great things about your women's ministry. Our men's ministry at church needs some help; I should meet with you for some ideas."

"I would be happy to share some ideas," Sally said. "Just send me an invitation."

"I will," he said. "You two have a great day!"

As Charlie headed down the hall, Susan said, "Well, I am off to the conference room. Have a great day Sally!"

Susan walked into the conference room and set her materials on a table. The team was not here yet, so she decided to fire up the coffee pot. She had considered bringing apple fritters, but it had slipped her mind while getting the kids off to school.

Just then the HR team walked into the room.

"We are here you lucky person," Mark announced.

"Well, welcome to each of you," Susan said. "As soon as you get your coffee we can review our check list. I want to make sure nothing slips through the cracks."

When the coffee cups were full and all were seated, Susan stood at the white board.

"Let's quickly check where we are on our list:

"Leadership Team informed as to top three—yes.

"Meeting planned with direct reports—yes.

"Interview locations set—yes.

"Interview day schedule complete—yes.

"Hosts have been prepared—yes.

"Situational activity ready—yes.

"Lunch locations—yes.

"Interview day date and time set.

"Candidates given date and time.

"Teams' and Ron's Interview."

"Mary finalizing travel arrangements for Laura and William.

"We are getting there!" Maria said. "And you have the interviews written, and we just need to review and give you some input."

"Yes, and we will review them shortly," Susan said. "First I want to show you the situational activity and get your opinion," Susan handed a copy of the activity to them. "As you will see, there are four topics. The candidates have to answer all four."

(1) On page 198 of the book, *The Power of the Other,* Dr. Henry Cloud writes:

TRUST

"It's hard to argue with the notion that trust is important. Nevertheless, it's not always clear when it's present, what actually builds it, and what it takes to keep it. While I find that everyone values trust, and everyone can feel when it's not there, many times we're not so clear on what it's made of. We don't know how to get to trust. To do so requires that we know what the ingredients are that build trust."

Please describe the following:

(a) What you believe to be the ingredients of trust?

(b) How you will build trust in our company?

(2) On pages 82–83 of the book, **Leaders Eat Last,** Simon Sinek writes:

SERVANT LEADERSHIP

"The rank of office is not what makes a leader. Leadership is a choice to serve others with or without any formal rank. Leaders are the ones willing to look out for those to the left of them and those to the right of them. Leaders are the ones who are willing to give up something of their own for us. Their time, their energy, their money, maybe even the food off their plate. When It matters, leaders choose to eat last."

(a) Please describe what servant leadership means to you and the behaviors the employees would observe in you as Operations Manager in our company.

 (b) Please describe how you, as a servant leader, will go about providing coaching and mentoring to the operations team.

(3) On pages 349–350 of the book, **Principles,** Ray Dalio, writes:

MISTAKES

"Mistakes will cause you pain, but you shouldn't try to shield yourself or others from it. Pain is a message that something is wrong, and it's an effective teacher that one shouldn't do that wrong thing again."

(a) Describe a time when one of your team members made a major mistake and how you handled it.

(b) Describe how to create a culture in which it is okay to make mistakes and unacceptable not to learn from them.

> (4) You and your team have completed several weeks of planning, developing the mission, vision, and purpose statements, as well as core values. It is now time to write the operating principles—those things that govern behaviors in relationships, communication, problem-solving, planning, issue resolution, and decision-making, for example.
> **OPERATING PRINCIPLES**
> (a) Describe in detail the operating principles that you believe would be most effective.

"Opinions?" Susan asked the team.

"I am glad I do not have to answer these," Mark said.

"These will really help us with our discovery," Cathy said. "I like the question about making mistakes. It really reflects our culture. Ron has really set the stage for this and it will be interesting to see how the candidates address it."

Maria spoke next. "I like the servant leader section. Servant Leadership is so important in our company. I want to see how they apply Servant Leadership to coaching and mentoring their team members."

"Then I assume we are okay with this," Susan said. All nodded.

Mary poked her head into the room. "We have set the date and time for the interview day, and I have sent an email to each candidate and told them to contact you, Susan, with any questions or special needs."

As she started to leave, Mary said, "If you need anything else from me, just let me know."

"Thank you, Mary," Susan said and turned her attention back to the HR Team. She handed a sheet of paper to each one.

"Here is how all three will begin their interview."

Candidate: _____

Interviewer: _____

NOTE: After greeting and introductions, tell the candidate you have prepared a list of questions and will begin with those shortly. Tell them that you will ask your questions for the first seventy-five minutes of the session and then will stop and turn the floor to them to ask questions.

Remember, the asterisk (*) is a stop sign. Stop and listen. The follow-up questions are optional, depending on the candidate's response to the main question.

1) Please take two or three minutes and tell me (us) what you most want me (us) to know about you.*

Why did you apply to this position with our company?*

This has been a long process. How do you feel about that?*

Susan said, "The interviews for the two teams and also for Ron, do not have any of the same questions on them except for the first and last question. Every main question is in bold type and followed by additional questions. The interviewer determines if there is a need to follow up with any of these, or to use the Hiring Tool Belt.

"The reason for this style is to have potential questions ready so the interviewer can focus on the candidate and not trying to write another question."

"Why do we ask them to tell you what they most want you to know about them?" Maria asked.

Susan responded. "It really serves two purposes. First, it gives the candidate a chance to breathe and hopefully relax. Second, it is really insightful to hear what is most important to them. Now here is the last question, which is the same for all three."

> ### *Conclude the interview with the following:*
>
> Based upon what you know now, and understand about our Company, do you have any reservations?*
>
> If you are offered, and accept this position, what can I (we) count on, from you, without fail?
>
> Is there anything I have not inquired about that you would like to share with me (us)?

"The consultant told me that he tells the interviewers to write down what they said you could count on and then pull it out ninety days later. Not a bad idea," Susan said.

"Is it a red flag if a candidate shares some reservations?" Cathy asked.

"Not really," Susan answered. "I would think a candidate might have some reservation. Usually not a major reservation."

"Does anyone really share more when asked for more information?" Mark asked. "I can't imagine what it would be, except, well, I got out on good behavior and did not serve the whole sentence.'" This got everyone laughing. "Or maybe, 'I didn't mean to embezzle; it was just an accident,'" Mark added.

"Actually, this series of questions brings a nice closure to the interview. Susan said. "I really like the 'count on' question a lot. Now here is how we set up the interview questions. This is our standard format."

> ### *Let's assume you are offered and accept this position. What actions will you take during your first few weeks on the job?**
>
> In previous positions, you probably initially faced some obstacles or challenges. What sort of obstacles or challenges have you faced and what did you do?
>
> Please describe the ideal on-boarding program for you if you are chosen as our new operations leader.*

As you will see shortly, when I give you copies of Ron's one-to-one, the Leadership Teams and the direct report teams, this is the style we use," Susan said. "The first question, the main question, is always in bold type. Depending on how it is answered, the interviewer uses one or more of the follow up questions. Questions?"

"I'm just wondering," Mark said. "Why have you used this style?"

"Good question," Susan replied. "First, we provide the questions to the interviewers because without our questions, I would be very concerned about the quality of the interview. And by having follow up questions in writing, it takes the pressure off of the interviewers and they can focus on listening to the candidate. We always stress to the team that when they are interviewing for other positions, regardless of the position, they must have their questions in writing, including the president or CEO."

"Do the interviewers always use all of the follow-up questions?" Maria asked.

"Actually, they do not," Susan replied. "Some times the follow-up question is already answered in their response to the main question. While we have made it easier by providing written questions, the interviewer must still listen intently to avoid using a follow up that is redundant or not using one that needed to be asked. Any more questions?"

"If you were asking this question to a candidate," Cathy asked, "what would you hope to hear from the candidate?"

"Great question, Cathy," Susan said. "I would be, for the main question, listening for a focus on having time to learn about the culture and time to get to know everyone in my circle. I would want to hear them describe a specific and clear plan.

"For the obstacles I would want to hear a specific and clear example of an obstacle and what they did to overcome it. As far as the onboarding, I would want to hear a detailed plan of learning and lots of time with people. I would also want to hear them talk about spending quality time in the various departments discovering responsibilities of each person and how the candidate would be interacting with them. Is that enough?"

"That is very thorough, Mark said. "I guess the interviewer better spend a lot of time in preparation."

"You bet!" Susan exclaimed. "Now, take the interviews with you, review them, and let me know if you have any questions. Also, please proofread them for typos, grammar, or spelling errors. I am going to go back to my office to prepare for the 'prep class' tomorrow."

As Susan walked to her office, Ralph stopped her. "Got time for a quick question?"

"Sure," she answered. "Come on into my office."

Ralph and Susan took chairs at her small, round conference table.

"Are you ready for the interview day?" Ralph asked.

"Just about. I have a few details to complete and the training sessions for all of the interviewers on Wednesday," Susan replied.

"Sounds good," Ralph said. "I notice two of the three candidates are marked relocation. I assume this means they would have to move to take the position. Correct?"

"Correct," she replied.

"A couple of questions come to mind. Are we paying their expenses to come to the interview day?" He asked.

"Yes," she said. "We told both of them we would pay lodging, meals, and transportation —either mileage or airfare."

"You need to give them the travel form to complete, and then they attach their receipts," Ralph instructed.

"Ralph, I have to admit this slipped my mind with everything else going on," Susan told him. "I assume it is the same form we use when we travel,"

Ralph nodded.

"Is there anything else I have forgotten?"

"Have we made any commitments regarding relocation expenses, assuming it is one of the candidates who is not local?" He asked.

"No," she said. "I never brought it up. What do we typically do?"

"We give them a moving allowance. We get an average cost from a mover to determine the amount. Also, if necessary, we can offer to pay temporary resident costs up to 90 days. We do not pay anything toward a house purchase," Ralph explained.

"I think I have it now," Susan replied. "Thanks for helping me."

"No problem," Ralph said. "I had a sneaky feeling none of this was discussed since you have been working day and night on this project."

Use a set interview style.

Chapter 23

FINAL PREPARATIONS

Susan stood in the conference room where the teams would soon gather. She wanted to brief everyone on all the details, as well as go over interviewing—including some skill building and review what she has written for each group.

Mary came in early and helped her get the room ready, setting out coffee, tea, donuts, and fresh fruit for the team members.

"Well I think the room is ready," Mary said. "Lots of choices for them!"

"Looks good," Susan replied, "and thank you for your help."

"My pleasure," Mary responded, walking toward the door. "I will be back when the meeting starts, and I can take any notes you want. See you in about thirty minutes."

"That would be great," Susan replied. She turned around to see Charlie.

"Got a minute, or do you need to keep preparing?" He asked.

"I am ready, thanks to Mary's help!" She said. "What's up?"

"I am not sure if I should participate in the interviews since it is my replacement," Charlie said. "It has bothered me for some time now. Is it standard for the outgoing person to be involved in the replacement's selection?"

"There is no set rule," Susan responded. "It depends on the company, the culture, the team's opinion, and the person leaving. All must agree.

"I know some of my HR peers say absolutely not. I do not agree with them. It also depends on the terms under which the person is leaving. For example, even with a person who resigns for a great opportunity, like you did, sometimes internal issues exist, and the person leaving should not be involved in any way in the selection process.

"In other words, sometimes a person's resignation makes people happy, even though they do not show it. In your case everyone is happy for you, but sad that you are leaving, and we all value your input."

"Thanks, Susan." he said. "I feel much better about being involved. Who all is participating today?"

"Let me begin with your team," she said. "Bonnie, Randy, John, and Michael have all confirmed. My HR team will be here—Maria, Cathy and Mark. And of course the Leadership Team—Ron, Bill, Sally, Ralph, Linda, Sam, you, and me. And Mary, who we could not live without."

"What a group!" Charlie said. "It will be fun to be with everyone one last time before I move on. I will miss this team and the whole company."

"Have you had a chance to meet the folks at your new company?" She asked.

"I have. I had dinner a couple of evenings ago with their leadership team. Very informal; just a get-to-know-each-other time. So far, so good," Charlie shared.

"I have been on some committees with their HR Manager, Barbara Knox," Susan shared. "I found her to be very friendly, and she knows HR backwards and forward. I think you will like working with her. Oh, and she brought the CFO, Marcus Baxter, with her to one of our meetings, and the guy is just like Ralph. I think that is good."

Laughing, Charlie replied. "It is good. Ralph and I have always worked extremely well together so that is a good omen. Well, I should let you finish prepping for the meeting, I am sure there are some last minute details."

Charlie left the conference room and Susan sat down to put her thoughts together. She had about fifteen minutes before the meeting would begin.

Just as she was thinking through the meeting, in walked the HR team. "We are here to help with anything we can," Mark said. "We are your loyal servants."

"Fantastic!" Susan said, "Actually, I think all is ready. Oh, wait. I forgot to put the name plates on the tables."

"Name plates?" Mark asked. "We all know each other."

"I am using name plates so I can make sure each person sits with his or her team. If I don't do that, the teams will be totally mixed up," she said. "The name plates are over next to the coffee pot, Mark. Please set them on the tables, creating team groups."

"Gotcha," Mark replied. "I am off and running, chief."

At that point, the team members started arriving and entering the room.

"Please, after you get your coffee," Maria said. "Take a seat next to your name plate."

The room filled quickly.

After everyone was seated, Susan began the meeting. "Thanks for taking time to meet with me this morning. This task ahead is very important to our company, and I need your full attention. I will go through all the details for our interview day and then work with each team on your specific interview questions. But, before I begin, I have asked Ron to say a few words."

"Thank you, Susan," he began. "I know how hard you and the HR team have worked to get us to this point. In the next couple of days we will make a decision that will impact all of us. We will replace our good friend, Charlie, and I, like you, know how much he has done for all of us. I am sorry to see him go, but he has a fantastic opportunity that he needs to take. Charlie, please stand up," Charlie stood, looking very humble. "Let's give Charlie a standing ovation!"

Everyone stood, clapped, and cheered.

When the cheers subsided, Ron said, "Charlie, we will all miss you, but I will miss you the most. And I so appreciate everything you have done for our company over the years. Finally, I really appreciate your participation in this process. You can help us make the best decision. Now, Susan, the floor is yours."

"My HR team will now distribute your packets. In the packets, you will find all you need to make this day successful. I will walk us through the packets, and then you will work in your respective teams, and I will talk about your interview questions.

"Okay, here we go! The first item is a copy of the resumes of our three interviewees: William Brown, Laura Clark, and Gregg Johnson. Don't be concerned about the resumes. We have gone through them with a fine-tooth comb, and there is no reason to dwell on them.

"If you want to read them that is fine. There is no need to spend time on resumes at this point. Your HR team interviewed the candidates, interrogated them about their resume, asked specific questions about responsibilities, and used a short behavioral interview to learn more about the person.

"Next, we had our consultant interview the top six candidates using their researched, validated process. They provided us with a behavioral study on each candidate. Then I did a one-hour one-to-one tele-meeting with each of the top six candidates.

"Once all of that was completed, we met and selected these three as our top candidates who appeared to be the best fit and match for us. At this point we are now ready to have interview day and select our new operations leader.

"Now let's take a look at the schedule for interview day. Please take a copy out of your packet," Susan paused and gave them time to retrieve a copy of the schedule.

Time Slots

Time Slots	William Brown (Mark)	Laura Clark (Maria)	Gregg Johnson (Cathy)
8:00 a.m. to 9:00 a.m.	Arrival and Tour	Arrival and Tour	Arrival and Tour
9:15 a.m. to 10:45 a.m.	OTO WITH RON	LEADERSHIP TEAM	REPORT TEAM
10:45 a.m. to 11:00 a.m.	BREAK	BREAK	BREAK
11:00 a.m. to 12:30 p.m.	REPORT TEAM	OTO WITH RON	LEADERHIP TEAM
12:30 p.m. to 1:45 p.m.	LUNCH	LUNCH	LUNCH
2:00 p.m. to 3:30 p.m.	LEADERSHIP TEAM	REPORT TEAM	OTO WITH RON
3:30 p.m. to 3:45 p.m.	BREAK	BREAK	BREAK
3:45 p.m. to 4:45 p.m.	SITUATIONAL	SITUATIONAL	SITUATIONAL
4:45 p.m. to 5:00 p.m.	DEBRIEF	DEBRIEF	DEBRIEF

"The day begins at 8:00 a.m. with the arrival of the candidates," Susan explained. "The HR team will serve as hosts for the day. Mark is with William, Maria with Laura, and Cathy is with Gregg. They will give a tour of our facilities, all going in different directions.

"At the end of the tour, the HR team will take their guests to the respective interview sessions and introduce them to the teams, or to Ron, who is doing a one-to-one.

"All interview sessions are ninety minutes. Of that time, you have seventy-five minutes to ask questions, and then the candidate has fifteen minutes to ask you some questions. Make sure to note what questions they ask, as that is part of our discovery process.

"During the day the HR team will spend the break times with their respective candidate and also take them to lunch. For the break times, feel free to stop in and chat with the candidates. Also, we will include a team member from each team to go to lunch with them. For the breaks, Mary will have coffee, tea, soft drinks, fruit, and donuts available."

Ron raised his hand. "Susan I would like to go to lunch with one of them."

"No can do, Ron," Susan said. "That is absolutely a no-no."

"Really?" He asked. "Why?"

"Let's say you go to lunch with Gregg Johnson," Susan said. "How would the other two feel? And if Gregg is hired, could they claim he had an unfair advantage due to the lunch with you?"

"Good point," Ron said. "I understand and agree with you. No lunch."

"All of you will be finished by 3:30 p.m. The situational activity is a written exercise, and a copy of it is in your packet. When the day ends, please review your notes in detail and be prepared to share your observations at the meeting the next morning. The debrief on the schedule is a time for the hosts to meet with their respective candidate and bring closure to the day. Any questions?"

"I see we have a long interview in our packet," Bill said. "Are you going to review that with us."

"Yes. As soon as I answer the last question," she said.

"When will we make an offer to one of them?" Ralph asked.

"We will all meet the morning after interview day, we will discuss the candidates in depth. Everyone will have a chance to share their observations. All of this is for the benefit of Ron. Ron will make the final call. This person reports directly to Ron, so he has the responsibility to make the choice.

"Of course, as you know, Ron values your input, and everything will be considered. It's like if Ralph were hiring someone for the accounting department, he would get input from others, but in the end, he makes the call."

"How soon will Ron make his decision?" Ralph asked.

"Ron, do you want to take this one?" Susan asked.

"Ralph, I hope to be able to make the call shortly after our group meeting, and after I review all of the information and the comments from all of our team members. Once I make my decision, I will invite that person back to our company to spend the day with us in an informal environment. We will have some of you go to lunch with the candidate, and then my wife, Cindy, and I will take the candidate to dinner. If the person is married, we will ask him or her to bring their spouse, not just for dinner, but the whole day."

"Thanks, Ron," Susan said. "That sounds really good and effective."

Ron said, "Based on all the things we are doing—and knowing the teams in this company—I am absolutely confident that we will make the right choice. I am really excited!"

"We are going to break into our team groups, and I will go over the interview with all of you and explain how it works," Susan said. "I know you will like and appreciate this process."

"Susan, I have a question." Sam said.

"You have not mentioned reference and background checks. Are you going to do them?"

"Yes," she answered. "All three candidates are currently employed so we will not do the reference and background checks on all of them. We are ready to conduct the checks as soon as Ron makes the call. We will check nine references. Three people the candidate has reported to, three peers, and three direct reports."

"I should have known you had it handled!" Sam added.

"I have a question." Sally asked. "Are you doing a Kolbe or some other assessment like that with the candidates?"

Susan said, "We will implement Lencioni's Working Genius Survey, so we had the three finalists complete it. This will not replace the Kolbe. We are also considering implementing EOS, and the KOLBE assessment is part of that process. In your packets you will find a thorough description of both Working Genius and the KOLBE."

"You mentioned EOS," Sam said. "I know we have briefly discussed it in our Leadership Team meeting, but can you provide a summary of EOS for the others?"

"We have Sam," Susan said. "In the packets is a complete explanation of EOS, as well as a citation for the book, *Traction*."

"As usual you are a step ahead of me!" Sam said.

"Any other questions?" Susan asked.

"Just one," Bill asked. "What is the dress code for the candidates and for us? I assume we will all wear three-piece suits and shiny black shoes, well polished."

"Ah, not exactly Bill," Susan said. "Did the suits come from Ralph?"

Bill hung his head and said, "You caught me,"

Susan shook her head and gave Ralph a stern look. "The dress code for all, including the candidates, is business casual.

"I want to work with each team now explaining how to use your interview. I will start with the operations team and then the Leadership

Team. Ron, I will meet with you in your office when the other two are completed.

"For the Leadership Team, if you want to take a break and check email and voicemail, please do. Mark will let you know when it is your turn. I want all of you to remember how important this day is for all of us.

"The consultant gave me a copy of the Candidate Rating Sheet they use," Susan said, "It is simple and concise and I think it would be helpful for us to use it. Mary please give everyone three copies of the form, one for each candidate. (See page 236.)

Susan added. "You will be meeting and hearing from three new people. Every time you interview someone you will learn something new. Pay attention and listen carefully. Okay, let's get into our teams."

Always do background checks and call references.

CANDIDATE RATING SHEET

Candidate: _____ **Evaluator:** _____

Immediately following the interview, each team member is to complete this rating form. The results will assist the team in selecting the right person. Use the key below to rate the candidates on each of the five categories. Be sure to note your comments justifying your ratings.

RATING KEY

Fully meets criteria/expectations	10
Generally meets criteria/expectations	7
Acceptable; need more information	4
Not acceptable	0

A. Professional Presentation	
B. Communication Skills	
C. Team Member Fit & Match	
D. Technical Experiencer/Competence	
E. People Person - Really Likes People	
COMMENTS	
TOTAL RATING	

PERCEIVED STRENGTHS	**PERCEIVED VULNERABILITIES**

Chapter 24

INTERVIEW DAY

The big day had arrived.

Mary was the coordinator for the day, as Susan needed to participate in the interviews. Mary had everything in place and ready for the day. She went through her check list just to double check. She had assembled information packets for each candidate, providing them with written copies of the company's mission, vision, and core values, as well as materials from the Chamber of Commerce about the community, including a list of government offices and churches.

Mary decided to walk to the lobby and put the packets on the reception counter, ready for the candidates. Maria joined her.

"I am sure you have everything in order and ready," Maria said. "You are so well organized."

"Thanks," Mary said. "Today is a real test of my organizing skills. I want this to be perfect."

"I am confident all will be perfect," Maria answered. "This is a major change for us in our whole hiring process, and I believe it is a great change. Is Susan here yet?"

"I have not seen her," Mary said. Just then Mark and Cathy joined them.

"Good morning!" Mark cheerfully greeted everyone. "This will be a great day for our company."

"I see you are your usual cheerful self, Mark," Cathy said. "I agree with you about this being a great day!"

"I love your attitudes!" Mary said. "I am sure it will have a positive impact on the candidates. By the way, I put together packets for them." She pointed to the reception counter. "Not sure if you want to give them to the candidates when they arrive or during your debrief."

"I recommend at the debrief," Maria said. "That way they do not have to carry them around to the various sections, breaks, and lunch. And, Mary, thank you so much for doing this. It is a great idea!"

"I would like to take credit," Mary said. "Susan asked me to do it. She has a comprehensive list of everything for interview day, and we now have a model to use for future hiring processes. Do you hosts need anything?"

"I don't think so," Mark said, "We are anxious and ready."

"Good," Mary replied. "I will stay in the lobby until the candidates have all arrived and you have gone on the tours. Susan told me to make sure we have introductions. She reminded me that all of the candidates were told the other candidates would be here at the same time, and while they would never be pitted against each other, they would probably meet the other candidates. So we are the welcoming committee."

"Speaking of which," Maria said, "I think the first candidate is coming up the sidewalk now. He entered the lobby and walked over to Mary at the reception desk.

"Good morning," the man said. "I am William Brown and I am here for an interview. Am I in the right place?"

"Yes you are," Mary responded, "I am Mary Foster, and I am the assistant to our president, Ron Howell. You will be with Mark Hart and here he is."

"Good morning, William," Mark said. "I am Mark Hart and will be your host for today, and welcome to our company, and thank you for participating. Let me introduce you to my HR team members Cathy Douglas and Maria Smith. Cathy and Maria will be the hosts for the other two candidates."

William smiled and shook hands with everyone.

Laura Clark and Gregg Johnson arrived as everyone was shaking hands. Mark jumped in and started the introductions again. He made sure everyone was introduced and thanked them for coming. After a few minutes, the hosts took their candidates on the tours, and Mary headed back to her office.

Susan caught up with Mary just as she reached her office. "How did the introductions go?" she asked.

"Really well," Mary said. "I think the fact they knew about the introductions before arrival made a big difference. Plus, Mark took charge and introduced everyone."

"That's Mark," Susan said. "He is a take-charge guy! He is a valuable member of the HR team."

"Susan go and enjoy the day. You have earned it," Mary said. "I will hang loose and be available for any needs people have today. I will walk around the building and check on the various sessions. I doubt if I will need to do much since the three hosts are super!"

The hosts stayed on schedule and took their candidate to their 9:15 a.m. interviews and were there to greet them when it ended. They did not need to knock on any doors since the first round ended on time—they were prepared to interrupt if the session ran over time. Probably the fact that each interview team had one member as the clock watcher made a difference.

After the second round, the hosts took their candidates to lunch.

The day went like clock-work. At 4:00 p.m. the hosts met in the debrief with their candidates and walked to the door with them when the session ended.

"What a day!" Mark said. "I am tired—and we didn't even have to do the interviews!"

"It was a great day," Maria said, "I have heard from several of the interviewers that the day was perfect, and the interviews went very well. It sounds like it will be a tough decision as all three presented themselves as competent leaders."

"I kept notes about my time with my candidate," Cathy said. "I am anxious to share them at the meeting in the morning, and I am really anxious to hear what all the others have to say about the candidates."

"Me, too," Maria said. "This was a great experience."

And all three of them headed to their offices to pack up and head home, knowing the next day would be a big day, too!

Interview day is a showcase for your company

Chapter 25

DECISION TIME

The meeting to discuss the three candidates was set for 10:00 a.m. in the conference room. Ron had asked Susan to meet with him early in the morning, as he had a few questions.

"Good morning. Thanks for getting in early," he said. "I just wanted to review our plans for the meeting so I know and understand my role. I assume I will lead the meeting."

"Good morning, Ron," Susan answered. "Yes, I did want to talk with you about the meeting."

"Great," he said. "I thought yesterday went extremely well, and I am anxious to get the feedback and compare it to my thoughts."

Susan said, "And Ron, that is why I will conduct the meeting and not you. You need to be able to sit and listen to all of the comments to help you make your decision. If you have to lead the meeting, you could possibly miss something key to your decision-making."

Ron sat silently. "After giving it some thought, I agree with you," he said. "I knew I could count on you to lead me down the right path!"

"I just want to make sure we get this right," Susan said. "I am sure you have some strong feelings about the candidates, and I want you to have all the information available to make the right call."

"Sounds good to me," he replied. "How will you organize the presentations?"

"I want to start with having our three hosts, my HR team share their observations after spending so much informal time with the candidates. The consultant told me that he calls the hosts his 'James Bond Technique.' In other words, he sees them as undercover agents. He told me about a time when feedback from one of the hosts actually ruled a candidate out."

"Really?" Ron said. "What did the candidate do? Confess to being a serial killer or a political assassin?"

"Not that dramatic," she replied. "But really significant. The host said whenever he introduced the candidates to a person with a manager title, the candidate he was super friendly, smiled a lot, reached out for a hand shake, and conversed."

"On the surface that sounds okay," Ron said.

"I agree," she said. "There is more to the story. Whenever he introduced the candidate to a person without a manager title, the candidate was not very friendly."

"How did the interview teams react to this information?" He asked.

"It opened a floodgate of people sharing concerns they had, but could not put a finger on until they heard this from the host."

"Interesting to say the least," Ron replied. "Wow. The more I learn about this system, the happier I am that we tried it and committed to moving forward with an agreement with the consultant. I'm glad we had the turmoil with Brenda Ross and her company that forced us to do something."

"Speaking of that," she asked, "did you hear any more from Brandon?"

"I did," he said. "I received an email yesterday. Remember the guy Brandon sent to us for an interview?"

"I do," she said. "If I remember, his name is Don Meyer."

"Correct," Ron replied. "He decided not to file a lawsuit against us. In the email, Brandon berated me and said we missed the boat by not hiring Don Meyer. He added that with Charlie leaving we are doomed. He said I had zero leadership ability and without Charlie, people will quickly see how incompetent I am. I guess he had a lot to get off his chest. Glad I got out of his group."

"Hopefully, that is all we will hear from him. Anyway, let me get back to the format of the meeting this morning."

"I am all ears," he said.

"After the hosts share, I will ask the operations team to share their information, followed by the Leadership Team. After that, I will ask you to make a few comments, but do not announce a decision at this time. Tell the teams how much you appreciate their efforts and you will be putting it all together to make the decision.

"Also, Ron, tell them you need to read the responses to the situational activity now that you have received all of their feedback. Tell them you intend to share your choice for number one within the next forty-eight hours. How does all that sound?"

"Makes sense to me," he said. "I assume you will be there to help me process all of the information and make the call."

"That is a given," Susan replied. "I will be there, but right now I need to go and make the final preparations for the meeting."

"Go get it done," he said. "And thank you!"

As Susan turned the corner to her office, she all but ran into Charlie.

"Oops," she said, "that was a close call!"

"My fault," he said. "I have a meeting with Ron, and I am running late. We need to go over all the final details for my departure."

"He has all the HR items," she said. "So it should be a short meeting."

"Good," he said. "Now that the time to leave is so close, I keep having second thoughts and wonder if I did the right thing."

"That's normal," Susan said. "You have a super opportunity, and it is a job that was made for you. We will miss you and probably struggle a little, but we will make it, and so will you."

"I know." he said. "I am glad you let me be involved in the interviews. Ron has three good candidates to consider. In fact, right now I am not sure whom I would choose. And I like how you are helping him. I love this system, and once I am settled into my new role, I will contact this consultant to get an agreement for the company."

"Sounds good, Charlie," she said. "Let me know if I can help."

" Will do," he said. "See you at the meeting,"

Charlie hurried down the hallway, and Susan made it into her office to find Mary waiting inside.

"Good morning, Susan," Mary said. "I wanted to catch you, so I waited here in your office."

"And good morning to you, too," Susan said. "What's up?"

"Nothing really," she said, "Just want to make sure you know I am ready to help in any way that is needed."

"That's great," Susan said. "I know I can count on you. Mary, probably the biggest help is for you to keep notes this morning. I have everything ready to go, but it would be great to have you taking notes along with me. That way we can limit what we miss."

"I can and will do that," Mary said. "If you need anything else just ask me. Now, I better get back to my office so if Ron needs something, he won't have to send out a search party," Mary smiled and headed down the hallway.

Susan took a deep breath, and settled into her chair. Across the hall, her three team members were talking about the search and the upcoming meeting.

"Are you prepared to talk about your candidate?" Mark asked Cathy and Maria.

Cathy spoke first. "I think I am. I have really good notes. How about you Maria?"

"The same," she said. "And since you asked us, what about you Mark?"

"I, too, have many notes," he said, "so I guess I am ready."

"You *guess* you are ready?" Maria asked. "Are you ready or not?"

"I am hoping no one asks if I think William is a fit and match," He replied.

"Well, is he?" Cathy asked.

Mark just stood there.

"Hello, earth to Mark, are you with us?" Maria asked.

After a short pause, Mark answered, "I really don't think so. He is a nice guy. And he has EOS experience, which could be valuable to the company. But I don't think he is a fit and match, but I cannot tell you why. I am frustrated."

"Mark," Maria said, "when you share with the teams, you need to be honest and tell them your feelings. Someone else might feel the same way, and your comments might trigger them, and they will connect some dots."

"I agree, Mark," Cathy said. "We must share our information and our feelings. Each piece of information adds to the others, and Ron will be able to sift through it and make his decision."

"Thanks," Mark said. "I feel much better."

"Good," Maria said. "Are we all ready for the meeting?" Both nodded.

"I want to just review my notes one more time," Cathy said. "Then I will be ready, and we can go to the conference room."

Bill and Sally were walking down the hallway to the conference room when Ralph came out of his office and joined them.

"Good morning all," Ralph greeted them. "Ready for the meeting?"

Bill answered, "Hi, Ralph. I am as ready as I ever will be."

"Me, too," Sally replied.

"I really enjoyed yesterday and the way Susan put everything together was just super."

"I also liked the questions she wrote for us to use," Ralph said. "I learned a lot."

"I think we all did," Bill replied. "It will be interesting to see how each of us perceived the three candidates. I have not zeroed in on one over the other two."

"Same here," Sally responded. "They all can do the job, but which one is the best fit and match for the team, and mostly with Ron?"

Bill said, "I am sure he will hear a lot from everyone and then he can put it all together and make the call."

All of a sudden Susan came down the hallway like a bullet train, full speed ahead.

"Everything okay?" Sally asked.

"Not really," Susan said, scurrying past them. "Can't stop to talk. I have to meet with Ron now."

"I hope she is okay," Sally said. "I suppose we will hear about it in the meeting. Let's go to the conference room."

Susan arrived at Ron's office and did not hesitate, but walked right into the office. Ron was at his small conference table with Mary.

"Ron," Susan began, "I have to talk with you now."

"Give me a second," Mary said, "and I can get out of the way."

"You can stay Mary," Susan said. "This involves a candidate."

"Take a deep breath, Susan, and slow down," Ron said. "Whatever it is, we can deal with it." He realized that tears were running down her face.

"I just spoke with William Brown's son. I called each candidate this morning to thank them for their time and remind them to submit the reimbursement forms. William flew home last evening, and when he arrived about 9:30 p.m., he told his wife he did not feel well. His wife called their son to tell him that she was taking him to the emergency room. On the way to the hospital, William experienced a heart attack.

Susan paused, took a deep breath and could hardly speak.

Mary walked over to her and held her hand.

Sobbing, Susan said, "William was declared dead upon arrival at the hospital."

Mary helped Susan to a chair.

Ron and Mary sat in silence as Susan gained control of her emotions. After a couple of minutes, Ron spoke to Susan.

"Did his son tell you anything else?" He asked.

Susan answered. "Only that he knew his dad was interviewing with us. His dad had spoken about how kind we were, and he had hoped to get the offer. He said that he was sure his father would want us to know."

"Susan, it is just about time for our meeting," Ron said. "Would you like to postpone the meeting?"

She sat still with her head in her hands, deep in thought. "I don't think we have time to postpone it," she said. "But how about if we delay the meeting until 1:00 p.m.?"

"I can do that," Ron said. "I think that makes a lot of sense. The meeting is set to begin in about five minutes. I want you to stay here with Mary, and I will go to the conference room and share this information and tell everyone that we will delay the meeting until 1:00 p.m."

Ron touched Susan on the shoulder and left the office, striding to the conference room, where everyone had already gathered. He walked to the front of the room.

"I have some sad news to share with you," he said softly. "One of our candidates, William Brown, died from a heart attack last evening."

Everyone in the room was still.

"Do you have any more information?" Charlie finally asked.

"Yes," Ron responded. "He was with his wife and they were driving home from the airport when he experienced the heart attack. He stopped on the side of the road and his wife took the wheel and drove to the hospital. He was pronounced dead upon arrival at the hospital."

"How did you find out so soon?" Charlie asked.

"Susan called William to thank him for participating in our process and learned from his son what had happened. Obviously, this news is tragic and Susan is very upset. She asked that we delay the meeting until 1:00 p.m., and I am sure you all understand."

"How is Susan?" Maria asked.

"Susan is a strong person," Ron said. "She needs just a little time to work through the emotions she is experiencing. She will recover quickly.

"I am sure those of you who spent time with William yesterday, like Susan, are feeling strong emotions. That is okay, and what you should be experiencing. I am going to say a prayer now for William's family, and then we will adjourn until 1:00 p.m."

Ron prayed from his heart, and then everyone quietly left the conference room.

When Ron returned to his office, he saw Mary and Susan sitting at the small conference table chatting quietly.

"She is doing much better," Mary said. "She has had a chance to process this tragic news, and we talked about it and prayed together for William's family."

Ron said. "We closed our meeting a few minutes ago in prayer for William's family. I could sense the sadness throughout the conference room. We only just met him, but he seemed to be a genuine and sensitive man."

"Thank you for handling the meeting for me," Susan said to Ron. "This call just hit me like a punch in the stomach. Out of nowhere.

I never expected to have a candidate die during our hiring process. I am okay now and ready to get back and focused on our tasks."

"Good," Ron replied. "I will meet you in the conference room about 12:45 p.m. just to touch base and talk about how we will approach the meeting now that we only have two candidates to discuss. Between now and then, why don't you and Mary leave the office and go to Mary's coffee shop and relax."

Susan and Mary headed out to the coffee shop and Ron walked to Ralph's office.

"Ralph if you have time now, we could review the financials," Ron said.

"Good idea," Ralph said. "I have to tell you that this event really shook me up. I just met the guy yesterday and had a great discussion with him about EOS and how it would impact me in accounting. He was so open and willing to listen. Now, today, he is gone. I have never experienced this before."

"It's not easy to understand," Ron said. "It must be heart-wrenching for the family. Just keep them in your prayers."

"I have, and I will," Ralph said. Ralph and Ron dove into the financials, and Ron was pleased with the results so far that quarter.

"Looks good, Ralph," Ron said, "thanks for taking some time. I need to make some calls so I will see you at the meeting."

As Ron left, Ralph sat still at his desk, deep in thought.

On his way back to his office, Ron encountered Sam and Linda in the hallway.

"Hey, Ron." Sam said. "We were just sharing about the information we received about William. Any time something happens like this, it is a tragedy. I had asked Linda if she ever experienced something like this during a hiring process."

"I told him not even close," Linda said. "He was so affable, happy, and fun to talk to yesterday, and now he is gone. Several years ago my sister and her husband died in an automobile accident. It has brought back memories."

"I did not know you then," Sam said. "But I remember you telling me about it. And you are raising your three nephews. Susan said his son told her. I don't know if William had other children or even grandchildren. I think he was in his mid-fifties."

"When I did my one-to-one with him," Ron said, "he mentioned that he and his wife were parents of three children and had four grandchildren."

"You had asked Linda if she ever had something like this happen during a hiring process," Ron said. "I also have not had this experience. Not to sound insensitive, but we do have two excellent candidates to consider, and we must push forward. Sam, you are on the worship team at your church. Please have them include William's family on their prayer list, and I'll see you both at the meeting."

At 1:00 p.m., everyone was in the conference room, ready to review the candidates. Ron started the meeting, thanking everyone for his or her flexibility in changing the time of the meeting, and he set the stage for Susan.

"I know the events this morning have impacted all of you in one way or another," Ron said. "We are reaching out to William's family and will keep you informed about what we can do for them. Now, we need to focus on the task at hand. I am turning the floor over to Susan, who will lead our discussion. I am taking a passive role so I can focus on what you share—to help me make the best decision for us in this hire. As Susan has said, I make the final call. However, I want you to know I could not do that without your input."

"Thank you, Ron, and thanks to all of you for letting me delay this meeting," Susan said. "Our hearts go out to William's family. However, as Ron said, we now have to focus. So, here is how we will proceed. The hosts, Cathy and Maria, will share with us what they saw and heard with their candidates and then the operations team will share with us, followed by the Leadership Team.

"I have given Ron the written situational activity documents, and he will review them, along with what he hears today. I have asked Mary to keep notes, which Ron will also have available to make the final decision. As a reminder, this is a new process for us. It is called a discovery process, and I believe it has lived up to its moniker. So, Cathy, tell us about Gregg Johnson."

Cathy summarizing her observations about Gregg Johnson, saying that from her perspective, he was a good fit and match. Maria talked about Laura Clark, who she felt did an excellent job, and ended with her opinion that Laura was a good fit and match.

The operations team had met and agreed on what they, as a group, learned about the two candidates. They obviously felt both candidates were possible choices. They saw both of them as having a similar personality, and believed that both of them would be sensitive and responsive to others' needs. In their opinion, both were called servant leaders. They all had completed the Candidate Rating Sheet and shared the combined results with everyone.

CANDIDATE COMPARISON CHART
Operations Team's Ratings

Category	Linda Clark	Gregg Johnson
Professional Presentation	10	10
Communication Skills	10	7
Team Member fit/match	10	10
Technical Experience/ Competence	7	7
People Person/Really Likes People	10	10
Perceived Strengths	Very Professional Servant Leader Excellent Communicator Rapport Builder Strong Values A Coach Accountable Well Organized	Professional Servant Leader Good Communicator Strong Values A Driver Objective Accountable Big Picture Person
Perceived Vulnerabilities	Tends to be soft spoken.	Can get in your face.
General Comments	Our team likes Laura and believes she is a good fit and match.	Our team also likes Gregg and believes he is a good fit and match.
Total Rating	47	44

253

Randy Young, speaking for the operations team, said, "We do not know if this is helpful Ron, because we sincerely believe either one would be a good leader for us. We were very comfortable with both of them, and believe it is up to you to select the one that fits and matches with you. We do appreciate being involved. Thank you."

"Well done," Susan said. "You have made me and the HR team feel great. We must have done a good job of selecting the finalists! Now let's hear from the Leadership Team and how they perceive the candidates. I believe Linda is speaking for them."

Linda stood up and said, "Thanks Susan. Yes, I lost, and I am the speaker for our group. I will do my best to represent the team. We also used the rating sheet, and we ended up with the same scores—Laura at forty-seven and Gregg at forty-four.

"We had similar observations about their strengths and vulnerabilities. We felt the biggest difference is very much like yours. We perceive Laura to be more laid back and, like the ops team said, soft spoken. Gregg tends to be more forward, and we agree he could get in your face. However, those are not deal breakers. Let me shares some comments from our discussions."

Linda read several comments that each member of the team had made about each candidate. While Linda spoke, Susan looked over and saw Ron listening intently. He was totally fixed on what Linda shared with the group. Linda ended her comments thanking the group for listening and thanking Ron and Susan for the new process for hiring.

Susan then said, "Thank you to all of you for helping us by participating in our new hiring process. And, thank you for your feedback. Ron, I am turning the floor back to you."

Ron stood and walked to the front of the room. "First, thank you to all of you for helping us find the right fit and match. All of your observations are so helpful to me. I have taken many notes. And I know Mary has been writing feverishly for me.

"I will sit down with all the information, and within the next twenty-four hours, I will announce my decision. I will have Mary call a meeting, as I want to tell you in person and not by email. I am sure you have a lot to do yet today, so this meeting has ended. Thanks again!"

All the staff members headed to their offices, except Charlie, who lingered to talk with Susan. "Great job. I am really impressed with the new process and I really enjoyed this feedback meeting. I assume this is part of the five-step system."

"It is," she replied, "and it is something many companies do not do in their hiring process. Ron is making the final decision, but if you work here, you have to feel really good about having the chance to be involved."

"I wonder if the candidates are always this close in other searches," Charlie reflected. "The quality of both of these people is fantastic."

"I asked the consultant what to expect," Susan said. "He clearly told me that the final candidates, if you do a good job of screening, would be quality. He added that most of the time, while all three will be well received, the best fit and match is usually clear. In our case we have two very similar finalists. If William had still been in the running, I wonder if it would have gone any differently."

"Probably not," Charlie responded. "I found these two highly competent, and both are without a doubt servant leaders. I can see myself in both of them, and I think that is why my team could not separate them."

"Interesting," she responded. "Now that you say that, I can see it. Well, now we just wait for Ron. I am actually very tired. I am going to go to my office and take care of two minor items, and then I am leaving early today."

"Go for it," Charlie said. "You deserve the rest. See you tomorrow."

"Thanks Charlie and have a good evening."

Down the hallway in his office, Ron was organizing all of the information.

"Here are my notes," Mary said. "I hope I captured everything. Oh, do you have the situational activity documents?"

"I do," Ron said. "I want to go through everything first and then read them last. Susan recommended that approach, as she said the consultant told her these documents can put the frosting on the cake."

"Ron you did a one-to-one with all of the candidates," Mary said. "How does that impact your decision-making?"

"Funny you should ask," Ron said. "After the one-to-one interviews were done, I have to admit I did have a preferred candidate. I still generally feel that way. However, the feedback session was fantastic, and is very valuable. It kept me comparing my thoughts to what I was hearing from the group."

"May I ask who is in first place?" Mary asked.

"No you may not." he said with a big smile on his face. "You will just have to wait until tomorrow with everyone else."

Ron spent most of his evening reviewing his notes and then he read the situational activity documents. The next morning, he arrived at the office early so he could put the finishing touches on his decision. He was sitting at his desk when Ralph walked in.

"I do not want to bother you, as I assume you are in the final stage of your decision- making," Ralph said, "but I have some information you will find interesting."

"Come on in Ralph," Ron said. "Did we break an all time sales record by so much that you got tired counting the money?"

"Not exactly," he responded. "I thought you would find it interesting that good old Brandon is out of his position."

"Seriously?" he asked in amazement.

"Yes.," Ralph said.

"Did he resign?" Ron asked.

"He was dismissed for unethical behavior," Ralph said.

"Makes me feel good. How about you?"

"Yes and no," Ron said. "I have already forgiven him, and now I will pray for him. I do not have time for vengeance in my life."

"I wish I could be like you," Ralph said. "I continually try to learn more from you. I go to church, but my faith is not as strong as yours. Next time you begin a new Bible study, please let me know."

"I will, Ralph," he said. "I am happy that you are interested. Have you made your decision?"

"I have," Ron said.

"I don't suppose you can tell me," Ralph said.

"Right," Ron answered, "I want everyone to hear the decision at the same time."

"I understand," Ralph said. "When will you meet with all of us?"

"Mary is sending an email as we speak," Ron told him. "Everyone is asked to meet in the conference room at 10:00 a.m."

Ralph said, "I am looking forward to hearing your decision."

As Ralph left, Ron leaned back in his chair with his arms behind his neck and took several deep breaths. In less than an hour he would share his decision.

Meanwhile in Susan's office, her three HR team members—along with Sam and Linda—speculated about Ron's choice.

"Anyone feel strongly as to which candidate he will choose?" Sam asked.

Susan spoke first. "I have worked closely with Ron for several years, and I usually can read him. On this one, I have no idea."

"He can't make a bad decision," Linda said. "I think both Laura and Gregg are great candidates and could do a great job. I think both fit our culture. I find few differences between them."

"I guess we just have to wait until he makes the announcement," Maria said.

Susan said, "I know he has spent a lot of time going over the screener summaries I gave him, the probe results from the consultant, the notes from my one-to-ones, the feedback discussion we had yesterday, the results of their situational activity, and the Working Genius reports."

"When you list all of that, I don't think I have ever had that much information to use in making a hiring decision," Linda said. "This new system is really impressive."

"Well, I have some things to take care of before the meeting so I am throwing all of you out of the office," Susan said. "I look forward to hearing Ron's decision very soon."

Susan turned to her computer to respond to some emails.

As 10:00 a.m. drew closer, team members headed toward the conference room. Ron took a deep breath and picked up his notes. Susan wondered if Ron would choose the one she had in mind. Linda and Sam were talking about who would be the new operations leader. Ralph was pretty sure he knew who Ron would choose. Bill shared with Sally that he had no idea who Ron would choose and Sally agreed. Charlie was thinking, *This brings several wonderful years to closure.* Mary was in the conference room making sure everything was in order.

As Ron entered the conference room, he noticed that everyone appeared to be present. He walked over to Susan and quietly said, "We have reached the finish line. You did a fantastic job getting the system working for us." And with that he stepped to the front of the room.

"Good morning," Ron said, "Thank you for taking time to meet with me. Yes, I have made a decision. Without your participation and input, I would not be confident in my decision. As Susan had shared— and by the way she did a great job working this system . . ." he paused as the coworkers applauded. "Now the way the system works the hiring manager, the person who will be the supervisor of the new hire, gathers input from all the stakeholders and then makes the call. If any of you have to hire a person who reports to you, this same system will be used, and we will give you input, but you will be the one making the final call."

Ron paused and took a sip of water.

"Here we are with the final decision being announced. We had planned to have three finalists to consider, but as you know, William Brown unfortunately passed away from an unexpected heart attack. While we only have two candidates at this point, it is not like having only two to consider. William went through the whole process, including interview day, so we really kept to the system. The two candidates under consideration are both highly qualified. The difference between Laura and Gregg is minor. It has been a challenge to select just the one. And, I hope all of our hiring processes in the future have the same result."

"I went through the results of the screener interview, the interview done by our consultant, the notes from Susan's one-to-ones, and I also watched the interviews since she was kind enough to record them. I did my one-to-one on interview day and kept good notes. I listened to the verbal reports during our meeting to discuss the candidates, and I talked off-line with several of you.

"And finally—and you know me well—I prayed for guidance in decision-making. With all of that said, Laura and Gregg came out just about equal on everything, including the result of the new assessment we are using, Working Genius.

"It came down to which candidate, in my professional judgment, is the best fit and match with the Leadership Team, the operations team, the HR team, and, last but not least, yours truly.

"When this meeting ends I will call Laura Clark and offer her a job."

Everyone was quiet for a second when Bill shouted, "Yes!" The other employees joined in cheers and applause.

"I think you all agree!" Ron said with a big smile on his face.

The final choice must be the top fit and match.

Chapter 26

MAKING THE OFFER

Ron walked back to his office with Susan. "I think everyone was okay with my choice," Ron said. "I do believe she had an edge, particularly with our culture."

Susan replied, "I agree. I am happy with your decision. I had hoped you would select Laura. My HR team loves her."

"Good," he replied. "I am going to call and give her a verbal offer and then follow up with the written documents. Are they ready?"

"All but putting her name on them," she answered.

"I am going to put the call on speaker so both of us can speak with her. Oh, as soon as we finish speaking with Laura, please call Gregg and let him know my decision."

"I will," she replied. "I like that we make a telephone call and do not send an email. He spent a lot of time with us and deserves more than an email."

Mary greeted them as they entered the office. "Great choice, Ron," she said. "She was my pick. also. Although, Gregg was right in there too."

"Mary we are going to call Laura and make the verbal offer," Ron said. "I am going to have it on speaker if you want to listen to the call."

"Thanks," Mary said. "I need to get the conference room ready for Linda and her team's meeting," Mary headed to the conference room.

"I have Laura's cell phone number from her resume," Ron said. "Is that the number you have been using?"

"It is," she replied. "Go for it."

Ron dialed the number. It rang three times.

"Hello," Laura answered.

"Hi Laura." this is Ron Howell, and I have Susan West here with me. How are you?"

"I'm good." she replied. "Thank you so much for the opportunity to be in your process. I enjoyed each step along the way, and I really liked interview day."

"Thanks," Susan said. "This is the first time we have used this system, and we are very pleased with how well it worked."

"You probably are wondering why we have called you," Ron said. "Let me get right to

it. We are giving you this verbal offer to join our team as our operations leader."

Laura did not immediately respond, but when she did, she said, "Wonderful. I really was hoping for the offer. I really like the people in the company. To be honest, I was really impressed with Mr. Johnson. I guess I expected him to get the offer."

"Well, this is a verbal offer," Susan added. "We will email you a written offer as soon as we end this conversation. The offer will include the base salary, benefits, and PTO summary. I think my team reviewed the benefits and salary range with you."

"They did," she answered. "If the written offer is consistent with what I have been told, I will accept it. I have to admit that I am anxious to join the team."

Ron then asked, "How long a drive was it for you to come to our offices?"

Laura answered, "It took me just under 4 hours."

"Many times we have the candidate come back to the office following the verbal offer to meet with us on an informal basis." Ron said.

"With your spontaneous reaction to our verbal offer this may not be necessary."

"It is not," Laura responded. "I am extremely comfortable with your company and people, and with a 4 hour drive, thanks, but the visit is not necessary."

"With the 4 hour drive, I assume this will be a relocation issue for you," Susan stated.

"Yes it is," Laura answered. "I checked real estate in your area and saw several good options. My husband is a self-employed consultant, so he can live just about anywhere."

"With a four-hour drive," Ron said, "until you find a house, we will secure and provide an apartment for you, so you do not have to commute."

"Thank you," she said. "That will be so helpful."

"Laura I need to run your references, and we do a standard background check," Susan explained. "Your offer will obviously be pending successful references and a clean background check."

"I understand and assumed that to be the case," she replied.

"For references please email me the following: Three people you have reported to, three people who were your peers, and three people who reported to you."

"I can do that quickly," she said. "I have my reference list prepared, and I will mark those people in the categories you stated."

"I will also email you the release form allowing us to do the background check," Susan told her. "Please sign and email back to me."

"I will do that," she said.

Ron then said, "For this position we put together a position profile. This was to guide our search. It is not a job description. I will, with Susan's assistance, prepare a proposed job description that you and I will then together put in final form, as an official job description. Our job descriptions are metric based. That will be included in the onboarding plan we have for you. Any questions?"

"Not now." she replied. "If I think of something I will send you an email with my questions."

"I would like to have all the necessary paperwork done by the end of the week. If it works in your schedule, I would like to have you begin next week," Ron said.

"I probably can do that," She said. "As I said during the interview process, my position is one of many that were eliminated. In fact, I just heard this morning that the company has been sold. and even more jobs are being eliminated."

Susan said, "I will get the ball rolling on this end. I am happy to have you joining our team. I will be in touch."

"Thanks, Susan," Laura said. "I am anxious to get started."

Once the call ended, Ron said, "That went well."

"It did," Susan responded. "I will finish all the details in the offer and have it for your review in about an hour. Once I have her references and signed background check authorization, I will get started."

"Sounds good," Ron said. "While you are handling the details, I will work on my draft of the job description, and I am making good progress on her onboarding plan. You know, when I was in the peer group, I was amazed that none of them used an onboarding plan with new managers. In fact, the attitude was that to put a manager in an onboarding plan was beneath them."

"That's fairly typical, Ron," Susan said. "Just think how many of them hire without a system even close to what we just used."

"That reminds me of Proverbs 26:10," he said. "'Like an archer who wounds everyone, is one who hires a fool or passerby.' That makes it very clear."

"I think I should paste a copy of that verse on my wall," Susan said. "Does Laura know that you share Scripture with us?"

Laughing, Ron replied, "She does. I had mentioned that I was an elder in my church, and she said that she was active in women's Bible studies at her church. You might want to key Sally in about that. Okay, then, let's get our tasks done!"

Susan said, "On it. I will keep you posted." And she left the office.

Always involve all stakeholders in the final hiring decision.

Chapter 27

ONBOARDING

Later that afternoon, Susan stopped into Ron's office. "Got a minute?"

Ron looked up, smiled, and said. "I do."

"You seem to be in a happy mood." she said.

"I am," he replied. "And to quote our consultant, happy in the Lord."

"I like that," Susan said. "I want to bring you up to date about Laura."

"I am ready to listen. " he responded.

"We have a complete signed offer letter, I have all of her references, and I have the signed release for the background check. I have already sent in the request for the background check, and my team will do the reference checks—two each. Mary found a short term apartment rental for Laura, and it begins now."

"That's great news," Ron replied. "Just curious. Maria, Cathy, and Mark each will do two reference calls. Correct?"

"Yes," Susan said. "We have a standard reference interview, but if you want, we can add to it."

"Nothing to add." he said. "I just did not actually know you had a standard reference interview."

"Would you like to see it?" She asked.

"Not necessary," he answered. "You can just tell me about it."

Susan explained the reference checking process.

"The first thing you have to know is that we ask positive questions.

At the end, rather than ask for the candidate's weaknesses, we ask if there is anything we have not inquired about regarding Laura that they would like to tell us.

"Nine times out of ten, they comment that we did not ask for weaknesses or areas of concern. The interviewer is instructed to thank the person for keeping them out of trouble for not asking about any concerns. This technique tends to make them comfortable and most of the time they really open up and share candidly about the person."

"I like that," Ron said. "What areas do you typically cover?"

"We ask how long they have known the candidate, how the candidate relates to others, communication styles, decision-making and problem-solving, for example."

Ron replied, "I like the reference interview. Let me know when it is done."

"I sure will. Should be done very soon," Susan said. "Before I go and leave you to get back to work, do you need any help with the onboarding plan for Laura?"

"Yes I would like some help," Ron said. "First, let me finish my draft outline and we can use that to prompt our discussion. Also, I was assuming, and I know I should not assume, that you will make sure that she gets our welcome packet, that her computer is set up, and that Sam will meet with her regarding password and programs. Will you send the welcome email to her?"

"I will," Susan said.

"Charlie's last day is tomorrow," Ron said. "Is everything set up for the farewell luncheon?"

"It is," Susan said, "and credit goes to Mary. I spoke with him, and he will have his office cleared out in the morning so I can begin preparing the office for Laura."

As someone tapped at the door, the two turned. "Can I join you?" Charlie asked.

"Come on in," Ron said. "I was going to ask Mary to set a time for us to meet, and now is as good a time as ever."

"I am on my way out," Susan said. "Charlie, I will check with you later because you and I have to do the formal exit interview."

"Just let me know when," he said, "I have a lot of time available. And I can hardly wait to share all the bad stuff stored in my memory banks!" Both shared a laugh.

"Probably early afternoon," she replied, and headed out.

"How is the new job shaping up?" Ron asked.

"I think it will be okay," he said. "Thanks for letting me spend some time over there checking everything out from head to toe."

"How do you feel about my decision to hire Laura?" Ron asked.

"You made the right call," Charlie replied. "She was my top choice. Please give her my number and she can call me anytime with questions. I don't think she will have that many. She is a professional and ready to take charge."

"Do you need anything from me?" Ron asked.

"Nothing comes to mind," he replied, "but I know your number."

"Thanks for everything Charlie," Ron said. "I will see you at the luncheon."

After Charlie left, Ron started working on the onboarding plan for Laura. He knew he needed to assign a buddy to her, and after going over the pros and cons of each team member, he decided on Linda. He jotted down some components of the plan so he could think it through and then get Susan's input.

As he thought about the plan he wrote:

1) Linda will be the assigned buddy. Meet with her to discuss the role.

2) I will have a set weekly meeting with Laura, not only for the onboarding plan, but also ongoing for coaching and evaluations.

3) Linda needs to spend at least half a day with each member of the Leadership Team to get to know that person and learn what he or she does.

4) Time for Laura and me to sit down and prepare her job description. Probably four hours initially, and then more time as needed.

5) Schedule time for her to meet with the three HR team members, at least half a day with each person.

6) Set up times with her in which she will lock her door and study all policies and procedures.

7) Have her spend extended time with Linda in the manufacturing area.

8) Have Mary tell her the history of the company and what family members are involved in some way in the company.

9) I will spend all morning with Laura on her first day—relationship building and establishing communication.

Ron felt good about the list and was anxious to review it with Susan. Ron knew most managers at his level did not help with new hires. Susan had mentioned this to him during the process. But Susan had also told him that studies show that onboarding plans significantly contribute to a new hire's success and makes the transition effective and successful. And Ron wanted Laura to succeed.

Susan had noted that while many companies have new employee orientation, it was seldom used for new management hires for fear of offending them with basic treatment.

"The hiring process does not end with acceptance of the offer," Ron murmured to himself, quoting Susan. "It continues through onboarding and through the first ninety days of employment."

"Now to prepare the remarks for Charlie's farewell luncheon. I'm really going to miss him!"

You cannot skip an onboarding plan for all new hires.

Chapter 28

THE OLD AND NEW

Ron was meeting with Susan prior to Charlie's farewell luncheon. "What is your opinion of my onboarding plan for Laura?" He asked.

"I like it," she replied. "I believe it covers all the bases. I like getting her out into all of the areas of the company. And Linda is a great choice to be her buddy. And I suspect the times you have for meeting with her will go well beyond your estimate."

"Probably." he answered. "She and I have a lot of ground to cover, and I want to make sure we do it right. I do not want to be one of those companies who, with a new hire, say 'Welcome aboard, and here are the keys to the office. Call me if you need me.' And guess what. No one ever calls."

"You have never been that way," Susan said. "Seventy-five percent of companies are like that, I would guess. I just do not understand them."

"Maybe that is why you are here," Ron said with a smile. "Other than the great pleasure of working with me."

"Of course," she said. "That is why I am here!"

They both laughed.

"I do want to take your onboarding outline and dress it up for Laura. Also, I invited Laura to come to Charlie's farewell luncheon, and she accepted. She said she and her husband would be in town checking out the apartment, so she is joining us today."

"That was a good call to invite her," Ron said. "Encourage her to speak to Charlie, and arrange a time when she can meet with him."

"Good idea," she said. "He can be a good resource as she learns the company."

"I know Charlie will be glad to meet with Laura," Ron said.

"I assume you have your remarks ready for the luncheon." She said.

"Now I am going to work on getting your onboarding ideas put together for Laura," "Thanks, Susan," Ron said. "I will see you at the luncheon."

Soon all of the Leadership Team, operations team, and HR team and many of their spouses gathered for Charlie's farewell luncheon in a private room at a popular downtown restaurant.

After everyone was seated, Sam, the master of ceremonies, welcomed everyone and asked a blessing for the meal. Sam then had everyone introduce themselves and spouses, if present, including the new operations leader, Laura Clark and her husband, Sean.

After everyone had eaten, Sam stood and introduced Ron. "It is my pleasure to introduce a man who needs no introduction, our leader, Ron Howell, who will deliver the tribute to our great friend, Charlie Richardson."

"Thank you for coming to this special event to give tribute to Charlie for his ten years of dedicated service to our company," Ron said. "As you know, he is leaving us for a great opportunity to be president of one of our community's other great companies, Specialty Products. I tried to change his mind, telling him it is lonely at the top, but he did not listen. Smart man."

Ron continued. "I know all of you will miss him, but not as much as I will. For ten years he has been at my right side, serving as a sounding board, giving advice, and keeping me focused on the goals.

"His accomplishments are too many to list. He was instrumental in preparing our mission and visions statements. He led our efforts identifying our core values. He never hesitated to challenge me, or any other team member, if he felt it necessary. He accepted criticism and believed it to be a chance to improve himself. And I want to mention one final improvement that was made possible because of Charlie."

Ron paused for just a moment. "In finding his successor, we used an entirely new system. The fact that he was leaving meant to replace him we needed a strong process and system to find the right fit and match. It is not easy to replace someone like him."

"Charlie and Connie, please join me here at the podium,"

As the two rose, Ron continued. "The people gathered here today will really miss you. And we are leaving the door open so you can stop in for coffee and a visit at any time. Connie, thank you for sharing Charlie with us these past ten years. I know at times he had to miss events to handle a crisis at the office. We want to send you to your new opportunity with a couple of things. Bonnie, Randy, John, and Michael, please join us up here." The four members of Charlie's team moved to the front of the room.

Bonnie said, "Charlie all four of us have enjoyed working *with* you, not *for* you, as you always emphasized. Your coaching and interest in us as individuals made all the difference.

"Recently, we noticed you stopped wearing your wrist watch. It seems that while you were in the manufacturing area, somehow it got smashed. I think that Timex was more than 20 years old. So, we have a replacement for you. Not a Timex, but the newest version of the Apple Watch."

She handed him the watch and hugged him, followed by the other team members. Once again applause broke out and the four team members returned to their seats.

Ron said, "Would the Leadership Team please come forward,"

Bill, Ralph, Sally, Susan, Sam, Linda and Mary stepped up to Charlie.

"Our team will miss Charlie's presence, advice, and logical answers," Linda said. "So that you will remember us, I have in this envelope tickets for an all-expense-paid ten-day cruise in the Caribbean, including airfare and all extras."

Again the room was filled with applause. Charlie hugged and shook hands with all of his team members.

"Finally Charlie," Ron said, "I have this plaque for you to hang on your wall at home or at work, in recognition of your ten years of service. And, in this envelope is a small gift of appreciation from the whole company. Now I will turn the podium to you Charlie."

"Thanks, Ron," Charlie began. "And thank you to everyone in this room for your kind gifts, and your support over the past ten years. And to Laura and Sean, you will find the same love and support for you from these folks that Connie and I have enjoyed for the past ten years."

Charlie continued. "I want to echo Ron about our new hiring system. It is thorough and challenging. It is consistent and fair. It proved to be what Susan told us it would be—a discovery process. As a company, overall we have done an okay job of hiring. Our turnover has been below national averages. With this new system, you will do even better. And just to let you know, my new company will implement the same system."

As everyone applauded, Charlie continued. "Now, as you use the system understand this. It is not perfect. It is not infallible. However, if you adhere to it and use it consistently, you will be very pleased with your new hires."

Charlie paused and took a deep breath. "I will now stop talking. However, I cannot thank everyone enough for your love and support all of these years. Connie and I will miss all of you." The people rose for a standing ovation.

Sam then returned to the podium. "Thank you everyone. Please feel free to linger and chat for a while, and come on up and share some hugs."

Ron found Laura and Sean and said. "Laura were you able to connect with Charlie?"

"I was, right before we all sat down for lunch," she said. "He will meet me for coffee on Friday the week after next at 3:00 p.m."

"Wonderful," Ron said. "I will see you on Monday, and we will begin with the onboarding process."

"Thanks Ron," she said, "I look forward to it. This is my, as you know, third management position, and my first onboarding plan. I really appreciate it that you are taking time to help me transition into my role and responsibilities here. All of my previous assignments I was left on my own. Thank you."

On Monday morning, Ron and Susan were in his office. Laura had arrived for the onboarding and she was given some time to organize her office. This gave Ron and Susan time to review the plan and get ready to meet with Laura.

"Do you have the onboarding plan in a professional format and not my notes? Ron asked."

"Sure do," Susan said. "Here it is." And she handed him the chart.

Laura's Onboarding Plan Category Details

Meeting with her buddy to discuss how they want to relate and meet with each other.	Initial meeting will be Monday afternoon. Time is estimated at up to 2 hours.
Weekly meeting with Ron.	Every Wednesday at 1:00 p.m. for 1 hour.
Half a day with each Leadership Team member for relationship building and gaining an understanding of their role in the company.	Each team member will reach out to Laura and set a mutually agreeable time for the half-day sessions.
Initial meeting with the HR Team and Susan.	Tuesday at 1:00 p.m.
First Day: relationship building with Ron	All morning.
Time with Linda in Manufacturing area	Linda to get with Laura and set the time.
History lesson with Mary.	Thursday - time to be set by Mary and Laura.
Study time	Daily for first week
Job Description with Ron	Friday morning

Ron reviewed the chart. "Looks good to me." he said.

"It provides the basics and allows for adjusted time as needed," Susan said. "The key is that we have identified specific activities and people. And we want her to not be involved in daily operations immediately.."

"Exactly," Ron agreed. "I will meet with her all morning. This will get us off to a good start. Thanks for your help."

Every new hire, regardless of position, needs an onboarding program.

Chapter 29

IT ALL BEGINS

Laura got to the company early. She was trying to contain her excitement. On the way to her new office, she saw Susan headed her way.

"Good morning, Susan," Laura greeted her. "How are you?"

"Really good," Susan said. "The hiring steps you went through were new for us. We really found it valuable and are getting trained on the Choosing Winners© system this week. When I say all of us, I mean myself, Maria, Cathy, and Mark."

"Is the training here in the office?" she asked.

Susan replied, "It is. We will be in training for two solid days. Say, let me ask you as one who just experienced the system, can you share some observations with me?"

"I would love to," Laura replied. "First, the communication with me was fantastic. When I was given a time, your team was prompt. I found the—I think you call it the screener interview—to be challenging in a positive way. The interview with your consultant was most interesting. It caused me to really think about my values, rapport with others, and effective coaching."

"I enjoyed the one-to-one with you a lot. The interview day was something totally new to me, but I loved it. It was different actually meeting the other candidates. I have been through interview processes before and nothing compares to this."

"Thanks," Susan said. "We are really happy with the system and look forward to completing the training, then implementing it into the company."

"If I can be involved in any way, just let me know," Laura responded.

"I will," Susan replied. "As you know, we narrowed the field to our top three, and I believe you met the other two?"

"I did." she replied. "Both gentlemen were very nice."

"Do you remember which one was William Brown?" Susan asked.

"I do," Laura replied. "He was very nice and pleasant. I really liked him."

"I need to tell you about Mr. Brown," Susan said. "After he got home from the interviews he and his wife were driving home from the airport when he felt ill and pulled the car to the side of the road. His wife took the wheel and drove to the hospital. Unfortunately, he passed away on the trip to the hospital. I wanted you to be aware of this in case you hear an associate talking about it."

"That is so sad," Laura replied. "Thanks for making me aware of it. He was such a nice man. Sean and I will pray for his family."

"Will you look who is here?" "Susan said as Sam approached them.

"Morning," he said. "Welcome aboard, Laura!"

"Thank you," she said. "The last time I saw you, your arm was in a sling."

"You are very observant." Sam replied. "I am all healed!"

"May I ask how you broke your arm?" Laura asked.

"Yes you may," Sam replied. "I was involved in a heated discussion with Susan, and she grabbed me and threw me to the floor breaking my arm."

Susan gave Sam one of her famous looks. "Sam, now tell Laura what really happened."

"If you insist," He replied. "I was in an automobile accident. Another driver ran a red light and hit my truck. My big truck was extremely damaged, but it protected me."

"You are fortunate to only have a broken arm." Laura said.

"I agree."

Sam said, "The Lord sent an angel to protect me."

"Laura was just telling me from a candidate's perspective that she liked our new interview process," Susan said.

"Hey guys," Bill said, as he joined them. "Welcome aboard Laura."

"Thank you Bill," she said. "I am anxious to get started. Susan and Ron prepared a great onboarding plan for me."

"Say, you remembered my name," Bill commented. "Impressive."

Before she could respond, Sally and Linda arrived on the scene.

"Welcome aboard Laura, "Sally said, "so happy to have you here."

Linda added, "I agree. And did you know that I would be your buddy?"

"I did," Laura answered. "I look forward to getting to know you."

Bill jumped back into the conversation, "Okay, test time. Laura, I see you remember

Linda, but tell me who is with her."

"Sally," she answered.

"Take that, Bill," Sam said, laughing.

"I think we better let Laura go since she is spending the morning with Ron," Susan said. "I trust she would like to take time to get her thoughts in order."

"Good point, Susan," Bill replied. "I am glad I could be on the welcoming committee this morning!"

With that, they all laughed and went their separate ways. Sam and Susan walked together, and Sam asked. "Did Ron hear any more from Brandon?"

"Not directly," she answered. "However, we learned that he was removed from his chair position. I also received an email from him telling me he was let go from his position and wanting to know if I knew of any job openings. True to his character, and lack of integrity, he wrote that his dismissal was Ron's fault, and he would never forgive Ron."

"That is Brandon," Sam replied. "A true loser."

"So sad," Susan said. "Well, I have to get ready for the training on our new hiring system. Have a great day, Sam."

Ron was in his office reviewing his weekly calendar with Mary. "Today I will spend all morning with Laura as part of her onboarding, so please, no calls—unless there is an emergency. Also, here is a copy of her onboarding plan."

"Thank you," Mary said. "I am really excited about Laura. She is a great addition to the Leadership Team."

Laura appeared in the doorway.

"Ready for me?" She asked.

"Oh, hi, Laura," Ron said.

"Welcome aboard, Laura," Mary said. "I am so happy that you have joined the team."

"Thank you," Laura answered. "And I am really happy to be here."

"Well, I will get out of here and let you and Ron get on with the onboarding," Mary said. "Please never hesitate to ask me for help."

"Thank you, Mary," she said.

Ron said to Laura, "Please join me at my conference table."

"Your team is a wonderful group of people," Laura said. "We just had an unplanned meeting in the hallway."

"Yes, our people really care about each other. I know you will enjoy being on this team. I would like to review the onboarding plan with you. Did you bring a copy?"

"I did." she replied.

"Good," Ron said. "I will start at the top and explain the items for you. Do not hesitate to ask questions. Your buddy is Linda, and she will meet with you later today to discuss how you will work together. You and I will meet all morning today, and then we will meet weekly. Mary is putting together a schedule for you to meet with the Leadership Team members. The purpose is to let them tell you about their roles and to just really get to know each other.

"Susan is setting up a time for you to meet with her and the HR team. Linda will take you through all of our manufacturing processes. Tomorrow, Mary will give you the comprehensive history of our company. Once you have completed all of these activities, you and I will meet to prepare your job description. Any questions?"

"Not right now," she replied. "Throughout the hiring process your team has been super."

"So, what did you think about our hiring process? Ron asked.

"I have never been through anything like that." Laura said. "I really liked it. Looking back, I think you have specific steps, like five or six?"

"I think Susan told you this is a new system for us," Ron said. "It passed the test, and we are now in training. We signed a license agreement with the Choosing Winners© organization. Let me give you a quick overview of the system," Ron explained the system to Laura and then asked, "Any questions?"

"Not right now," she replied. "I hope I will have an opportunity to learn more about it."

"You will," Ron said. "Once the training is done with the HR team, Susan will educate the whole Leadership Team. I am looking forward to this.

"Okay, let's share about ourselves so we can know each other,"
Ron said. "How do you prefer giving information to others and myself?"

"I prefer one-to-one sharing," she said. "I use email primarily to document something we agreed to or to just share basic information."

"We are of the same school," Ron said. "I want to have personal one-to-one time with you and the other team members. I agree that email works well to document agreements reached in a meeting. So, how do you prefer receiving information?"

"I prefer one-to-one, but I will discover the other person's preferences and adjust to meet his or her needs. And I do appreciate email follow ups."

"I am with you on that," Ron said.

Ron and Laura spent the balance of the meeting building rapport by sharing their life histories, likes and dislikes, goals, dreams, and their value systems.

Laura worked her way through the onboarding, and after ninety days was fully up to speed. The team had found their fit and match!

A few weeks ago the Leadership Team took on the task of finding a replacement for their operations manager, Charlie Richardson. They decided to use a new system, the Choosing Winners© System. You have now completed your journey through the system with them as they successfully hired Laura Clark to take Charlie's place.

You are now aware of the value of a hiring system. What you do with this information is up to you.

If you would like to know how to implement the Choosing Winners © System in your company, contact Bob Spence at 614-787-6502 or bobsp@mac.com.

Chapter 30

CLOSING THOUGHTS

The president and leader of Howell Manufacturing, Ron Howell, is a good example of involving people in all aspects of the organization. He is a humble leader and is not prideful.

What about pride?

The Bible gives us numerous examples of pride and its consequences on the lives of leaders and followers. Over the years, I've worked with hundreds of leaders, interviewing over 6,000 of them.

In that process, I have seen so many leaders who were like those noted in the Bible. I have witnessed their disgrace, as written in Proverbs 11:2 (ESV), "When pride comes, then comes disgrace, but with the humble wisdom."

In *Mere Christianity*, C.S. Lewis wrote, "Pride leads to every other vice; it is the complete anti-God state of mind."

And pride prevents you from serving God.

If you are a leader, and you like the spotlight and think, "I have arrived," it might just be time to do a self-analysis. Do you feel entitled to all the trappings of your position? Have you stopped listening to others? Proverbs 13:0 (ESV) notes, "By insolence comes nothing but strife, but with those who take advice is wisdom."

If pride is consuming your life, whom do you turn to for counsel and advice?

The Apostle Paul wrote in Philippians 2:3 (ESV), "Do nothing from selfish ambition or conceit, but in humility count others more significant than yourselves."

Several years ago, I was coaching a young, first-time manager. I quickly discovered that his perception of his role was that of the leader who sat on a pedestal, and others bowed to him daily. His team members were coming to me, sharing their frustration with a leader who did not listen, took personal credit for all achievements, and lacked personal accountability.

In our next coaching session, I told the team manager what I was hearing from his team members. He became defensive, rejected every concern, and took no responsibility for his behavior. Pride was alive and well in him.

Then I shared Servant Leadership with him. I used the inverted pyramid as an example. I explained how he must step off the pedestal and begin to serve others. His nonverbal behavior showed me that I was not close to breaking through his self-pride.

I would like to tell you this ended up as a success story, but I cannot. His pride was so strong that he was totally blind to reality. His insolence caused strife in the organization and destroyed the team. What about you and your pride?

Ron Howell, unlike many leaders did not experience being "lonely at the top" because he met people where they are, involved them, and coached them. What about being "lonely at the top"?

Stop and think about it. Who helps you see the blind spots? Who gives you honest feedback? Who is willing to disagree with you? Who will ask you the right questions to help you process a decision or a problem?

I have been where you are. I know how lonely it can be.

It is difficult to place a monetary value on having someone you can turn to who will help you eliminate that empty feeling of loneliness.

Maybe you have an assistant you trust and share some information with at times. However, can you be totally open with this person about your innermost thoughts? Can you share your deepest worries and concerns about the business with the assistant? Probably not.

An article in the *Harvard Business Review* reported that fifty percent of CEOs reported feeling lonely at work. And, about sixty percent believed the feeling of being alone hindered their performance. For the first time, the numbers in both areas were seventy percent.

Being at the top can easily result in isolation and becoming out of touch with the business. If you are isolated, how do you really lead, create a motivating environment, develop people, innovate, evaluate, and assess needs for individuals and the business—and manage productivity and profitability? Let me answer for you: You don't.

If you feel lonely, and even isolated, this can lead to poor decision-making, inept problem-solving, frustration, dysfunctional teams and team members, and even the internal stress that builds and eventually causes negative behavior, or even major health issues.

Why? As the CEO, president, or business owner, you receive less feedback and information, and the information is filtered.

Do loneliness and isolation have to be an inevitable part of your leadership? No. You can take steps to reduce the risk of isolation.

First, how about your walk with the Lord? Who in the Body of Christ do you turn to on a regular basis, one who encourages you to love and trust God more?

Proverbs 3:5–6 (ESV) admonishes, "Trust in the Lord with all your heart, and do not lean on your own understanding. In all your ways acknowledge him, and he will make straight your paths."

Sounds simple enough. Your relationship with the Lord makes all the difference!

For several years, I served as the CEO/superintendent of public school districts. I dealt with the public, elected officials, union members, thousands of employees, thousands of young lives and their parents, special interest groups, court decisions, legal issues, and all the politics that went with it.

Believe me, in that scenario you can feel very lonely and isolated. Here is what I did to reduce loneliness and isolation, and I offer these ideas for your consideration.

- Prayer. Developing and building my relationship with Jesus, putting my trust in Him by being in prayer and the Word.
- Visibility. Every day I was out in the organization and the community, speaking with people, asking lots of questions, and getting to know as many as I possibly could on an individual basis.
- Boundaries. I set and was clear with everyone about my boundaries and expectations, as well as about my values.
- Involvement. I prioritized getting people involved in processes—decision-making, problem solving, communication, and training. I made sure we put decision-making at the knowledge base.
- Coaching. I worked closely with my direct reports, setting clear and achievable goals, conducting regular and consistent performance reviews, and developing a mentoring relationship, using Jesus as a personal role model.
- Collaboration. I met with every department once a month to listen to them and their concerns, as well as to share information with them. I learned so much!

Many leaders struggle with having a healthy work–life balance. In our story, Ron Howell, was comfortable with who he was, and he had good balance—having time for his family, social time with friends, and serving his church as an elder.

What About Work–Life Balance?

What is balance in life? Sounds like a simple enough question. However, if you ask ten different people, you will get ten different answers. In Luke 10:38–42 (ESV) is this story about Mary and Martha:

> Now as they went on their way, Jesus entered a village. And a woman named Martha welcomed him into her house. And she had a sister called Mary, who sat at the Lord's feet and listened to his teaching. But Martha was distracted with much serving.
>
> And she went up to him and said, "Lord, do you not care that my sister has left me to serve alone? Tell her then to help me."
>
> But the Lord answered her, "Martha, Martha, you are anxious and troubled about many things, but one thing is necessary. Mary has chosen the good portion, which will not be taken from her."

Are you most like Martha, or Mary?

Many assume that Mary is the right one and that Martha is the wrong one. Jesus let Martha know about her busyness, but he did not blame her for being a hard worker and efficient. Jesus did not want Martha to be "like Mary," but rather to stop worrying about doing things for him, rather than experiencing the intimacy of being with him.

Do you have a Martha spirit or a Mary spirit?

Are you that hard-charging leader who is totally consumed by the business, always working in it and not on it, afflicted with the need to always over-achieve and reach the mountain top regardless of the cost? Or are you a leader who is clear about priorities.

As Romans 12:2 (ESV) advises, "Do not be conformed to this world, but be transformed by the renewal of your mind, that by testing you may discern what is the will of God, what is good and acceptable and perfect."

That is what Jesus meant when he spoke to Martha.

Want a role model for work–life–balance? Look to Jesus. He is the perfect example of effectively balancing both halves of life. Ron Howell, in our story, looked to Jesus.

How about focusing your thoughts on honoring Jesus with your life and work? How about not seeking your own personal wants and desires?

As Paul wrote to the Philippians in chapter 2:3–4 (ESV): "Do nothing from selfish ambition or conceit, but in humility count others more significant than yourselves. Let each of you look not only to his own interests, but also to the interests of others."

Charles Spurgeon once said, "The best work is done by the happy, joyful workman. And so it is with Christ. He does not save souls as of necessity, as though He would rather do something else if He might, but His very heart is in it, He rejoices to do it, and therefore He does it thoroughly and He communicates His joy to us in the doing of it."

Our lives consist of many parts: faith, family, friends, job/career, our health and well- being, personal development, and our finances, to name a few. The balancing act is knowing your core values and priorities and recognizing when some areas need more attention from you than the others.

Talk with, and listen to, God, seeking his path for you. "Let the word of Christ dwell in you richly, teaching and admonishing one another" (Colossians 3:16, ESV).

I believe that a balanced life is one in which you use your talents and gifts to glorify God; you focus on learning and growing in the Spirit; you intentionally give back through His church; you practice sound stewardship with your time and resources; and you know your core values and priorities and use them with discernment. And remember this: "Whatever you do, work heartily, as for the Lord and not for men" (Colossians 3:23, ESV).

In our story, Ron Howell demonstrated excellent decision-making skills. He was known as a very good decision maker. Why? He involved others!

What About Making Effective Decisions?

Decision-making is a key skill in the workplace and is particularly important if you want to be an effective leader. However, regardless of your job, you always face important decisions. Whether you're deciding which person to hire, which supplier to use, or which strategy to pursue, the ability to make a good decision with all of the available information is vital—including input from those impacted by the decision.

It would be easy if there were one formula you could use in any situation, but there isn't. Each decision presents its own unique challenges, and we all have different ways of approaching problems.

So, how do you avoid making bad decisions—or leaving decisions to chance? You need a systematic approach to decision-making so that, no matter what type of decision you face, you can make decisions with confidence. No one, regardless of their role in the company, can afford to make poor decisions.

Too often decisions in organizations are made at the wrong level. And, in most cases, they are made without enough information and a lack of input from those affected by the decisions. I firmly believe in putting decision-making at the knowledge base. Empower people to make decisions and give them the training and tools necessary to be effective decision-makers.

With decision-making in a company, you have to be consistent with the core values and the mission statement. Remember in our story how Ron Howell turned to the core values to make a major decision? When I was superintendent of schools, I made it clear that I would not approve any proposals that did not clearly state how the proposal was in the best interests of the students.

The director of maintenance came to me with a new and innovative preventive maintenance proposal. I was impressed with his ideas.

"Jeff, I like what I see," I told him. "Now, tell me how this is in the best interests of our students."

He struggled with words and then said, "What do the kids have to do with maintenance?"

I paused and then said, "When you can answer that question, come back with your proposal, and we will discuss it."

Within a week, Ralph came back and answered the question. He gave me an excellent summary of how preventive maintenance is vital to the well being of our students. I decided, after using my systematic process, to recommend his proposal to our board.

What does a systematic decision-making process include?

(1) Cross-check your pending decision to your mission statement and core values. Good decision-making requires consistency with your mission and core values.

(2) Gather all of the available information before making your final decision. However, do not overload with information or you will never make a decision.

(3) Determine who should have input and whom you need to speak with before making the decision. Always involve those who will be impacted by the decision.

(4) Test your decision by asking yourself the future impacts and consequences of your decision. Take time to anticipate what you believe will be the consequences.

(5) Good decisions are made when you remain calm and patient throughout the process.

EPILOGUE

Thank you for reading my book, and I sincerely hope this was a learning experience for you. In closing, I want you to know that I am happy in the Lord—yesterday, today and tomorrow!

The first time I heard this was when I was seven or maybe eight years old. My Dad's mother, Lola Spence, managed her sister's photography studio on Lorain Avenue in Cleveland, Ohio.

Mom and Dad went Christmas shopping in Cleveland and left me with Grandma at the studio. During the morning, after sharing many Bible stories with me, Grandma said, "Bobby, let's take a walk."

She took my hand and we left the studio and walked down Lorain Avenue. A man approached from the other direction. He said, "Good morning, Lola. How are you on this beautiful day?"

I looked up at Grandma. She had a great big smile on her face, and she said, "Happy in the Lord."

Over time I shared this experience with others and was asked, "What do you think she meant by happy in the Lord?"

The best way to answer that is to share what she wrote on June 29, 1950:

> "I am happy in the Lord, light as a feather, free as a bird, happy as a lark—today and everyday because He is in my heart to stay. I am fully surrendered to do His will instead of my will and everything is smooth and harmonious. The

harmony, tranquility, peace and joy that I now have is what I wanted all my life. It is heaven on earth."

I believe my grandmother meant that to be happy in the Lord means that we live by and walk with the Spirit. As Paul wrote in Galatians 5:25–26, "If we live by the Spirit, let us also keep in step with the Spirit. Let us not become conceited, provoking one another, envying one another." Remember Ron Howell and his team and how they related to each other.

As Christian business leaders the way we walk, talk, and treat others must be like Jesus. Business leaders must be Servant Leaders. And, as a Servant Leader, according to Proverbs 3:27, "Do not withhold good from those to whom it is due, when it is in your power to do it."

Amen.

Appendix

FOUNDATIONAL FACTS ABOUT HIRING:

- **Finding candidates** requires a clear company culture, a mission and vision, a positive reputation in the community, networking, specific job postings, and input from current employees.

- Clear, specific and agreed-to **Core Values** is critical to success in hiring the right people—those who are a fit and match with your culture.

- Hiring must be a **planned process**. You must have a system, and the system must be part of your company policy with specific consequences for those who fail to follow the policy.

- **Training managers** how to interview is not optional. The training must include not only interview techniques, but also how to prepare effective questions.

- **Involving the stakeholders** in developing position specifications, as well as participating in actual job interviews with the top candidates, will have a definite, positive impact and reduce the number of mis-hires.

- **Desperation hiring** is a guaranteed, 100 percent chance of having a mis-hire. A word to the wise is, "Hire slow and fire fast"—and totally reject desperation hiring.

- **Never conduct a blind search.** This is unethical and in no way demonstrates integrity on the part of your company.

- **A hire does not end** when the new employee reports to work. You absolutely *must* have an effective and comprehensive orientation and on-boarding program.

- **Weekly one-to-one meetings** between the new hire and the supervisor are mandatory. These meetings begin at hire and continue throughout employment. They should range from thirty minutes to one hour and always have an agenda.

- **There is no magic potion.** There is no "single test" or program that will tell you who to hire. It is a myth.

Evaluate your current hiring process.

Take a few minutes to check your current hiring process.
1. Is your hiring system part of policy and consistently enforced?
2. Does your application meet all legal standards and EEOC rules?
3. Do you involve all stakeholders in planning and final interviews?
4. Do you focus on cultural fit first, technical competence second?
5. Do you have a process to score resumes accurately and consistently?
6. Do you use effective telephone screening to narrow the field?
7. Do your interviewers know the EEOC "do not ask" list of questions?
8. Have your managers been trained on basic interview techniques?
9. Do you have your interview questions prepared and written?
10. Do you use a situational activity/skill test as part of your process?
11. Do you have an offer letter that has been reviewed by legal?
12. Do you have a legal plan for background checks & drug tests?
13. Do you have a consistent procedure for checking references?
14. Do you have a planned process for on-boarding new employees?
15. Do you have comprehensive job descriptions with specific metrics?

How did you do? If you want to have hiring success, you need to have all fifteen items marked yes!

I find it interesting when managers tell me that hiring is different than everything else they do. They view hiring as something foreign. This attitude can be changed through effective training and a systematic method.

A Final Word

If you would like to learn more about the Choosing Winners© and learn more about getting training on the system, or having assistance in a key leader search, email Bob Spence at bobsp@mac.com or call 614-787-6502.

ABOUT THE AUTHOR

Bob completed his Bachelor's and Master's Degrees at Bowling Green State University in Ohio, and also has done Ph.D. work at BGSU. (ABD) At BGSU he received the Distinguished Service Award. He spent the first 20 years of his career in public education as a teacher, coach, principal, and as a school superintendent. He has also worked in construction, manufacturing, insurance and retail. Bob founded Creative-Leadership Consultants in 1988, a human resources company, in San Diego, California, serving clients with the Choosing Winners© system.

Bob has given more than 400 presentations to business groups and companies in the United States and Canada, and numerous other presentations for select conferences, conventions, and other business meetings, many times serving as the Keynote Presenter. Bob is a Christian Abstract Artist using ink on paper to draw free-hand abstract designs based on various passages from Scripture. He has also published a book of some of his designs, "In the Beginning...The Art of Bob Spence" under the label Adonai Art Designs LLC.

Bob lives in Davenport, FL, with his wife Joan. Both are active in their church, he serving in mens' ministry and she leads Prayers and Squares, a quilt ministry.

BOB SPENCE CONSULTING

www.ingramcontent.com/pod-product-compliance
Lightning Source LLC
Chambersburg PA
CBHW060328200326
41519CB00011BA/1873